THE TRUTH ABOUT HITLER'S ELITE

•**Rudolf Hess**—Why did he *really* make that historic flight to Scotland?

•**Martin Bormann**—Did he *really* escape during the last hours of the war?

•**Ilse Koch**—Called "The Bitch of Buchenwald" because she had a penchant for lampshades made from human flesh.

•**Ernst Roehm**—An avowed homosexual, the Night of Long Knives ended both his influence and that of his Storm Troopers.

•**Julius Streicher**—A pornographer and sadist, his vicious anti-Semitism earned him a noose at Nuremberg.

•**Josef Kramer**—The "Beast of Belsen," he never missed a mass execution.

•**Rudolf Hoess**—The mastermind of Auschwitz, he designed the gas chambers to streamline human slaughter.

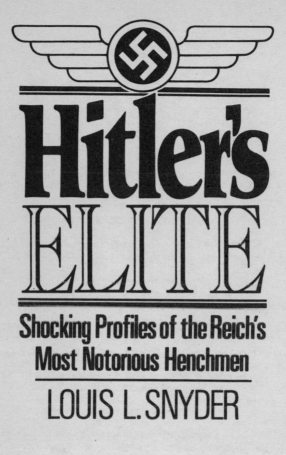

Hitler's ELITE

Shocking Profiles of the Reich's Most Notorious Henchmen

LOUIS L. SNYDER

BERKLEY BOOKS, NEW YORK

This Berkley book contains the complete text of the original hardcover edition. It has been completely reset in a typeface designed for easy reading and was printed from new film.

HITLER'S ELITE

A Berkley Book / published by arrangement with
Hippocrene Books, Inc.

PRINTING HISTORY
Hippocrene edition published 1989
Berkley edition / December 1990

ISBN: 0-425-12449-5

A BERKLEY BOOK ® TM 757,375
Berkley Books are published by The Berkley Publishing Group,
200 Madison Avenue,
New York, New York 10016.
The name "Berkley" and the "B" logo
are trademarks belonging to Berkley Publishing Corporation.

PRINTED IN THE UNITED STATES OF AMERICA

10 9 8 7 6 5 4 3 2 1

For
MALLON ANDREW
and
KAREN ANN SNYDER

And sovereign law . . . sits empress,
crowning good, repressing ill.

Sir William Jones (1746–1794)

CONTENTS

PREFACE

Power, like a desolating pestilence,
Pollutes whate'er it touches; and obedience,
Bane of all genius, virtue, freedom, truth,
Makes slaves of men, and of the human frame
A mechanized automaton.

With these words—"power" and "obedience"—English poet Percy Bysshe Shelley caught the essence of the quality that later was to characterize Adolf Hitler and his lieutenants.

Ambitious thugs have always gravitated to a repository of power and they sense the necessity of obedience to its source. They seek fame and fortune, glory and prestige, but more important, they court a share of the golden trappings of power. The process is familiar in any milieu—from that of sun-king Louis XIV in seventeenth-century Versailles to gangster Al Capone in Chicago during the prohibition era.

From its beginnings the Nazi movement attracted more than its share of such unprincipled hangers-on at upper- as well as lower-class levels of Party administration. Hitler also took a number of them into his personal retinue. Mostly inefficient mediocrities, they fitted well into his design of ethical and political nihilism, rejection of customary morals, and a desire to destroy established institutions—political, social, economic, and cultural—to make way for a society of his own conception. The leader's subordinates accepted without question his violent revolutionary tactics, including an accent on terrorism.

The Nazis in this gallery are the worst of the lot. Another book could be written about the scores of lesser rogues who infested the body politic of Nazi Germany.

For many of the facts presented here I am indebted to the Wiener Library, a treasure trove of material on National Socialist Germany. My thanks are due also to the New York Public Library and I am also grateful to the efficient staff of the Princeton Public Library, especially Eric Greenfeldt.

Every author must undergo agonies of production. For this book as well as those published in the past, I thank my better two-thirds, Ida Mae Brown Snyder. I can only express my amazement at the number of times she found the exact word and phrase while I floundered through Webster's *Unabridged*. She has been more collaborator than editor.

"*If ever the taming talisman, the cross, should shatter, primitive fury will be loose once again . . . , the senseless frenzy of the Berserk, of which the Nordic poets sing and tell so much. That talisman is decaying and the day will come when it will fall miserably to pieces. The old stone gods will then rise from their long forgotten rubble and wipe the dust of a thousand years from their eyes; and Thor will leap up in the end and shatter the Gothic cathedrals with his giant hammer.*"

—Heinrich Heine, *On the History of Religion and Philosophy in Germany* (1835)

INTRODUCTION

"What a dreadful thing it is," wrote Horace Walpole in 1778, "for such a wicked little imp as man to have absolute power." Famed for his tales of horror, that English writer would have been intrigued by the monster of Berchtesgaden and his praetorian guard.

Like other mortals, dictators are known for the company they keep. The *Fuehrer* of the Third Reich surrounded himself with as obnoxious a cast of characters—from toadies to charlatans to psychopaths—as ever appeared on the stained pages of history. Such people are common in any country at any given time, but to find them in such large numbers in positions of power in a modern state is unique.

Here they are in all their grotesque behavior—the jovial but vicious would-be Falstaff, Hermann Goering; little mouse-general Dr. Goebbels; dim-witted Rudolf Hess; pornographer Julius

Streicher; and Buchenwald's lamp-shade maker, Ilse Koch. All rose to important posts and left their mark on that brown society that disgraced the land of Beethoven, Goethe, and Schiller, and that throttled European civilization for too many grim years.

These were truly evil characters in a country that adopted as its symbol the crooked cross. They set themselves apart by their nihilism and racism, as well as their fondness for the occult. Above all, they reflected the personality of their half-demented leader. The syndrome was not new. As early as 42 B.C. Roman Publius Syrus recognized it: "He who is bent on doing evil can never want occasion."

The great German poet Johann Wolfgang von Goethe described the clash between good and evil in his literary epic *Faust*. He contrasted the good in God's servant Faust with the evil of satanic Mephistopheles. Along with the good in the world, the poet saw irrational and violent evil, both of which served to illuminate the human condition. The characters described in the following pages bear witness to Goethe's Mephisto in action.

Still another variation between good and evil was presented by Nobel Laureate William Golding in his *Lord of the Flies*. His tale concerns a group of schoolboys left to their own devices on an otherwise uninhabited Pacific island. The circumstances forced them to form a sort of community and the frightening result was that primitive instincts surfaced and the boys became barbarians.

The parable of the clash between good and evil is clear, if gloomy. Evil is within man himself. It cannot be eliminated, but merely recognized for what it is. Man is condemned to a battleground of a clash between meaning and madness.

The analogy is not precise, but Hitler's National Socialist revolution brought to power men as immature as Golding's young boys on their Pacific island. In the heat of ideological battle, Hitler's comrades reverted to primitive behavior of mythical configuration. They acted like immoral zombies. Consumed by ambition, they clawed their way to the top of the Nazi jungle. They harbored no sentiment beyond their immediate families, and some threw off even that.

How can one explain the lives of these characters? The psychiatric community has tried for decades with little success. Diligent search into childhood patterns and environmental conditions has yielded little enlightenment. One can only look on and wonder.

And what about the German people, themselves victims of the *Fuehrer*? Characterized by an unwillingness to dissent against political dictation, and with a few democratic forms but little disposition to use them, they had to be rescued eventually by a global combination of outraged peoples. It was a tragedy in German history.

At the base of German behavior was the obedience syndrome, a characteristic that called for subservience to the *Obrigkeit*, the legal authority in the state. Do what you are told—and keep your mouth shut! Hitler had won his way to power by legal means and that was all that was necessary. One did not challenge authority. If there were rumors of excesses in concentration camps, it was the duty of the citizen to turn away.

Some see a parallel on a national scale with the kind of minor phenomenon later revealed by the Kitty Genovese case, a truly shocking symbol of apathy. On the night of March 13, 1964, the 28-year-old woman was stalked and stabbed again and again as thirty-eight of her neighbors silently turned away from her cries. "Oh, my God, he stabbed me," she screamed into the early morning stillness. "Please help me!" Many people listened or watched but failed to call the police. Behaviorists could not explain satisfactorily the inaction of witnesses to this savage murder, this bad Samaritanism. "Nonrational behavior," said one sociologist.

Just as frustrating has been the effort to explain the conduct of German bystanders during the Holocaust. The reaction of most was to remain silent. Do not become involved. Those who did, placed themselves in jeopardy and many paid the price of imprisonment or death.

Among the more sensitive there was a residue of guilt. "I didn't speak up," said German Lutheran pastor Martin Niemoeller, who was arrested by the *Gestapo* in 1938 and sent to Dachau concentration camp until he was freed by Allied forces in 1945. He described his sense of guilt in a memorable passage:

In Germany, the Nazis first came for the Communists, and I didn't speak up because I wasn't a Communist. Then they came for the Jews, and I didn't speak up because I wasn't a Jew. Then they came for the trade unionists, and I didn't speak up because I wasn't a trade unionist. Then they came for the Catholics, and I didn't speak up because I was a Protestant. Then they came for me, and by that time there was no one left to speak for me.

A parallel book could be written and certainly will be, to record a Roll of Honor of Germans who opposed the Nazi regime at the risk of their lives. There were heroes who did speak out in Naziland, among them Pastor Dietrich Bonhoeffer, army officer Ludwig Beck, student Sophie Scholl, and others. One should bear in mind that the excesses of those in the following pages are not an accurate reflection of the whole German people, a people held in bondage by a gangster chieftain and his retinue of assorted rogues.

1

HERMANN GOERING: GERMANY'S DEADLY FALSTAFF

The Ruhr will not be subjected to a single bomb. If an enemy bomber reaches the Ruhr, my name is not Hermann Goering—you can call me Meier!

Sir John Falstaff is one of Shakespeare's most comical figures. He was "that father ruffian, that vanity of years," and in his own imagination, "that kind Jack Falstaff, valiant Jack Falstaff." Father substitute for King Hal, he was a gross, ale-swilling libertine. Dr. Samuel Johnson described "unimitated, inimitable Falstaff" as "thou compound of sense and vice, a character loaded with faults—a thief and a coward and a boaster, at once obsequious and malignant."

Equally obese, reckless, and egotistical was Hermann Goering, Nazi Germany's Falstaff. A giant, with ruddy face and piercing eyes, he appeared before his adoring public and strode the halls of power as a licentious rake, a proud cynic who cared nothing for convention or moral codes.

Like his fictional English counterpart, Goering was loaded down with heaps of flesh. His countrymen joked that "he sat down on his stomach and wore corsets on his thighs.'' He was not sensitive about his size. For him it was a badge of distinction.

In one respect Goering differed from Falstaff. Where Shakespeare's comic character was noted for his discreet cowardice, there is no doubt about the extraordinary, almost fanatical courage of Goering when he was a slender young combat pilot in World War I. That sort of bravery would later be dishonored by his growing brutality.

Behind the jovial exterior one can trace the evolution of a thug. A legitimate war hero, he turned into a savage killer. At the time of the German invasion of Soviet Russia in June 1941, he announced: ''This giant area must be pacified as soon as possible. The best solution is to shoot anybody who looks at us sideways.''

Sir Nevile Henderson, British Ambassador to Germany, caught the essence of the man: ''Goering is a typical and brutal buccaneer but one who has certain attractive qualities. For the German public those engaging characteristics were sufficient to win him esteem as a veritable national treasure.''

It was a meteoric career from poverty to fame and wealth. Along the way Goering won the confidence of Adolf Hitler, a multitude of high offices as No. 2 Nazi, a huge fortune, and the amused tolerance of his countrymen. He also managed to attract the contempt of millions of non-Germans disgusted by his flamboyant lifestyle.

Most of those in this survey of important Nazis were motivated by the obedience syndrome and their overweening ambition—in that order. Highly disciplined, they took their personal oath to Hitler seriously. They remained faithful to him because he was the fountainhead of authority. They would nourish their ambitions inside a framework of blind obedience.

In Hermann Goering the motivations were exactly reversed. He would put on a careful show of loyalty, but ambition was his own true master. In the climactic days of the Berlin bunker, when Hitler was reduced to a quaking shadow of himself, Goering finally achieved his goal—he announced himself as successor to the *Fuehrer*. It was too late.

Ambition was the key to Goering's life. In Nazidom he saw the Elysian fields in which he could operate as a giant among pygmies. He cast aside any sentiment of ordinary decency and accepted the coarse savagery that became the hallmark of Hitler's Reich. If a gangster code of violence, vengeance, and genocide was necessary, then so be it.

For Goering the comedy changed into tragedy. Fate decreed an unhappy end for him. He presupposed it. On the dark side of his manic-depressive personality was a cynical attitude to the business of living. During his last days in his cell at Nuremberg, he expressed a contempt for life and indicated that he was indifferent to the way he would die.

Hermann Wilhelm Goering was born on January 12, 1893, in Rosenheim, Upper Bavaria, one of the few Nazi leaders who came from a distinguished family. His father, Dr. Heinrich Ernst Goering, was the first governor of the German Protectorate of West Africa, and in that post had connections with British statesmen Cecil Rhodes and Joseph Chamberlain. Young Hermann spent his early days in the mountains and forests of South Germany. "I was bored by school," he said later. "All I wanted to be was a soldier."

The youth achieved his first goal when he attended the cadet college at Karlsruhe. When the World War began in August 1914, he was a lieutenant in the 112th Prinze Wilhelm Infantry Regiment, and took part in border battles in Alsace-Lorraine. In October 1914 he was made a flying observer. In June 1915 he became a pilot, at first in a reconnaissance role and then with a fighter unit.

The young Bavarian had an impressive war record as combat pilot. He became an "ace", with many planes shot down to his credit. In 1917 his hip was hit by a bullet, a wound that was to trouble him for the rest of his life. Returning to action, he was appointed leader of a fighter squadron. In June 1918, after the death of Manfred Freiherr von Richthofen, the famed Red Baron, Goering was given command of Richthofen's squadron, the Flying Circus.

There is no doubt about the distinguished combat record of the slender young pilot. Goering was awarded a chestful of decorations, including the order *Pour le Mérite*, one of Germany's highest awards. By the end of the war he was a national hero, enjoying popularity as a knight of the skies.

Immediately after the end of the war, Goering was ordered to surrender his flying machines to the advancing Americans. He defiantly refused and flew them back to Germany, where they were destroyed. Already he was showing that independence of spirit that was to characterize his later career.

On his return to Berlin, still wearing his uniform, Goering was attacked on the streets and the insignia torn from his uniform by a band of leftist revolutionaries. It was an experience he never forgot. He had risked his life and limb in defense of his country, and now some Communist goons had humiliated him—war hero—in broad daylight. He would get even with them.

As did other German officers in a similar predicament, Goering found it difficult to adjust to civilian life. For two years he held a job with the Fokker Aircraft Works. He then took a succession of positions: first as an advisor to the Danish government, then a stunt pilot, and then a commercial pilot for *Svenska Lufttraffik* in Sweden. There he met Carin von Katzow, who became his wife after divorcing an older man.

By this time the dashing war hero had put on a great deal of weight but lost little of his energy and zest for life. With his wife he returned to Germany in 1922. He rejected an invitation to join the *Reichswehr*—he would not defend the Weimar Republic, which he despised for its role in accepting the Treaty of Versailles. Instead, he enrolled at the University of Munich to study history and political science. But he soon grew contemptuous of the intellectual life and he attended few classes.

Goering went to Berlin, where he settled down in a bachelor's flat. His wife, Carin, who was epileptic and also suffering from tuberculosis, had returned to Sweden. It was a tragic separation because they were deeply in love. In Berlin, Goering worked as an advisor to *Lufthansa*, the commercial airline.

Goering also made it a point to cultivate social contacts. It was easy to use his past popularity as a war hero to move in the same circles as the eminent. He met the former Crown Prince and members of his entourage, as well as many others, including Prince Philip of Hesse, who had married the daughter of the King of Italy. He also made contacts with barons of the business and industrial worlds, connections he was later to exploit.

Unhappy with the Weimar administration, which he dismissed as "the Jew Republic," Goering began to search for political connections. In October he heard Hitler speak and he was enormously impressed. Later, for public consumption, he said of his reaction: "The convictions [of Hitler] were spoken word for word as if from my own soul. Now, I finally saw a man who had clear and definite aims. I just wanted to see him at first to see if I could assist him in any way. He received me at once and after I had introduced myself it was an extraordinary turn of events that we should meet.''

Extraordinary, indeed. There began a liaison that was to last nearly twenty-three years. The enlisted dispatch bearer and the glamorous pilot hero of the World War I went on to become the two most powerful men in Germany.

For budding politician Hitler it was an important conquest. He was delighted. In his view it was a splendid acquisition, a war ace with the *Pour le Mérite*. This was superb as a propaganda tool. Moreover, Goering probably had money and he did not cost the new Party a *Pfennig*.

Hitler was wrong about the expected source of new income for his movement. Actually, Hermann and Carin were living on the proceeds and sale of her jewels and on money they borrowed. They knew people of wealth but had little money themselves. Unaware of that, Hitler decided in December 1922 to give the war hero the important post of Supreme Leader of *Sturmabteilung, (SA)*, the brown-shirted Storm Troopers.

Always the cynic, Goering, nevertheless, was impressed by the energetic Hitler, but he was not thoroughly convinced by the loudly proclaimed philosophy. When on trial at Nuremberg after the war, he said that he had joined the Party not because of its "ideological stuff," but merely because it was revolutionary. For the decorated combatant of the World War, the association with Hitler and the Nazis promised action, even if the clashes were to take place in the streets in the battle against communism.

Goering was very much aware of Hitler's colossal vanity and he made sure to play upon it as often as possible. He proclaimed that "the law and will of the *Fuehrer* are one." And again: "If Catholic Christians are convinced that the Pope is infallible in all religious and moral matters, then we National Socialists proclaim with equal strong conviction that for us, too, the *Fuehrer* is completely infallible in all political and other matters which concern the national and social interests of the people." And still again: "God gave the savior to the German people. We have faith, deep and unshakeable faith, that he was sent to us by God to save Germany." This sort of praise assured Goering's rise and his retention of a power base. Other Nazis used the same technique.

Goering was present at all the milestone actions of the early movement. In the November 1923 beer-hall *Putsch* in Munich, Captain Goering issued commands to his *SA* lieutenants: "The revolution will break out. Make yourselves respected by unprecedented terror. In every locality at least one man must immediately be shot dead to frighten the people." There he set the standard of brutality for the rest of his career.

On the night of November 8, when Hitler was having trouble with the crowd in the Munich beer hall, Goering mounted the podium and quieted the spectators. "You have nothing to fear. You have your beer!" The next morning Goering marched forward with, among others, General Erich Ludendorff, in a major Nazi street demonstration. Facing the police at the Ludwig Bridge, Goering suddenly rushed toward them and shouted that he would shoot his hostages who were in the rear lines, if the police opened fire. The threat worked. The column was allowed to proceed to the Marienplatz. There Goering was wounded severely by the bullets of other policemen who would not stand aside. Arrested, he managed to escape to Austria and then returned to his wife's homeland.

In September 1925 Goering was admitted to the Langbro Asylum in Sweden diagnosed as "an extremely dangerous asocial hysteric." He became for a time addicted to morphine, apparently because of the pain caused by his war wounds. For the rest of his life he was accused of being a permanent slave to drugs, but there is little evidence to prove that charge. His claim to have been cured of his addiction at Langbro Asylum is probably accurate.

After the political amnesty of 1926, Goering returned to Germany and immediately resumed his contacts with Hitler. He spent the next year reorganizing the *SA* and trying to mold it into an effective fighting organization for use against the Communists. In 1928 he was elected to the *Reichstag*, was one of the first Nazi deputies, and was re-elected in 1930. After the surprising outcome of the elections of July 1932, when the Nazis won 230 seats in the *Reichstag* and the National Socialists became the largest political party in Germany, he became President of Germany's law-making body.

Meanwhile, Goering was beginning to build his personal fortune. He became head of a motor works in Munich. In this capacity he tried with some success to persuade industrialists that when Hitler came to power, the *Fuehrer* would immediately institute a rearmament program that would mean great financial gain for them.

Goering was also instrumental in the political machinations that finally won the chancellorship for Hitler. In January 1933 he informed senile President Paul von Hindenburg that General Kurt von Schleicher was conspiring to dispatch troops to arrest the President. This report was among the pressures that led the credulous old man to sign the decree appointing Hitler as Chancellor.

The grateful *Fuehrer* named Goering to the post of "Minister Without Portfolio," one of the three Nazis in Hitler's first cabinet. Goering's next step was to assume the office of Prussian Minister of the Interior, which gave him control of the Prussian police. He also persuaded the old President to give him special police powers.

Goering now went to work eliminating dissenters and even lukewarm supporters. He replaced Weimar officials with *SA* Brown Shirts, and used every means, including blackmail and even more serious steps, to get rid of enemies of the Party. To those who offered the least objection, he replied: "Get used to the idea that I am not in office to dispense justice but to destroy and exterminate."

Goering was now in the hurricane eye of Nazi politics. He was one of the first on the scene at the *Reichstag* fire on the night of February 27, 1933. To the press he condemned the conflagration as "a Communist outrage," and that became the official Nazi explanation. In his capacity as police chief of Prussia, he took the drastic action, approved by Hitler, of arresting a hundred Communist *Reichstag* deputies as well as many others. He proclaimed a virtual state of siege because of "this monstrous act of terrorism."

How the fire started remains a mystery. Goering himself was accused of having planned the arson; a tunnel from his office to the *Reichstag* would have made this possible.

At the *Reichstag* fire trial held later in 1933, Goering engaged in a heated courtroom encounter with Georgi M. Dimitrov, a Bulgarian Communist who had been arrested as a suspect. The dramatic face-to-face confrontation attracted global attention. To

Dimitrov's taunting, Goering reacted with fury: "You are a Communist crook who came to Germany to set the *Reichstag* on fire. In my eyes you are nothing but a scoundrel, a crook who belongs on the gallows." The press reported "a moral whipping for Goering." Dimitrov was acquitted for want of evidence.

On April 20, 1933, Hitler appointed Goering to the post of Prime Minister of Prussia. In this capacity Goering founded the *Gestapo (Geheime Staats Polizei)*, the secret police that carried out the twelve-year reign of terror that followed the burning of the *Reichstag*. "The first prerequisite," Goering said later, "was to create along new lines that instrument which at all times and in all nations is always the inner endorsement of power, namely the police." His *Gestapo* agents tracked down opponents, took them to headquarters, and subjected them to interrogation and beatings that were often fatal. The dreaded knock on the door late at night struck fear into the hearts of most Germans. They knew only too well about family members or neighbors who had disappeared into *Gestapo* dungeons.

Hitler had a comrade he could trust. Goering took part in the Blood Purge of June 30, 1934, during which Hitler eliminated those who challenged his leadership. Before the event, Goering denounced *SA* chieftain Ernst Roehm and Gregor Strasser, both of whom championed a "Second Revolution." He drew up a list of traitors to be liquidated when Hitler would give the order. On Bloody Saturday, while the *Fuehrer* was directing executions in southern Germany, Goering led the operation in Berlin. Not only political enemy General Kurt von Schleicher, but even the general's wife, fell victim.

At Orienberg, Goering also set up the first concentration camp. Later, at his Nuremberg trial, he explained that he was interested only in the principle of "protective custody" to prevent the possibility of traitorous acts. "This was nothing new," he explained, "and not a National Socialist invention. Prisons were not available for that purpose. I want to stress that from the very beginning that was a political action for defense of the State." He insisted that he was in charge of the camps for only a short while in 1934 and had no responsibility for the later campaign of mass extermination.

At the same time, Goering worked energetically to advance Hitler's vast rearmament program. The Treaty of Versailles had forbidden the construction of military aircraft, a provision that

Hitler intended to ignore. He ordered Goering, his Minister of Aviation, to begin the training of thousands of young men in "glider sport clubs." Appointed *Oberbefehlshaber der Luftwaffe* (Commander-in-Chief of the Air Force), he revived the German aviation industry as well as the training of pilots and bombardiers. The veteran commander of Richthofen's Flying Circus was now in his element. His superbly trained pilots in their screaming *Stuka* dive bombers were to play an important part in Hitler's opening series of *Blitzkrieg* campaigns in World War II.

By then, Goering was second in power to the *Fuehrer* himself. Carin was not there to enjoy it. Critically ill, she had died on October 17, 1931. Goering was crushed. Later he brought her body to his sumptuous new estate in the Schönheide, north of Berlin, which he named Karinhall in her honor. In 1935 he married actress Emmy Sonnemann. Because Hitler was a bachelor, Emmy became the unofficial first lady of the Third Reich and took over the direction of the Party's social affairs.

The Goerings lived in luxury at their palace in Berlin and at their elaborate country home. At the estate Goering kept his huge collection of uniforms, many of which he designed himself, as well as an enormous number of military decorations. It was rumored that he once went on a hunting expedition carrying a spear, wearing a bearskin, and topped by a Wagnerian headgear. One gossip sheet reported that he wore an admiral's uniform while taking a bath.

At his country estate Goering kept young lion cubs as pets in his private zoo and delighted in having his picture taken romping with one cub, Caesar. He employed a huge staff of foresters and huntsmen at public expense. Notables from all over the world came to visit the Goerings, including American hero Charles A. Lindbergh, who, apparently to avoid insulting his host, accepted a decoration from the former German war ace. Years later, many of Goering's visitors were astonished by his private collection of Rembrandts, Raphaels, and El Grecos expropriated from countries occupied by German troops after the start of World War II.

Basking in luxury, Goering frequently boasted of his closeness to the public. He was proud of being their revered hero. "The *Fuehrer* is too often too far removed from the masses. That is why they cling to me."

Goering was right. The German people were proud of their

jovial Hermann. Corpulent and magnetic, he was the charmer with impeccable public manners who gave tone to an otherwise rough Nazi movement. They delighted in this adventurous clown who strode ponderously through the streets of Berlin with naïve joy in his power. They were inclined to agree with the massive egoist who described himself as "the last Renaissance man." Delighted German burghers, with their own protruding beer bellies, found Goering irresistible. They were entranced by his love for uniforms and medals and by his often infantile behavior. They identified with this jolly, lusty extrovert.

Most of all, the German public liked to repeat jokes about the "fat one." They happily pointed out that Goering roared with good humor when he heard stories about himself. The jokes came tumbling over one another.

—Goering was late for a meeting with an English friend for luncheon. He apologized, explaining that he had been out for shooting. "Oh!" exclaimed the poker-faced Englishman, "animals, I presume." Goering dissolved in laughter on hearing that one.

—Goering was sent to Rome to negotiate with the Pope. Within a short time he reported back to Hitler: "Mission accomplished. Pope unfrocked. Tiara and pontifical vestments are a perfect fit."

—Goering arrived at a naval inspection ahead of Hitler and Goebbels. He boarded a flagship and went below to look out a porthole. Goebbels, catching sight of Goering from shore, said to Hitler: "Look at Goering! He's draped a whole battleship around his neck!"

—Official announcement in Berlin: "*ACHTUNG!* IT IS HEREBY MADE KNOWN THAT NO GASOLINE WILL BE AVAILABLE TO MOTORISTS FOR A WEEK. *REICHSMARSCHALL* GOERING IS HAVING HIS UNIFORMS CLEANED."

—The controlled Nazi press reported that a water main had burst in the cellar of the Air Ministry. When told of the mishap, Air Minister Goering instantly issued out an order: "Bring me my admiral's uniform."

All this was acceptable—except when the jokes got out of hand. Goering was not amused when told of a rumor popular in the armed forces: "He is one of us. He likes his food, his women, and his graft—especially his graft."

Goering's gargantuan greed matched his girth. From 1933 on, he carved out a private empire for himself. The arms magnates, aware of the individual who sponsored the appropriations that filled their own coffers, whispered to one another: "He accepts gifts." He held iron deposits for his own gain and founded the enormously profitable Hermann Goering Works. He acquired coal fields, lignite mines, gravel pits, and other sources of raw materials, and established businesses and shipping companies. He held directorships in many industrial enterprises, including Daimler Benz and Bayerische Motorwerke (BMW), as well as in aircraft firms. When industrialist Fritz Thyssen, angered by excesses of the Nazi regime, left the country in 1937, Goering was quick to take over his holdings, including the largest steel mill in Germany. In addition to the income from his many offices, he also accumulated substantial book royalties. Once an impoverished veteran, Goering was now one of the richest men in the world.

Hitler was content with the situation. He was willing to let the fat associate, with his bizarre eccentricities and puerile antics, have whatever he wanted. A master of crowd psychology, the vegetarian *Fuehrer* saw in his corpulent Goering one who appealed strongly to the masses. Though lacking a sense of humor himself, Hitler saw a precious Party and national asset in Goering. Many Germans could not identify with the fanatical Goebbels or with one-time chicken farmer Himmler, but they could identify with Goering.

In April 1936 Dr. Hjalmar Schacht persuaded Hitler to appoint Goering as Commissioner for Raw Materials and for Foreign Exchange. The economics expert hoped that in this post Goering would put an end to Goebbels's spendthrift ways as Minister for Public Enlightenment and Propaganda. Goering, who envied Goebbels for his access to the *Fuehrer*, was delighted.

The difficulty was that Goering knew little or nothing about economics. Yet, the following September Hitler made him Plenipotentiary for the Four-Year Plan, a scheme to make Germany self-sufficient in event of war. Dr. Schacht, by this time finally aware of the depth of Goering's ignorance of economics, was appalled.

Goering went ahead with his own plan for autarky—to make the Third Reich independent of imports. He controlled the country's gold supplies and foreign exchange. As Germany's economics czar, he announced his goal: "Guns instead of butter":

> Party comrades, friends, I have come to talk to you about Germany, our Germany. *Germany* must have a place in the sun. Rearmament is only a first step to make our people happy. . . .
> I must speak clearly, There are those in international life who are hard of hearing. They listen only if the guns go off. We have no butter, my good people, but I ask you, would you rather have butter or guns? Should we import lard or metal ores?
>
> Let me tell it to you straight—preparedness makes us powerful. Butter merely makes us fat.

Goering also made his presence felt at every important meeting of the top Nazi leadership. He was one of five influential leaders present at the Hossbach Conference of November 5, 1937, at which Hitler spoke of Germany's need for *Lebensraum*, her necessary living space, and his plan to win territory for "the solid core of the German people."

It was Goering who engineered the proceedings resulting in the February 4, 1938, Blomberg-Fritsch crisis, by which the German Army's two leading generals were dismissed. The outcome enabled Hitler to solidify his control over the army and embark upon his program of aggression.

And the Jews? Like Goebbels, Himmler, and Streicher, Goering was aware that he had to cater to Hitler's monomania. In the Nazi environment he knew that his rapid promotion depended upon how thoroughly he could satisfy the *Fuehrer's* fanatical anti-Semitism. Every top Nazi, including those who personally shared Hitler's hatred of the Jews, felt the same way.

When Herschel Grynszpan, a young Polish Jew, killed Ernst vom Rath, embassy secretary in Paris, the assassination was followed by the *Kristallnacht*, the Night of Broken Glass, during which synagogues were burned, Jewish stores ransacked, and Jews attacked. Goering denounced what he alleged was Jewry's hostile attitude toward the German people, and he held all Jews responsible for the assassination. "Foul murder calls for decisive defense and harsh atonement. I order Jews of German nationality to pay a contribution of one million reichmarks to the German Reich.''

To please his master, Goering went even farther. He required Jewish shopkeepers to repair at their own expense all the damage done to their stores in the riots. He banned Jews from walking on certain streets, using park benches, and driving automobiles. He forbade them use of public markets, playgrounds, and winter resorts. As a crowning insult, he ordered that all Jews wear the yellow Star of David on their clothing as identification.

Goering was a central figure in negotiations for the *Anschluss*, Germany's annexation of Austria in March 1938, for which he later took responsibility at his trial in Nuremberg. He ordered Artur Seyss-Inquart, Nazi puppet in Austria, to telegraph the German government requesting troops "to restore order." Later, he threatened to bomb Prague if the Czechs did not accept the Nazi proposed protectorate over their rump state.

On May 23, 1939, Goering was present at the Reich Chancellery when Hitler informed his military leaders that "there is no question of sparing Poland." He was at the important Obersalzberg meeting on August 22, 1939, when more detailed plans were made for that invasion.

On August 30, 1939, just before German troops marched over the Polish border, Hitler appointed Goering chairman of the Cabinet Council for Defense of the Reich. The next day the *Fuehrer* made a speech designating Goering his successor in the event that Hitler met death in the uniform he intended to wear until victory. "If anything should happen to me, my successor will be Field Marshal Goering." It was a designation the frantic *Fuehrer* was to forget in his subterranean bunker under blazing Berlin in the closing days of the war.

Despite his boasting about the power of his *Luftwaffe*, Goering was not altogether confident at the outbreak of the war. When informed that Britain had entered the conflict, he said: "If we lose this war, then may God have mercy upon us." He sensed that Hitler had gone too far too fast.

Still, the field marshal sent his planes to bomb Rotterdam as part of successive *Blitzkrieg* attacks. After the fall of France in 1940, a grateful Hitler rewarded Goering with the title of *Reichsmarschall*, and with new decorations for his many uniforms. From then on Goering carried a baton to show his exalted rank.

Then came the crucial Battle of Britain. Hitler counted on the

Luftwaffe to smash British will in preparation for Operation Sea Lion, the intended cross-Channel invasion. The would-be conqueror received a total and unexpected setback when the Royal Air Force, Churchill's "so few" brilliant pilots, blasted much of the *Luftwaffe* out of the skies and delivered a staggering blow to the whole technical structure of Goering's vaunted air force. In June 1941 the *Luftwaffe* commander received another setback when his air force failed to smash Soviet resistance. The days of boasting were over.

At one time Hitler had tolerated Goering's weaknesses. "In time of crisis he is brutal and ice-cold. I've always noticed that when it comes to the breaking point, he is a man of iron without scruple." The failure of his *Luftwaffe* finally discredited Goering in Hitler's eyes. The two met in angry confrontation. Hitler accused *Luftwaffe* pilots and bombardiers of cowardice as well as incompetence, and he blamed Goering, accusing the *Reichsmarschall* of being taken in by his *Luftwaffe* officers.

Goering was crushed by his stormy quarrels with Hitler. The old fire-breathing confidence was gone as he saw his relations with his master steadily deteriorate. His prestige in Party circles sank as that of Goebbels, Himmler, and Bormann, his longtime rivals, grew. Even his sense of humor withered.

The discredited *Reichsmarschall* lapsed into subservience and tried to carry on as best he could. He worked for the recruitment and allocation of manpower. He signed a directive for "special treatment," euphemism for the slaughter of Polish workers in Germany. Against international law, he ordered Russian and French prisoners of war to work in armaments factories, and even forced Soviet prisoners to man anti-aircraft guns.

The bloated voluptuary retreated to Karinhall, where, somewhat subdued, he appeared at dinner dressed either like an Oriental Rajah or in white silk like a Doge of Venice. Here he entertained his guests in fantastic surroundings, including a domed book room in imitation of the Vatican Library, a 25-foot long desk encrusted with jewels and swastikas, Gobelin tapestries, and works of art taken from museums all over Europe.

Meanwhile, Berlin was being smashed into rubble by Allied airpower and eventually by Soviet artillery. Before the war, Goering had boasted "You can call me Meier" if a single bomb fell on Germany. Berliners now wryly called their pitiful air-raid sirens "Meier's bugle horns."

Living the life of a troglodyte in his Berlin bunker, Hitler raged in anger: "The entire *Luftwaffe* should be hanged." He shouted that he had been deserted by traitors. Everything was finished! On April 20, 1945, an embarrassed Goering left the bunker to a cool farewell.

Now at his retreat in Obersalzberg, Goering thought about Hitler's speech at the beginning of the war naming him as successor "should anything happen to me." Something, indeed, had happened. The *Fuehrer* now said: "All is finished. There is nothing left to fight for. Goering can now operate better than I can."

To Goering this was a clear-cut invitation. He sent a carefully worded telegram to Hitler:

My Fuehrer! In view of your decision to remain at your post in the fortress of Berlin, do you agree that I take over, at once, the total leadership of the Reich, with full freedom of action, at home and abroad, as your deputy in accordance with your decree of 29 June 1941? If no reply is received by ten o'clock tonight, I shall take it for granted that you have lost your freedom of action and shall consider the conditions of your decree as fulfilled, and shall act for the best interest of our country and our people. You know what I feel for you in this gravest hour of my life. Words fail me to express myself. May God protect you, and speed you quickly here in spite of it all.
Your loyal

—Hermann Goering

The telegram was given to Martin Bormann, now Hitler's closest confidant in the bunker. For years Bormann had hated Goering. Now he had exactly what he wanted. Triumphantly, he took the telegram to the shaking *Fuehrer*. He pointed to the ultimatum—"ten o'clock tonight." Not only had the fat clown traitorously tried to open negotiations with the Allies but now he wanted the *Fuehrer's* sacred post.

Hitler exploded with animal rage. Send a telegram, he ordered Bormann, informing Goering that his action represented high treason to National Socialism and its leader, that the penalty was death, but that Goering would be excused from this extreme punishment because of his earlier services to the Party. He must resign at once. Answer yes or no.

The next day came the official announcement from the besieged bunker—the *Reichsmarschall* had resigned from all his offices. Goering was arrested and taken to the fortress at Obersalzberg.

Bormann, highly satisfied, sent an order to the fortress commander urging him to execute "the traitors of April 23." He told the man to do his duty—his life and honor depended on it. But the commandant refused to recognize Bormann's authority.

Goering was spared but he was disconsolate. He apparently believed that he was only fulfilling the *Fuehrer's* orders when he sent his fateful telegram.

In the second part of his Political Testament, dated 4:00 A.M., April 29, 1945, Hitler started with the bitter words:

> Before my death I expel the former *Reichsmarschall* Hermann Goering from the Party and deprive him of all rights which he may enjoy by virtue of the decree of June 29, 1941, and also by virtue of my statement in the *Reichstag* on September 1, 1939. I appoint in his place *Grossadmiral* Doenitz, President of the Reich and Supreme Commander of the Armed Forces.

When Goering heard of Hitler's suicide, he exclaimed to his wife: "He's dead, Emmy! Now I shall never be able to tell him that I was true to the end."

On May 9, 1945, Goering was captured by troops of the United States Seventh Army. Expecting to be treated as an honorable foe, he demanded a "man-to-man talk" with Gen. Dwight Eisenhower. Instead, he was astonished to be brought to Nuremberg to stand trial before the International Military Tribunal as a war criminal.

In custody at Nuremberg, Goering tried to rehabilitate his role as Hitler's loyal champion. At the same time he attempted to pull rank on his fellow prisoners, insisting that they obey him. He, Goering, was in charge now. His response to the Tribunal's indictment was: "The victor will always be the judge, and the vanquished the accused." He was being tried, he complained, only because Germany had lost the war.

In his cell Goering protested to prison psychologist G. M.

Gilbert: "*Gott in Himmel! Donnerwetter nochmal!* I can't stand there like a louse and call the *Fuehrer* a millionfold murderer. He was more than a person to us. I swore my loyalty to him and I cannot go back on my word."

Aggression? "Certainly, I rearmed Germany until we bristled. I'm only sorry that we did not rearm still more. Of course, I considered our treaties as so much toilet paper. I wasn't running a girl's finishing school. The Nazi Party was the only one to say, 'To hell with Versailles!' while the others were crawling and appeasing. Sure, I was willing to go to war to restore Germany's power."

Atrocities: "I just want to defend myself on one point where my honor is involved—I never gave command for these atrocities. Do you suppose that I'd have believed it if somebody came to me and said there were freezing experiments on human guinea pigs—or the people were forced to dig their own graves and be mowed down by the thousands? I would have said: 'Get the hell out of here with that fantastic nonsense!' My God! I shrugged it off as enemy propaganda."

Patriotism: Whatever he did, Goering insisted, he did for his country.

Morality? Code of honor? "Sure, you can talk about one's word of honor when you deliver goods in business. But when it is a question of the interests of the nation? Phooey! Then morality stops. That is what England has done for centuries; America has done it; and Russia is still doing it. *Herr Gott!* When a state has a chance to improve its position because of the weakness of a neighbor, do you think it will stop at any squeamish consideration of keeping a promise? It's a statesman's duty to take advantage of such a situation for the good of his country." So much for the Nazi code of morality.

In the witness box, Goering's nervous tension betrayed itself by trembling hands and jerky facial expressions. He now played the role of martyred patriot. He refused to recognize the authority of the court. "Whatever happens in our country does not concern you in the least. If five million Germans were killed, that is a matter for Germans to settle and our state policies are our own business. This is presumptuousness unique in history."

After describing his early life, Goering told how he had helped build the Nazi Party and promoted its political and military power. He described how Hitler solved unemployment, rearmed the country, and annexed Austria, for all of which he, Goering, claimed a major share of credit and responsibility. He testified about his role in the Czechoslovak affair and in the Polish and Norwegian campaigns. He claimed that the *Luftwaffe* attacks on Warsaw, Rotterdam, and Coventry were simply necessary and fully justified acts of war.

On cross-examination by Prosecutor Robert H. Jackson, Goering claimed that he was a moderating force on the Jewish question. He denied looting art treasures from occupied countries by the trainload: he was only building a collection for the future cultural interest of the State. Use of slave labor? Confiscation of food and property? He was only working for the good of his country.

The judgment of the Court was explicit: "The evidence showed that after Hitler, Goering was the most prominent man in the Nazi regime. Until their relations deteriorated, he had tremendous influence with Hitler. There is nothing to be said in mitigation. For Goering was often the moving force, second only to his leader. He was the leading war aggressor; he was the director of the slave labor program and creator of the oppressive program against the Jews and other races, at home and abroad. All these crimes he has frankly admitted. On some specific cases there may be conflict of testimony, but in terms of the broad outline his own admissions are more than sufficiently wide to be conclusive of his guilt. His guilt is unique in its enormity. The record discloses no excuses for this man."

Verdict: guilty on all four counts—conspiracy to prepare aggressive war; crimes against the peace; war crimes; and crimes against humanity.

Sentence: death by hanging.

It was midnight, October 15, 1946, at the prison in Nuremberg. Within an hour after the scheduled reading of the sentences to eleven condemned Nazis in their cells, Goering was to be led out to a nearby small gymnasium building in the jail yard. He would lead the parade to the scaffold. Neither Goering nor any of the other condemned prisoners had been told previously that they were going to be executed that morning.

Colonel Burton C. Andrus, American officer in charge of security, walked across the prison yard to read the sentences of death. How Goering knew that this was to be his last day on earth and how he managed to conceal a poison vial on his person remain mysterious. Although watched by a guard, he bit the hidden cyanide capsule and fell dead seconds before Colonel Andrus reached his cell.

Psychohistorians and specialists in the behavorial sciences do not find it easy to assess the character of this extraordinary human being. There was a combination of many different motivations, including greed, overweening ego, and a don't-give-a-damn syndrome. A distinguished war hero, revered by his people, turns political gangster and earns global scorn. Captured by his enemies, he bellows his hatred at them, and then in a final gesture of contempt, cheats them of the satisfaction of delivering him to the hangman.

Hitler's No. 2 man remains the perfect example of ambition gone berserk. Goering would allow nothing to stand in the way of his inordinate desire for power, wealth, and fame. Along the way he rejected any sense of morality or decency. His ambition fed on strange stuff. He would live the life of a power broker and a luxurious Sybarite and heaven help any mortal who stood in his way. Gustave Naudaud recognized the syndrome in his homily: "Ambition ruins all mankind."

At the same time, the obese one remained a confirmed cynic. He had contempt for anyone and anything in what he regarded as the higher comedy of life. Unlike the fanatical Goebbels or the addlepated Hess, who saw Hitler as a Teutonic god, Goering's sense of loyalty to the *Fuehrer* was artificial and strictly practical. He was skeptical of Nazi ideology but he was willing to go through the motions of *Fuehrer*-worship to nourish his own ambition.

Prone to the pendulum of euphoria-depression, Goering was a man of psychic contradictions. He could enthusiastically shoot animals at his hunting lodge, and then react with horror when a visiting royal guest insisted on having the beasts crowded together for better targets. He could become Grandpa Charm in the presence of children, but then lapse into cold detachment when Jewish boys and girls were herded off for "special treatment." He could utter praise about German honor, and then loot the museums of Europe for precious works of art. He could appear before the public as a gentle war hero, and then push his ample weight around as a brutal buccaneer.

When trapped in his cell at Nuremberg, Goering revealed the extent of his own cynicism and simultaneously the nature of his character. When architect Albert Speer testified about a possible attempt on the life of Hitler, Goering dropped his usual pose of jocularity and exploded in venom: "Damn that stupid fool, Speer. Did you see how he disgraced himself in court today? How could he stoop so low as to do such a rotten thing to save his lousy neck? To think that Germans will be so rotten to prolong this filthy little life—to piss in front and crap behind a little longer! *Herr Gott! Donnerwetter!* Do you think I give that much of a damn if I get executed or drown, or crash in a plane, or drink myself to death?"

Goering answered his own question when he bit the cyanide capsule.

2

MASS MURDERER
HEINRICH HIMMLER

*What happens to a Russian or a Czech does not interest
me in the slightest.*

—Heinrich Himmler

Greek philosopher Diogenes Laertius said it: "If appearances
are deceitful, then they do not deserve any confidence when they
assert what appears to them to be true." The words are precise
when applied to the case of Heinrich Himmler, twentieth-century
mass murderer extraordinary.

Heinrich Himmler looked for all the world like a stereotypical
schoolteacher or filing clerk, his pince-nez spectacles hiding
beady eyes, a weak chin, and vacuous expression defined on a
most ordinary face. His benign appearance and inane manner
seemed to mandate a destiny of anonymity.

But behind the bland exterior was one of the most cold-blooded
personalities of all time—the architect of the Holocaust. A one-
time chicken farmer and fertilizer salesman, Himmler was more
responsible than any other member of Hitler's court for the death
of millions. He was head of the notorious *Gestapo*, the Secret

State Police, and later established and commanded the concentration and extermination camps in which those declared enemies of the Reich were imprisoned and liquidated.

Ironically, Himmler could not stand the sight of human blood. On an inspection tour of one of the death camps he became nauseated and excused himself from witnessing the mass executions. He was wracked by spasms of stomach colic that incapacitated him for a time, but he remained fanatically committed to the task he and Hitler had set for the nation.

What possible explanation can there be for the character and career of this callous murderer? What motives can be found in his early life that led to crimes that stagger the imagination? What was the origin of the instinct for destruction that led this man to supervise the killing of millions of human beings?

Unfortunately, here again the search for motivation in Himmler's early life by experts in abnormal psychology has led to no satisfactory conclusions. There is little clarification to be found in the various schools of psychoanalysis, either in Sigmund Freud with his theories of consciousness, intrapsychical conflict, or infantile sexuality; in Carl Jung with his synthetic psychology; in Alfred Adler's concept of the neurotic's inferiority complex; or in harry Stack Sullivan's generalized idea of interpersonal relations.

This kind of search leads into essentially abstract soil from which only doubtful conclusions can be drawn. The man seemed normal enough in his early days. There were no discernible neurotic mechanisms. Like millions of other young Germans, his early life conformed to accepted standards. There was no apparent motivation in his youth toward mass murder.

On his part, the psychohistorian, without scientific tools, must search elsewhere in environmental conditions, always with the danger of passing beyond the canons of science and entering the realms of both philosophy and mysticism. He finds one overwhelming fact emerging from the complex of influences working on this seemingly colorless young life. Himmler was the ultimate product of a system that produced the unthinking robot, the perfect yes-man.

That necessitates a brief journey through the halls of recent history. The eighteenth-century "Enlightenment," the Age of Reason, centering in the Western world, rejected the medieval Age of Faith and its union of church and state and opted in its place a new society based on liberty, equality, fraternity, constitutionalism, parliamentarianism, and sovereignty of the people. This last item—*sovereignty of the people*—was of critical importance in setting a way of life for democratic peoples.

But not in Germany. Here the waves of the Enlightenment moved harmlessly across the disunited German states. The men who guided German destiny turned down Rousseau's sovereignty of the people as impractical and turned instead to the Hegelian concept of primacy of the state. The German philosopher saw the state as the consummation of man's goals. The state, he said, was the necessary starting point whence the spirit rises to an absolute existence in the spheres of art, religion, and philosophy.

Unfortunately for Germans, and tragic in its implications, the interpretation of Hegel's glorification of the state took on a quality that was bound to cause trouble. Germans began to worship the state as the be-all and end-all of existence. They had no understanding of, or special desire for, sovereignty of the people. Both the German educational system and family home life were geared to this kind of state worship. In the late nineteenth and early twentieth centuries the German educational system, from kindergarten to universities, was controlled by Hegelian-trained teachers and professors.

In the German society in which Himmler grew up, obedience was a prime virtue. To be a good citizen meant to do what one was told. Problems could be solved only by listening to the *Obrigkeit*, which was authoritative, magisterial officialdom. Obedience to proper authority was considered an absolute necessity.

Himmler was a product of this system. But in his case the reaction went far beyond the normal process of doing what one was told to do. For him, obedience as a tool of law and order was perverted somewhere along the line into an indifferent willingness to go far beyond the boundaries of normal human conduct. In his macabre job of extermination, Himmler saw himself only as following the orders of Adolf Hitler, the proper, lawful authority. He felt no sense of brutality, no feeling of horror or guilt. He was only performing his duty and the responsibility was not his concern. His was not to reason why. Hitler would decide. The *Fuehrer* had spoken and he, Himmler, was only the *Fuehrer*'s right arm. He would have done the same if he had been ordered to kill his grandmother, or all bald-headed men, or those whose names began with an A or a Z. The man-god of

Berchtesgaden was always right. It was Himmler's job, as he saw it, to carry out Hitler's order to the best of his ability. One did not question the master. When his henchmen rebelled at the gruesome task of mass murder, Himmler insisted that they not betray their *Fuehrer*.

This obedience syndrome presented by psychohistorians is one possible explanation for Himmler's behavior. There may well be other reasons beyond wild guesswork, but they are difficult to find. We have the annoying case here of the transformation of what seemed to be a young man of normal habits into a ruthless, efficient engineer of death, without pity and indifferent to cruelty.

Heinrich Himmler was born on October 7, 1900, at Landshut, near Munich, the son of Bavarian schoolmaster Gerhard Himmler. It was said that his parents were well-liked and enjoyed the respect of their neighbors. The senior Himmler had been tutor to one of the members of the royal Bavarian court. With the prestige of this connection and with his lectures at the University of Munich, Gerhard Himmler won the deference and esteem of the people in his community.

Heinrich, the second son between Gebhard and Ernst, was a shy, introverted child with weak eyes and a tender stomach. He was known for his kindness to little old ladies and often helped them with their shopping packages. He was brought up as a devout Catholic, like young Hitler, and he was careful to attend mass regularly. He received an ordinary education and seemed to be a bright student much the same as others of his status. He was, however, a loner, who never aspired to be a leader among other boys. This characteristic carried over into his adult life. Later, when he was thrust into posts of important leadership, he preferred to delegate responsibility to others.

There were other signs of personality traits that were to emerge considerably strengthened in adulthood. As a youngster, Heinrich showed signs of persistency. Without any musical talent, he spent ten years during his early life trying to learn to play the piano, with no success whatever in solving the mystery of black and white keys. A precise and fussy youth, he paid close attention to his stamp collection and regularly used dumbbells to strengthen his weak muscles.

How and why young Heinrich developed a hatred for Jews remains a mystery. It is a major task to understand human behavior, which is as inexplicable as life itself. Himmler's later urge to kill Jews may well have stemmed from atavistic causes, a reversion to primitive behavior. We do not know. Certainly there was little in his youth to explain his later conduct as executioner of designated human beings. He was to share Hitler's compulsion to rid the world of what he saw as a pestilential enemy.

A clue may be found in the anti-Semitic atmosphere of the Munich cafes where Heinrich, even as a young man, acquired a sense of contempt for the Jews he saw around him. Like other Bavarian boys, he used the term "Jew louse" or other insults when he saw an elderly Jew in caftans walking down the street. His attitude, again like that of Hitler, was later transformed into cold hatred.

Most of all—and this was an accurate signal for his future—young Heinrich was motivated by a fanatical regard for order and discipline. As a boy he always played according to the rules of the game. One always did what one was told to do and one must be obedient to authority. This trait, which he saw as absolutely necessary for a decent life, became his guide for the rest of his life.

Heinrich was a student at a lower level when the Great War began in 1914. He was too young to serve when hostilities began, but after three years he was assigned to the 11th Bavarian Infantry Regiment until November 1918. For most of the time he was an officer-cadet, but the Armistice came before he could be commissioned. He was happy in his military service. The kind of order he craved was to be found within the strict discipline of army life. As an orderly room clerk, he seemed to find his true vocation. He could deal with thick card index files and compile thorough case histories of his comrades. It was effective basic training for the later Grand Inquisitor of the *Gestapo* and the driving force behind the Holocaust.

After the war Heinrich enrolled at Munich Technical High School as a major in agriculture. He later enrolled at the University of Munich. He studied chemistry, soil fertilization, and plant biology, subjects he was later to use in his genocidal extermination of "inferior races." Because of his weakened body, he avoided most sports, but he did manage to win the respect of his fellow-students by taking part in duels, which left him with a small but coveted scar. He bore that facial disfigurement proudly for the rest of his life.

On leaving the university with a diploma in agriculture, Himmler bought a small chicken farm and worked on the side as a fertilizer salesman. Meanwhile, like others who became leaders in the Nazi movement, he joined a rightist paramilitary organization in the *Freikorps* as a member of the *Reichskriegsflagge* (Reich War Flag). In the unstable early days of the Weimar Republic even the Allied Control Commission tolerated these secret units because they were useful in combatting continued revolutionary threats to the Weimar regime.

In early 1923 Himmler had his first contact with the Nazis when he met Ernst Roehm, who had been delegated to spread the doctrine of National Socialism among susceptible students. Roehm was also interested in acquiring homosexual partners, but was not attracted by the straight-laced Himmler. Thus far, Himmler had indicated little interest in politics other than a desire for an end to what he saw as the iniquitous Treaty of Versailles. But now he was drawn to the Hitler movement, which to him meant salvation for his Fatherland.

Himmler took part in the famous first episode in Nazi history—the Munich Beer-Hall *Putsch* of November 8 and 9, 1923. While serving as a salesman for the fertilizer factory of Stickstoff located at Schleissheim, a few miles north of Munich, he joined the march of the attempted *Putsch*. Eyewitnesses described how he stood behind wire barricades with the Nazi standard in the crook of his arm and a belligerent frown on his ordinarily passive face.

Losing his job with the Stickstoffs, Himmler turned to minor work with the Nazi Party. He now began to dream of political advancement. He tried to get Hitler and one of the leader's most bitter enemies, Gregor Strasser, interested in him. His persistence was rewarded. Strasser, who had set up an office in a single room in Himmler's native town, took Himmler on as an office assistant. In this post Himmler began to collect confidential reports made by spies on party members.

The ambitious Himmler began to see opportunity for himself in the differences between boss Strasser and Hitler. He began to transmit confidential information about Strasser and other party members to Hitler. At the same time he transferred his interest in hatching chickens to Hitler's scheme of breeding a Nazi elite and a super-race of Aryan Nordics.

Meanwhile, unsuspecting Strasser had appointed Himmler his deputy as district organizer of the party in Bavaria. Himmler was delighted by his new title of *Ortsgruppenleiter* (local branch leader). He was also given the post of second-in-command of a unit of the *SA* called the *Schutzstaffel*, or *SS*, the Shock Troops or Elite Guards who originally were assigned to protect Hitler and other Nazis.

In his post with the *SS*, Himmler told an interested Hitler: "If I had the power to rule this magnificent body of men, I could help perpetuate the Nordic race forever. They could become the bulwark against that wave of Jewish influence which threatens to drown our beloved German people."

That was the kind of language Hitler wanted to hear. On January 6, 1929, to the astonishment of everyone in the party, he appointed the colorless Himmler *Reichsfuehrer-SS* (Reich Leader *SS*), one of the most important posts in Nazi officialdom. A kind destiny had propelled the pedantic little poultry farmer to the top of Hitler's movement.

At the time the *SS* was still subordinate to the *SA*, the Storm Troopers. It numbered fewer than three hundred members, but Himmler proceeded to build it into a combined private army and police force. By 1933, when Hitler became Chancellor of Germany, it reached a strength of 52,000.

Himmler was rapidly becoming known not only in party circles but throughout the Reich. Until 1934 he had worked under the shadow of Ernst Roehm, but when the purge of June 30, 1934, meant death for Roehm, Himmler rapidly augmented his own power. Within a month he had made the *SS* independent of the *SA*. This was Hitler's way of rewarding him for carrying out executions in the Roehm removal.

Even before the purge, Himmler began to take an interest in a police apparatus. In April 1934 he took an important step in his drive for power when Goering appointed him chief deputy of the Prussian *Gestapo*. He would not build up a police empire of his own. He would utilize the *Gestapo* and make it a machine of terror as well as the scourge of Europe.

Meanwhile, Himmler's personal life was taking on a complexion far removed from the prissy character of his youth. In 1928 he married the daughter of a West Prussian landowner. Margarete Boden, seven years his senior, awakened his interest in homeopathy (doctrine of curing disease with very minute doses of medicine that in a healthy person would produce a condition like that of the disease treated), mesmerism (hypnotism or animal magnetism), and herbalism (knowledge of plants). On his own part, Himmler neglected both wife and family and fathered several illegitimate children. Apparently his early concept of the moral life was changing. As a youth he had written his brother: "I am determined to remain chaste until marriage, however much I might be tempted. A real man will love his woman as his wife whose feet he longs to kiss and who gives him strength never to falter even in the worst strife, the strength she gives him, thanks to her childlike purity." Himmler was an obstinate stickler for purity.

As he ascended the Nazi ladder, Himmler surrounded himself with a crowd of astrologers, masseurs, and fake anthropologists who bolstered his idea of racial supremacy. Until his suicide in 1945 he believed that the mass slaughter of human beings and the breeding of a new Teutonic race would result in the creation of a Nordic race of supermen.

At first the *Gestapo* was controlled by Goering, but when the rotund one was named Minister of Aviation, the unit became an arm of the *SS* under the seemingly mild-mannered Himmler. However, there was nothing soft about the chicken farmer turned Nazi professional. Under Himmler's guidance, the *Gestapo* became an instrument of terror. It was supposed to be concerned with the detection and prevention of crime, but in Himmler's hands it was used to destroy dissent and opposition to the Hitler regime. Himmler's secret police tracked down and eliminated all complainers and dangerous opponents. This was standard operating procedure in the Nazi world.

Himmler organized the *Gestapo* until it extended throughout the country. Autonomous, with its own legal system, its powers exceeded that of any law court. It controlled the lives, freedom, and property of everyone. It hunted down Jews, Marxists, and Bolsheviks. It snatched unfortunates who dared tell an anti-Nazi joke. The German public lived in dread of its agents, who could knock on the door in the middle of the night and take terrified prisoners to headquarters for interrogation and torture in its cellars.

Himmler's *Gestapo* brought crooked cross, double cross, murder, and blackmail to the German people. After the war, the International Military Tribunal at Nuremberg declared Himmler's organization to be criminal because of its participation in war crimes and crimes against humanity.

Meanwhile, Himmler went about the business of methodically building up and training the *SS*. He rejected any member suspected of racial impurity and insisted that every *SS* man produce documentary evidence of his Aryan forebears for three generations. The former army clerk was euphoric with his filing cabinets and card indexes. What he needed now was a proper source of help. Although in a position of authority in the Nazi world, he set out on the task of finding an assistant on whom he could rely for the dirty work of his beloved *SS*. For him, young Reinhard Heydrich was a fine specimen of the Teutonic hero of impeccable Aryan purity. The man was tall, handsome, and sadistic. He knew exactly what Himmler wanted and he was prepared to give it to him.

What Himmler did not know at the time was that Heydrich was besmirched by an indelible stain—he was suspected of having Jewish ancestors. Later the boss would have to make herculean efforts to remove Heydrich's sullied ancestry. In an interview with Hitler, both agreed that this "highly gifted man" must be retained. In this case, his non-Aryan origins were extremely useful. He would always be grateful that he had not been expelled and he would follow orders blindly. So much for Hitler's boasted Aryan-Nordic "racial purity."

Together the fussy dove-turned-hawk and his power-hungry assistant made the *SS* the most powerful organization of its kind in the Third Reich. Himmler and Heydrich, devotees of *Gründlichkeit*, German thoroughness, accumulated a vast number of dossiers in their filing cabinets.

Himmler saw his *SS* men as breeding bulls for the improvement of the race. In a speech he delivered in the midst of the war he told of his heartfelt wish: "It must be a matter of course that the most copious breeding should be by our *SS* Order, by this racial elite of the German people. In twenty or thirty years we must really be able to furnish the whole of Europe with this leading class." Heydrich, unfortunately, could not be utilized for the program: he had already been assassinated by Czech patriots.

By 1936 Himmler had engineered the absorption of the *Ge-*

stapo into the *SS*. Soon he was in control of the entire police apparatus. In June 1936 Hitler appointed him chief of the German police, which included not only the *Gestapo* but all uniformed police, a total of nearly three million men by the end of 1942. This was something unique in German history. The entire police force had been placed under Himmler's *SS*, now virtually a state within a state.

The little man with his index cards was now, after Hitler, one of the most powerful men in the Nazi Reich. In his office of *Reichsfuehrer-SS* and as police chief he held control over the entire German people.

Secure in his post of authority, Himmler began to ape his *Fuehrer* by mounting the lecture platform. He would pay homage to the leader and to his own *SS*. In a long rambling speech delivered on National Farmers' Day in Goslar in November 1935, he spoke at length on the "principles and virtues" of his *SS*. His "great corps" could only fulfill its duty if it understood and carried out all the measures set up for it by the *Fuehrer*. The speech was a revealing index of what went on in Himmler's mind.

Himmler began his talk by denouncing Bolshevism as organized and led by Jews. He described the competition between humanity and subhuman life, between human beings and Jews. It was a struggle between life and death, as natural a law as any other plague, such as the battle between the pest bacillus against the healthy body. The Jew, Himmler went on to say with a bow in Hitler's direction, was the eternal enemy, no matter what mantle he wore or what organization he operated. "We always see it in his bloody hand. We see it when mothers and daughters were burned into ashes after witch trials. We see it in the Inquisition when the Spaniards were depopulated. We see it in the terrible Thirty Years' War, when twenty-four millions of Germans were cut down to a hungry four million."

Himmler's interpretation of history was unique. He saw the Reign of Terror in the French Revolution as the work of Free Masons, "that excellent Jewish organization." The Russian Revolution of 1917, he charged, was triggered by the Jew Kerensky, who went on to overthrow the last Czar and prepared the way for Bolshevism. The way Kerensky was treated, said Himmler, illustrated Aryan decency. Kerensky's Jewish mother had been condemned to death because of her anarchistic activities, but she was given her life by the mother of the last Czar because she was pregnant with this Kerensky. That was it—Aryan decency spared Kerensky.

After this extraordinary lesson in history, Himmler went on to discuss his sacred *SS* and the measures set up for it by the *Fuehrer*. He described its first guiding principle as "the knowledge of the true value of the blood and the elite race." It was necessary to concentrate on the choice of physical specimens who came closest to the goal of Nordic-oriented humans. It was important to consider physical characteristics such as height and outward appearance. This principle had become sharper as the years went by. Himmler made it plain that he would not remain inactive in promoting this concept.

Himmler's second principle was that his *SS* men retain as their current and permanent characteristic the will to freedom [*sic!*] and the will to fight. (Himmler was proficient in Nazi double-speak.)

The third principle—*SS* men must be imbued with the ideas of loyalty and honor. Both were inseparable. The *Fuehrer* had provided a guiding light: "All honor comes from loyalty." Many things, as they concerned the *SS* man, could be forgiven on this earth, but never violations of loyalty. "He who injures the concept of loyalty cuts himself off from our society. For loyalty is a matter of the heart, never of the brain. The heart must continue to beat, and when it stops, man dies, just as a people dies when it loses its sense of loyalty."

The fourth principle, Himmler told his audience, was obedience, which was absolute and came from the free will. Obedience was the key to National Socialist *Weltanschauung*, its world view, a way of life that never hesitated for an instant but blindly followed every order of the *Fuehrer*. Score again for the Nazi obedience syndrome.

Himmler reminded his hearers about the oath taken by all *SS* men as well as by the military forces: "I swear before God this holy oath, that I shall give absolute confidence to the *Fuehrer* of the German Reich and people, Adolf Hitler, the Supreme Commander of the *Wehrmacht*, and as a courageous soldier will be ready at all times to lay down my life for this man."

Himmler closed his speech by boasting that "We, the *Schutzstaffel*, have come to life on the *Fuehrer's* command, and we have grown and prospered. Every one of us who wears the black tunic, no matter what his station in life—worker or sportsman or official or soldier—understands this. Everyone of us knows that he does not stand alone but represents the will of 200,000 men. He knows that he represents this black corps and its sense of nobility and honor. Bolstered by our principles and laws, we march forward as a soldierly National Socialist order of Nordic men, and as a sworn community of racial comrades who believe in their future. We want to be the forerunners of those who work for the eternal life of the German people."

This sort of speech, with its grotesquely inaccurate history and its appeal to nobility and honor, was again exactly what the master wanted to hear. In every detail it mimicked Hitler's own ignorance of history and his blurred code of honor. When the war began in 1939, the *Fuehrer* appointed "faithful Heinrich" *Reichskommisar für die Festigung deutschen Volkstums* (Reich Commissar for the Consolidation of German Nationhood). The gentle little ex-fertilizer salesman was now at the apex of his power. He was in charge of concentration camps administered by his *SS* men. He organized a supply of expendable labor for the camps. He was responsible for fifth-column activities of *SS* units in occupied countries. After the German invasion of the Soviet Union in June 1941, Himmler was given control over the political administration of occupied areas. He expanded his *SS* from three to thirty-five divisions until it rivaled the *Wehrmacht* (the regular army) itself. On August 25, 1943, he was made Minister of the Interior, with a strengthened grip on civil service and courts.

Most important was the new office at the top of the Nazi world. It had been a long pull—from Bavarian chicken farmer to grand inquisitor of the *Gestapo* to *Reichsfuehrer-SS* to Lord High Executioner for the *Fuehrer*. Himmler was to head the rationalized extermination process with the task of eliminating those "racial degenerates who stood in the way of Germany's regeneration." It was a post of honor in which Himmler would purge the Aryan-Germanic-Nordic race of its tainted elements. It was an "honorable and noble" task to which he would devote all his organizational ability. He took delight in the *Fuehrer's* gratitude for a task well done.

This was the Holocaust, the slaughter of millions of human beings in the most extraordinary race-cleansing process ever attempted in the recorded history of man. Heinrich Himmler, the

Fuehrer's loyal paladin, was in control of the gruesome proceedings.

Himmler had already gained experience as master of concentration camps set up in the early days of the Nazi regime—the first at Dachau near Munich in the south, the second at Buchenwald near Weimar in central Germany, and the third at Sachsenhausen near Berlin in the north. At first the camps were regarded as correction institutions where enemies of the state would be rehabilitated. They would be trained to conform.

Hitler changed his mind in the crucible of war. He would purge his Third Reich of its internal enemies by transforming concentration camps into extermination centers. He advocated terror to gain his end and he would allow no stupid bourgeois mollycoddlers to stand in his way. He designated Auschwitz, Birkenau, Treblinka, and Maidanek in Poland as death centers. Himmler's *SS* guards would reduce the inmates to subhuman conditions, work them beyond their capacity, and starve, humiliate, and torture them beyond endurance before sending them to gas ovens.

At the Wannsee Conference held on January 20, 1942, in a Berlin suburb, fifteen Nazi bureaucrats, chaired by Himmler's deputy Reinhard Heydrich, gathered to discuss the *Endlösung* (Final Solution). IT was planned to destroy all Jews in Europe, many of whom were already incarcerated in concentration camps. Caught in a struggle to the death with the Soviets, Hitler saw Jews as a hindrance to victory. He would eliminate them and in the process cleanse the Aryan "race."

Responsibility for the project was placed in Himmler's hands. Under his guidance, camps in Poland began to operate at full blast as Jews were sent in increasing numbers to the gas ovens. Victims were transported to what they believed were shower baths (*Brausebäder*). As they entered, amethyst-blue crystals of hydrogen cyanide were dropped through chamber vents to form hydrocyanic or prussic acid fumes. The special gas, known as Zyklon-B, was derived from an I.G. Farben patent of a strong disinfectant.

Order-minded Himmler decreed that careful records be kept of clothing, shoes, women's hair, and other by-products of the slaughter. Thousands of inmates—Communists, liberals, and Gypsies as well as Jews—died of disease and starvation in the camps. Horror and bestiality. Human beings were turned into scarcely living robots before being hustled off to the gas chambers.

Himmler was pitiless in his cruelty. He saw all Europe as a neglected animal farm that needed the elimination of poor and unhealthy stock by better reproduction methods. He would apply the fundamentals of chicken breeding to the human condition. "We Germans," he said, "are the only ones in the world who have a decent attitude to these human animals (*Menschentiere*), but it would be a crime against our own blood to worry about them." On another occasion he was even more specific: "Don't bedbugs, rats, and other vermin have to fulfill a purpose in life, too? And yet, don't human beings have the right to defend themselves against such vermin?"

The gentle soul visited one camp after another to see what liquidation was really like. On one occasion he spotted among the victims a man of about twenty with blue eyes and blond hair. Immediately before the executions were to begin, Himmler walked up to the doomed young man and asked him if he was a Jew.

"Yes," was the reply.

"Were both of your parents Jewish?"

"Yes."

"Do you have ancestors who were not Jews?"

"No," said the youth.

"Then I can't help you."

The man was led off to execution.

Himmler decided to make a speech to the SS guards assembled to greet him. "You *Einsatztruppen* (task forces)," he said, "are called upon to fulfill a repulsive [*sic!*] duty. But you are soldiers who have to carry out every order unconditionally. You have a responsibility before God and Hitler for everything that is happening. I myself hate this bloody business and I have been moved to the depths of my soul. But I am obeying the highest law by doing my duty. Man must defend himself against bedbugs and rats—against vermin."

After his speech Himmler visited a barracks of insane inmates and ordered his SS officers: "Do the humane thing and end the suffering of these people as soon as possible." He suggested the use of dynamite instead of shooting. Humane mind at work! The order was carried out with frightening results.

The extensive killings had a chilling effect on SS guards, many of whom drank themselves into insensibility before and after performing their gruesome tasks. Himmler made special efforts to console these men. Again and again he repeated one theme to his subordinates: there was an absolute need to overcome humanitarian instincts. They must relentlessly root out all opposition. They could remain "decent" in the process. "Most of you SS men will know what it means when a hundred corpses of executed persons lie there, when five hundred lie there, or when a thousand lie there. To have remained unrelenting and—apart from human weakness—to have remained decent, that has steeled us. This is a glorious page in the book of our history which has never been written and is never to be written."

Glorious page! Himmler pursued this lunatic notion throughout his career as Hitler's mass murderer. He would lead a complete biological reorganization of the German people on the basis of Mendelian law. He would breed a super race in an atmosphere of chivalry and discipline. It was a crime against German blood to worry about subhumans or assume that they were human.

German historian Joachim Fest gave this estimate of Himmler: "Crazy ideas of this sort exist on the lunatic fringe of every society in almost every epoch. Stable societies absorb those who hold them to a certain limited field of activity as founders of sects, quack doctors, or pamphleteers. It is only in a hopelessly disrupted society that a figure like Heinrich Himmler can acquire political influence; and only under a totalitarian government offering universal salvation could he come to hold the power that offered some prospect of putting his ideas into practice."

Fest's judgment is correct. Here was a sober man of meek demeanor and boasted common sense, qualities which, strangely, made it possible for him to reach the highest level of power in the Third Reich. His real nature emerged in his post of authority—a certified evil monster. Wherever he went he left behind him a bloody trail of misery and death. Fest labels him "the most dreadful combination of crackpot and manipulator of power, of quack and inquisitor, that history has ever known."

On one occasion, in late August 1942, Himmler attended a mass execution in an extermination camp to see firsthand the results of his campaign of "special treatment, sanitary measures, and natural diminution." The self-admitted champion of decency fainted on the spot, and subsequently suffered a hysterical fit. And Himmler, in his own view, was an honorable man.

As the war went on and Germany suffered one reverse after another, there was a shortage of labor for the war machine. Himmler now started a plan for "The Delivery of Anti-Social Elements to the *Reichsfuehrer-SS* to Be Worked to Death." He ordered privileged prisoners from concentration and extermination camps to labor on road construction, burying the dead in bombed-out cities, and the like. The victims were to work until they dropped dead from exhaustion and starvation.

At the same time, Himmler instructed his secretary to send a thousand toy balloons to Auschwitz to issue to incoming children before they were to be injected with phenol. The good family man would give the children pleasure before they went to their death.

By early 1945 Himmler was beginning to have doubts about his adored *Fuehrer*, now ensconced in the cloud-cuckoo land of his bunker under the Chancellery in Berlin. After an unsatisfactory conference on April 20 in the *Fuehrerbunker* (leader's bunker), Himmler went to his headquarters and began to negotiate with members of the International Red Cross about the Jewish question. At breakfast he met Count Bernadotte of Sweden. He assumed that he could have presented himself as the *de facto Fuehrer* of Germany in view of Hitler's incapacity, but he did not. He simply discussed technical details such as the release of Polish women from Ravensbrück concentration camp; even then he would have to obtain Hitler's approval. Indecisive, he was trying to save his own life in a delicate situation.

In another interview with Count Bernadotte on April 22, Himmler told his host: "The *Fuehrer's* great life is drawing to a close." Hitler was in Berlin to perish together with its inhabitants. The city would fall within a matter of days. Until then, Himmler had been unable to break his oath to the *Fuehrer*. The situation was now changed. He urged Bernadotte to pass along his offer of surrender to the Swedish government for submission to the Western Allies. On no account would he give up to the Russians. He wrote a personal letter to Bernadotte to take to Stockholm as proof of his offer.

On April 27 Bernadotte brought news that neither Himmler nor a limited surrender was acceptable to the Allies. Himmler was crushed. He saw himself as the heir-apparent to Hitler's throne. As *Reichsfuehrer-SS* he had his own private army, he held important offices, he had a record of long service to the *Fuehrer* in absolute loyalty, and he had even a program for peace. Now all was lost.

That same day the news of Himmler's negotiations with Count Bernadotte was brought to Hitler. Hugh R. Trevor-Roper recorded the terrible reaction: " 'He raged like a madman,' says Hanna Reitsch; 'his color rose to a heated red, and his face was almost unrecognizable.' This was the last, the unkindest cut of all: *der treue Heinrich*—faithful Heinrich—had betrayed him; the one Nazi leader whose loyalty had always been above suspicion had stabbed him in the back. As the news spread around the bunker, the obedient chorus again echoed the voice of its leader, and men and women competed to denounce the traitor."

For Hitler the report on Himmler was a signal for the end. He ordered the arrest of his once faithful paladin. "A traitor," he shouted, "must not succeed me as *Fuehrer!* See to it that he does not." In the second part of his Political Testament he made it official: "Before my death I expel from the Party and from all his offices the former *Reichsfuehrer-SS* and Reich Minister of the Interior Heinrich Himmler. . . . Goering and Himmler, by their secret negotiations with the enemy, without my knowledge or approval, and by their illegal attempts to seize power in the state, quite apart from their treachery to my person, have brought irreparable shame on the country and the whole people."

The chastened Himmler offered to serve under Grand Admiral Karl Doenitz, named by Hitler as his successor. The suggestion came from one who had hopes of supreme power for himself. Response negative.

On May 6, 1945, Doenitz dismissed Himmler from his government in a move that was calculated to win favor with the Allies. The former *Reichsfuehrer-SS*, who for so many years had held the power of life and death over millions of Europeans, wandered in a daze around the vicinity of Flensburg. The once-proud Nazi leader looked ill and was shabbily dressed. On May 21 he set out with eleven other *SS* officers to try to pass through the British and American lines and get to his native Bavaria. He shaved off his mustache, wore a black patch over his left eye, and donned a mended army uniform. With this disguise he hoped to avoid capture. Hitler's high priest had become a wandering shadow.

It did not work. The party was stopped the first day by British guards at a control point between Hamburg and Bremerhaven. The captain in charge reported that a small man who was being questioned removed a patch from his eye and put on a pair of spectacles. ''His identity was at once obvious and he said 'Heinrich Himmler' in a very quiet voice.''

Himmler was stripped and searched for concealed poison. Nothing was found. But he had hidden a vial of cyanide in a space between too teeth.

When a doctor who was examining him saw the black projection in Himmler's mouth, seemingly a carious tooth, the self-confessed champion of decency reacted with the most decent act of his entire life. He bit down on the capsule and swallowed the cyanide.

For twelve minutes there were frantic efforts to save Himmler's life by use of stomach pumps, emetics, and artificial respiration. Nothing was successful.

Reichsfuehrer-SS had tricked his captors and escaped Allied retribution for his crimes. In death, his face bore the same contortions of agony he had inflicted on countless victims in the extermination camps of Nazi Germany.

3

JULIUS STREICHER:
PORNOGRAPHER AND SADIST

"Purim Fest, 1946!"

—*Streicher on the gallows*

Decent Germans were not amused. They said of Julius Streicher that it was impossible to understand him if one had no sense of smell.

He was a short, squat, fiercely ugly little man with an obtrusive beer belly and totally bald head. He was seldom seen in public without a whip in his hand, and he was fond of boasting about the countless lashings he had meted out. Those who knew him spoke of the half-crazed look in his piercing eyes.

Blustering street-corner agitator, his raucous obscenities appalled many Germans unfortunate enough to cross his path. This depraved sadist was one of the most unsavory characters among the gang of disreputable misfits gathered around Adolf Hitler.

Julius Streicher, semi-literate, ignorant Jew-baiter and pornographer, rose to the top of the Nazi hierarchy. He became *Gauleiter* (district chief) of Franconia, was elected to membership in the *Reichstag*, and in the early days of the Hitler movement was named an honorary *SA* general. Anyone who dared to challenge the "King of Franconia" became eligible for prison and torture.

He was born in the village of Fleinhausen, Swabia, on February 12, 1885, the ninth child of a Roman Catholic primary school teacher. Little is known of his early life beyond the fact that he, too, became a teacher in a Nuremberg suburb. Before World War I he served as a one-year volunteer in the army, but behaved so badly that an entry was made in his paybook to the effect that he was never to be given a commission. Despite this warning, his combat record in a Bavarian unit during the war was so impressive that he was given the rank of lieutenant and awarded the Iron Cross, First and Second Classes, for bravery in action.

After the war, Streicher returned to Nuremberg to teach again in an elementary school. Limited in education and ambitious, he was dissatisfied with boring work in the classroom and began to turn to politics as more suitable for his energies. In 1919 he founded the German Socialist Party in Nuremberg, nominally a branch of a party founded by Alfred Brunner. He had finally found the right outlet for his talents in political agitation and organization. He lost no chance to speak before a crowd wherever he could find one.

Streicher's main interests were anti-Semitism, hatred of the Treaty of Versailles, and political power. In these goals he had a rival in Adolf Hitler, who had become member No. 55 of the German Workers' Party, and who had transformed that group into the *NSDAP*, the National Socialist German Workers' Party.

At first a bitter rival, Streicher changed his mind in the fall of 1922 when he first heard Hitler speak:

When he finished his speech, an inner voice had me get up. I arose and forced myself in the crowd to the speaker's desk. I went toward him and introduced myself. I spoke to him. *'Heil Hitler!* I heard your speech. I can only be the helper but you are the born leader. Here is my movement in Nuremberg.' On that evening I gave the movement which I created in Nuremberg to Adolf Hitler.

The gift doubled Hitler's following.

From then until 1939, when his star finally faded, Streicher was one of the most important men surrounding the *Fuehrer*. Hopelessly outstripped by Hitler in mass appeal, he gave up competition and became a loyal supporter.

Hitler was grateful. In *Mein Kampf* he praised Streicher as solemnly convinced of his mission and the future of his movement. "However, he came to recognize the greater power and stronger growth of the *NSDAP*. He ceased working for his own party and demanded that his followers join the victorious ranks of the NSDAP and to fight for the common cause. This was personally a hard but reasonable choice."

Streicher played a role in the Beer-Hall *Putsch* of November 8–9, 1923, when Hitler and his new Nazi Party attempted to seize political power. As soon as he heard of the coming *Putsch*, Streicher, unwilling to be left out of the revolution, rushed to Munich. On November 9, relays of speakers, Streicher among them as roving agitator, were haranguing clumps of people in sections of the Marienplatz. When Streicher, who had the largest audience, saw Hitler and his cohorts marching by to meet the police in a bloody encounter, he jumped to Hitler's right side and was there when a hail of bullets cut down the marchers. Streicher was arrested as one of the conspirators.

The collapse of the 1923 *Putsch* resulted in the temporary disintegration of the Nazi movement but Hitler, released from Landsberg Prison under an amnesty in December 1924, was soon hard at work reconstructing his Party. Streicher hailed Hitler's return to politics as a "gift of God," a judgment the *Fuehrer* never forgot.

By this time Streicher was *Gauleiter* of Franconia for the Nazi Party, a reward for his loyalty. Although he tried to hold on to his teaching post, he was having increasing difficulties. He insisted that his pupils greet him each day with *"Heil Hitler!"* and the Nazi salute. Later, in 1928, when charges were brought against him for conduct unbecoming a teacher, he was dismissed. He expressed great pride in this "achievement."

Meanwhile, Streicher acquired a reputation as an eccentric. With whip in hand, he strode through his district like an avenging master. He took pleasure in beating people in the presence of witnesses. On one occasion he visited the Nuremberg jail, where before two friends he administered a severe beating to a young prisoner. He reveled in such "exploits." He boasted of his skill as a fornicator, who took pleasure in blackmailing the husbands of women who were his mistresses. He was obnoxious by any standard. Brutish and violent, he advocated use of force as solution for any problem. A master rabble-rouser, he heaped scorn on his enemies both inside and outside the party.

Most of all, he wanted money. Dishonest and corrupt, he had no use for laws that barred his path to riches. He was to find the way by means of a notorious scandal sheet. The tradition was there. In the early days of the Weimar Republic, scandal magazines provided a lucrative source of income for journalists who cared little for the ethics of their profession. The pages of these sheets were filled with anonymous attacks on public officials and entertainers, with lurid accents on their sex life. This was for Streicher. Pornography paid off. Yellow journalism meant easy money.

In 1923 Streicher emerged as editor and publisher of *Der Stürmer (The Stormer)*, a weekly newspaper with its base in Nuremberg. It was journalism at its worst. Columns were filled with reports on sex scandals as well as almost hysterical paeans of praise for Hitler and Nazism. Illustrations invariably included cartoons of Jewish faces with grossly exaggerated features, or drawings of such subjects as blond Christian girls being raped by evil looking dark-haired Jewish boys.

At the top of his front page, Streicher gave title and subtitle: NUREMBERG WEEKLY DEDICATED TO THE STRUGGLE FOR TRUTH. A typical issue, June 1, 1934, had the headline:

JEWISH MURDER PLAN
Against Non-Jewish Humanity Discovered

Across the bottom of the page was Streicher's favorite aphorism:

DIE JUDEN SIND UNSER UNGLÜCK
(THE JEWS ARE OUR MISFORTUNE)

Another issue was devoted to Ritual Murder, with a front-page drawing of Jews slaughtering helpless Aryan infants. Streicher was an enthusiastic advocate of the allegation that Jews murdered non-Jews in order to obtain blood for the feast of Passover. Lurid articles featured a complex of deliberate lies, trumped-up accusations, and popular beliefs about the murder-lust of Jews and their bloodthirstiness. The charge was that Jews hated Christianity and mankind in general.

Der Stürmer went to grotesque lengths in its attacks on Jews. It attributed the destruction of the Zeppelin "Hindenburg" on May 6, 1937, in Lakehurst, New Jersey, to a Jewish plot. Editorials announced the discovery that Christ was not a Jew but an Aryan. No opportunity was missed to stir up the German public against what was called the Jewish menace.

Anti-Semitism was not new in Germany. Throughout the Middle Ages it flourished on German soil. In early modern times the great German theologian Martin Luther was noted for his strictures against the Jews. At the late nineteenth century, German political parties had anti-Semitic planks in their platforms, the only political parties in the world with such stated goals. But Streicher's brand of anti-Semitism went far beyond that of his predecessors.

Again and again *Der Stürmer* featured the *Protocols of the Elders of Zion*, a forgery professing to contain the minutes of a secret Zionist Congress aiming at the overthrow of Christian civilization. It was charged that an international Jewish government had met in Basel, Switzerland, simultaneously with the First Zionist Congress in 1897, and that the delegates had entered into a conspiracy to blow up major buildings in the capitals of Europe, destroy the Aryan race, and initiate a Jewish world-state.

It made no difference to Streicher that the *Protocols* were proven to be a forgery, that most of the document was copied from a French pamphlet published in 1864 as a polemic against Napoleon III. It was enough for him that the *Protocols* had been published in every European language as well as Japanese, Chinese, and Arabic. Henry Ford, the great American industrialist, printed the *Protocols* in his *Dearborn Independent*. That Ford ceased publication after a lawsuit was unimportant to Streicher. In his view, Nazi Germany knew what it was doing—the *Protocols* were officially recommended by authorities in the Third Reich for use in schools.

The pages of Streicher's paper consisted of one long diatribe against Jews. As early as 1938 he began to call for their total annihilation. At first he merely conducted a hate campaign against Jews and Jewry, but gradually his articles and editorials began to call for extermination of "root and branch." One leading article in September 1938 called the Jew a germ and a pest, not a human being but "a parasite, an enemy, an evildoer, a disseminator of disease who must be destroyed in the interests of mankind." Streicher had chosen the way of destruction.

Other articles in *Der Stürmer* charged that only when world Jewry had been eliminated would the Jewish problem be solved. Streicher printed a letter from a reader who compared Jews with a swarm of locusts that must be destroyed completely. Editorials predicted that fifty years hence the Jewish graves "will proclaim that this people of murderers and criminals has after all met its deserved fate."

The columns of *Der Stürmer* were specific. In May 1939, even before the outbreak of World War II, a leading article expressed this goal:

A punitive expedition must come against the Jews in Russia. A punitive expedition which will provide the same fate for them that every murderer and criminal must expect. Death sentence and execution. The Jews in Russia must be killed. They must be exterminated root and branch.

Between August 1941 and September 1944 *Der Stürmer* published many articles, including twelve by Streicher's own hand, calling for annihilation and extermination of Jews. Streicher was adamant:

If the danger of the reproduction of that curse of God in the Jewish blood is finally to come to an end, then there is only one way—the extermination of that people whose father is the devil. . . .

Whoever does what a Jew does is a scoundrel, a criminal. And he who repeats and wishes to copy him deserves the same fate: annihilation, death.

All this from a man who at his Nuremberg trial vehemently denied any knowledge about mass executions of Jews, and defended himself by insisting that the solution of "the Jewish problem" which he favored was strictly limited to the classification of Jews as aliens.

Week after week, month after month, the pages of *Der Stürmer* infected the German mind with the virus of anti-Semitism. The paper reached a circulation of 600,000 in 1935 and even more after that year. The obscene Nuremberg weekly, with its combined anti-Semitism and pornography, reflected the cultural atmosphere of the Third Reich. Readers were entranced with gory details of supposed Jewish ritual murders and unfortunate German girls violated by Jewish rapists.

For Adolf Hitler, who much preferred to talk rather than read, *Der Stürmer* was favorite reading matter. He went through each issue carefully, reveling in its dismal tales about Jewish sexual excesses and ritual murders. According to Konrad Heiden, Streicher spoke and acted aloud what Hitler secretly thought and desired. "Streicher was the embodiment of Hitler's subconscious."

For Streicher himself, the man who wallowed in filth and who made libertinism his religion, *Der Stürmer* was a golden sheet, an open sesame to fame and fortune. He did everything he could to promote the success of his paper. He used public health boards to publicize the more defamatory material. His paper made him an important man in the early days of the Nazi movement. Indeed, he became valuable to Hitler because he was raking in money from *Der Stürmer* as well as from various forms of blackmail. He had accumulated a fighting fund which, for practical purposes, meant the success or failure of the Nazi movement.

One issue of *Der Stürmer*, plus several pages of Hitler's *Mein Kampf*, should be enough to convince any skeptic as to what happened to German culture in the Third Reich.

In all his activities Streicher remained consistent on only two points: his loyalty to Hitler and his virulent anti-Semitism, from which he never retreated. His aversion was of monumental meanness. In a speech delivered before the Hitler Youth in 1935, he did all he could to infect the minds of his youthful listeners with hatred for Jews.

Only the Jews, he shouted, had remained victorious after the dreadful days of World War I. These were the people, he charged, of whom Christ said, "Its father is the devil." But young people, he said, should take heart. Hitler had appeared on the scene and the entire world took courage in the thought that the human race might be free again from this people, marked with the sign of

Cain, a people who had wandered around the world for centuries and millenia.

Streicher asked his boys and girls not to believe that the Jews were a chosen people because "a chosen people does not slay and torture animals to death." "A chosen people does not live by the sweat of others. A chosen people joins the ranks of those who live because they work. Don't ever forget that." Germans must fight Jews, "that organized body of world criminals against whom Christ, the greatest anti-Semite of all time, had fought."

And Pope Pius XI? Streicher claimed he had it "on good Italian authority" that Pius XI had Jewish blood.

The Jews, Streicher claimed, were fighting Germany. Foreign statesmen, he said, who were not friendly to the Third Reich were Jews, part-Jews, or somehow dominated by Jews.

Speaking at dedication ceremonies for the Wilhelm Gustloff Bridge in Nuremberg (Gustloff had been assassinated by a Jew), Streicher said: "Look at the path which the Jewish people has traveled for millenia: Everywhere murder, everywhere mass murder."

The moral? War to the death against Jews plotting the destruction of Germany.

In 1929 Streicher was elected to the Bavarian *Landtag* (Legislature) as a Nazi delegate from Franconia. In 1932 he was given the important post of preparing the annual Nuremberg rallies, also called the *Parteitage* (Party Days), designed to impress both the German public and foreigners with the strength and prestige of the Nazi movement. It was his task to persuade the world that National Socialism was the one true German religion and that Adolf Hitler was the messiah of the German people.

But things were not going well for Streicher in Franconia in the immediate days before Hitler's assumption of power. In the Bavarian province of Franconia, Streicher's domain, nearly the whole of the *SA* mutinied, after accusing *Gauleiter* Streicher of embezzling funds owed to the Storm Troopers' leadership. There was much criticism of his "nude culture" and his friendship with ex-convicts.

Streicher's behavior was causing much embarrassment. He was pitiless in his treatment of Jews. He had the hair clipped of girls who had been friendly with Jews and put the couples on display in amusement parks. He forced Jewish prisoners to eat grass which had previously been defouled. Even fellow Nazis were not amused. Despite the criticism, Streicher was returned to the *Reichstag* in the elections of January 1933. For him, this was reward for his efficient conduct in Franconia.

Soon after Hitler's assumption of power, a worldwide boycott of German goods began. Hitler replied by setting up a Central Committee for Counteracting Jewish Atrocity Tales and Boycotts. He made Streicher its chairman. Other members included Robert Ley, Heinrich Himmler, and Hans Frank. The idea was to strike back at German Jews for what was regarded as a global economic conspiracy against the Third Reich.

Streicher acted swiftly. On April 1, 1933, he ordered *SA* Storm Troopers to do sentry duty in every town and village in Germany, holding placards, challenging citizens, and with threatening looks cautioning them not to patronize Jewish stores. These "defensive guards," recruited from the brown-shirted *SA* and the black-shirted *SS*, were ordered to inform the public that the proprietor of the establishment was a Jew. Many eager guards smeared shop windows with swastikas and the word *"Jude!"* ("Jew!")

Jewish businessmen were frightened into selling their holdings at whatever price they could get. But the boycott was never really effective. Nazi harassment of Jewish business became a feast for the cameras of foreign reporters. The action was hurriedly called off when it became obvious that boycott was a double-edged economic weapon. Streicher's day of glory did not last long.

Streicher's campaign against the Jews prepared the way for the Nuremburg Laws of Citizenship and Race, also called the Ghetto Laws, by which the status of Jews in Nazi Germany was defined. German citizenship was withdrawn from all those "of non-German blood." The result was that Jewish physicians were excluded from hospitals, Jewish judges dismissed, and Jewish students thrown out of universities. Streicher took great pleasure in presiding over the destruction of Jewish synagogues, even before *Kristallnacht*, Crystal Night, the Night of Broken Glass, November 9, 1938, when terror attacks were made against synagogues and Jewish stores throughout Germany. The next day Streicher publicly justified the atrocities committed on that tragic night.

By this time Streicher's behavior was becoming even more embarrassing for the Nazi hierarchy. Though he still held Hitler's confidence, and though he was esteemed in some academic circles for his "scientific" support for anti-Semitism, he was loathed for his bizarre and eccentric personality. Despite all his titles, he had no real influence on policy making. Many party leaders thought it best to remove him from the limelight.

Accordingly, in 1939 he was dismissed from his post as *Gauleiter* of Franconia and was allowed to retire to his estate at Pleikersdorf. He still retained his editorship of *Der Stürmer*.

In exile Streicher continued his attacks on Jews and Judaism, for which Hitler was grateful. In December 1941, as revealed in his *Table Talk*, the *Fuehrer* went out of his way to express his gratitude to Streicher. He was pleased that Streicher, despite his many faults, had contributed much to the Nazi conquest of the masses. *Der Stürmer*, in Hitler's view, did a good job in exposing Judaism, but actually it did not go far enough. The Jews, Hitler said, were far more diabolical, unruly, and ignoble than Streicher had described in his paper.

As the war went on, Streicher was bored by lack of action. In the spring of 1945 as the Nazi war machine was lumbering to a halt, he sent a letter to Goebbels asking for some assignment in the Fatherland's extreme emergency and saying that he could no longer endure just to remain in his own house in the country. Goebbels went to Hitler on Streicher's behalf. The *Fuehrer* asked the Propaganda Minister whether he could give Streicher something to do. Perhaps he could be used in the *Werwolf*, the organization of guerrilla fighters then being set up in Germany in the closing days of the war. After all, said Hitler, Streicher was a man of great energy.

Goebbels wrote about it in his *Diaries*: "Streicher could make five-minute speeches which, however, I would have to revise beforehand. I will get in touch with him. In any case the *Fuehrer* would be happy if I could give Streicher some employment. At heart the *Fuehrer* is somewhat uncomfortable since Streicher is a man of stature who only once went off the rails. . . . He is more loyal than many people working in influential positions in the party and state today." It was too late. Nazi Party and Nazi State were approaching their death throes.

Streicher was brought before the Nuremberg Military Tribunal between November 1945 and October 1946. The blustering street bully, deprived of his riding whip, was changed in appearance. At the age of sixty, he gave the impression of a decrepit old man, perspiring profusely and muttering under his breath. But much of the old bravado was still there. He complained angrily to his guards that all his judges were Jews. His sense of brass-knuckled anti-Semitism was very much alive. He would never change his mind about what he called the Jewish menace.

Prison psychologists who examined the accused found that Streicher had an IQ of 102, the lowest intelligence of the twenty-one defendants. This was one of the few men Hitler addressed with *"Du"* ("thou"), the expression of familiarity Germans used when speaking to a friend.

The prematurely aged defendant was indicted on Count One: Crimes Against Peace, and Count Four: Crimes Against Humanity. He was accused of writing and publishing his "propaganda of death": "Streicher's incitement to murder and extermination, at the time when the Jews in the East were being killed under the most horrible conditions, constitutes persecution on political and racial grounds in connection with war crimes and constitutes a crime against humanity."

Who, me? The prisoner found himself charged with crimes of which he claimed he was completely innocent. In his defense Streicher insisted that it was all the *Fuehrer's* fault: Hitler had such a power of hypnotic suggestion that the entire German people believed in him. In his final speech before the court, he denounced Hitler's "mass killing of Jews." Sudden end to Streicher's oft repeated pledge of loyalty to the *Fuehrer*.

Among the twenty-one shattered defendants in the dock, only two could be regarded as clinically abnormal—Rudolf Hess and Julius Streicher. Both, Hess with his real or feigned amnesia, and Streicher, the rabble-rousing, whip-carrying pornographer, had failed even in Nazi society.

Streicher was a restless prisoner in his cell at Nuremberg. In captivity he reacted like a caged lion. Even before receiving his death sentence, he had terrible nightmares and shouted imprecations in his sleep. Other prisoners in nearby cells complained again and again about his behavior. The caged animal struck back furiously. He denounced the trial as "a triumph for World Jewry." He harangued his guards about the injustice being done to him. He repeated all the old accusations. The Jews always lived from the blood of other peoples. They were in desperate need of ritual murders. It was absolutely necessary to free the European continent from Jewish destroyers of people. The Jewish world tormenters, he said, must be eliminated. He saw it as a matter of self-preservation.

Yet, to his judges Streicher indicated that he hoped for acquittal on charges that he denounced as ridiculous. He was only a cog, he said, in a gigantic machine.

The angered prisoner was aware that his days of power were long past. It now became apparent that he had to face retribution for his behavior in a swastika-oriented society. Something had gone deadly wrong in his life.

Justice Robert H. Jackson, chief American prosecutor, described Streicher as a venomous vulgarian who "manufactured and distributed obscene racial libels which incited the population to accept and assist the progressively savage operations of 'race purification.'"

The verdict was delivered by Lord Justice Geoffrey Lawrence, British President of the Tribunal.

Concerning Count 1: Conspiracy—Lawrence stated that Streicher was a staunch Nazi and supporter of Hitler's main politics. There was no evidence to show, he said, that he was ever within Hitler's inner circle of advisers, nor during his career was he closely connected with the formulation of policies which led to war. He was never present, for example, at any of the important conferences when Hitler explained his decisions to his leaders. Although he was a *Gauleiter*, there was no evidence to prove that he had knowledge of these policies.

In the opinion of the Tribunal, Lord Justice Lawrence stated, the evidence failed to establish Streicher's connection with the conspiracy or common plan to wage aggressive war as that conspiracy had been defined in the Judgment.

The Tribunal found Streicher not guilty on Count One. If there was any joy in the prisoner's heart, it was soon dispelled. The Judge then turned to the Count Four: Crimes Against Humanity.

This was an entirely different matter. Judge Lawrence spoke softly and clearly. For twenty-five years of speaking, writing, and preaching hatred of Jews, Streicher had become widely known as "Jew-Baiter Number One." In his speeches and articles, week after week, month after month, he had infected the German mind with the virus of anti-Semitism. Streicher, said the judge, had charge of the boycott of April 1, 1933. He advocated the Nuremberg Decrees of 1935. He was responsible for demolition of a synagogue in Nuremberg on August 10, 1938.

Justice Lawrence then quoted liberally from the pages of *Der Stürmer*, which injected poison into the minds of thousands of Germans and which caused them to follow the National Socialist policy of Jewish persecution and extermination.

With knowledge of the extermination of Jews in the Occupied Eastern Territories, the Justice went on, the defendant continued to write and publish his propaganda of death. In his defense he had vehemently denied any knowledge of mass extermination of Jews. But the evidence made it clear that he continually received current information on the progress of "the Final Solution."

Streicher, said the Justice, had sent his press photographer to visit the ghettoes of the East in the spring of 1943, the time of the destruction of the Warsaw ghetto. The Jewish newspaper, *Israelitisches Wochenblatt*, which Streicher received and read, carried in each issue accounts of atrocities on Jews in the East, and gave figures on the number of Jews who had been deported and killed. For example, issues appearing in the summer and fall of 1942 reported the death of 72,729 Jews in Warsaw; 15,542 in Lodz; 18,000 in Croatia; 125,000 in Romania; 14,000 in Latvia; 85,000 in Yugoslavia; 700,000 in all of Poland.

In November 1943 Streicher quoted verbatim from an article in the *Israelitisches Wochenblatt* which stated that the Jews had virtually disappeared from Europe, and commented: "This is not a Jewish lie."

In December 1942, referring to an article in the London *Times* about atrocities aiming at extermination, Streicher said that Hitler had given warning that the Second World War would lead to the destruction of Jewry.

In January 1943 Streicher wrote and published an article which said that Hitler's prophecy was being fulfilled, that World Jewry was being extirpated, and that it was wonderful to know that Hitler was freeing the world of its Jewish tormentors. It was idle to suggest, the Justice added, that Streicher's solution to "the Jewish problem" was limited strictly to classifying Jews as aliens.

Justice Lawrence concluded: "Streicher's incitement to murder and extermination at the time when Jews in the East were being killed under the most horrible conditions clearly constitutes persecution on political and racial grounds in connection with War Crimes, as defined by the Charter, and constitutes a Crime Against Humanity."

The verdict: Guilty on Count 4.

Punishment: *Tod durch den Strang!* Death on the gallows!

End of the line for the Pornographer of Nuremberg.

At twelve and a half minutes after two o'clock in the morning of October 16, 1946, Julius Streicher appeared in Nuremberg's execution hall, which only a few nights previously had been used for a basketball game by American security guards. There was a warning knock at the door by a guard outside as Streicher entered through the middle of the hall.

An American lieutenant colonel had fetched the condemned man from his cell block. Two Americans sergeants stopped Streicher as he entered the hall and closed in on him. They held his arms while another sergeant removed his manacles and replaced them with a leather cord.

In his threadbare suit and well-worn bluish shirt buttoned to the neck without a tie, Streicher stared at the three wooden scaffolds in front of him, of which two were being used alternately for the hangings while the third was held in reserve. There were eight newspaper correspondents in the room, two each from the United States, Britain, France, and Soviet Russia.

Streicher's hands were then tied behind his back. Guards directed him to No. 1 gallows.

Kinsbury Smith, European general manager of International News Service, reported that Streicher walked steadily the six feet to the first wooden step. His face was twitching nervously. As he was stopped for official identification, he uttered a piercing scream:

"Heil Hitler!"

As the echo died away, an American colonel spoke sharply: "Ask the man his name."

Streicher glared at him defiantly, and shouted: "You know my name well."

After the interpreter repeated the question, came the yell: "Julius Streicher."

As he mounted the platform, Streicher cried out: "Now it goes to God!"

The condemned man mounted the thirteen steps to the eight-foot high and eight-foot square platform. He was pushed two steps to the spot beneath the hangman's rope, suspended from an iron ring attached to a crossbeam resting on two posts.

Master Sergeant John G. Woods, United States Army official

hangman, held the rope. Streicher was swung around, face front. He glanced at the Allied officers and newsmen lined up against the wall behind small tables directly in front of the gallows. The condemned man's eyes burned with hatred as he looked down at the witnesses. He then screamed at the top of his voice:

"*Purim Fest*, 1946."

(*Purim* is a Jewish holiday, celebrated in the spring to commemorate the hanging of Haman, biblical oppressor of the Jews.)

When asked if he had any last words, Streicher shouted: "The Bolsheviks will hang you one day!"

As the black hood was being adjusted to his head, Streicher was heard saying: "Adele, my dear wife."

As the trap was sprung and the rope snapped taut, Streicher's body swung wildly on the gallows. A groan could be heard distinctly inside the dark interior of the scaffold.

There was one additional morbid detail. As Streicher was audibly strangling, the hangman disappeared into the interior of the scaffold. The groans ceased at once.

No one explained it. The hangman may well have grabbed the swinging body and pulled down on it.

4

ERNST ROEHM: BULLY BOY OF THE STREETS

Because I am an immature and wicked man, war and unrest appeal to me more than good bourgeois order.
—Ernst Roehm

There are scoundrels and scoundrels. Some operate within the boundaries of civilized behavior and broadcast their behavior in a devil-may-care fashion—directed mainly at themselves. These social rogues cause little damage beyond their immediate environment. From libertine Giovani Giacomo Casanova to his scandalous current counterparts, their name is legion.

Then there are the dyed-in-the wool scoundrels who by accident or by some lenient fate are propelled into positions of great authority. Unfortunately for Germans and the rest of the world, there was a surplus of these rascals in the immediate entourage of Adolf Hitler, head villain of them all.

Rotund Goering, arrogant Ribbentrop, foul-mouthed Streicher—these characters in Hitler's court were unprincipled knaves, dangerous to the lives of millions of innocents. There was nothing amusing about them.

Among the meanest of the dissolute lot was Ernst Roehm, a thug who rose to prominence in the early days of the Nazi movement. In true gangster fashion he was to lose his life in confrontation with the *Fuehrer*. "Let me speak to Adolf," he cried out as he fell victim to Nazi bullets.

He was a squat, obese, thick-necked little man with a slightly red, bullet-scarred face and a gruff manner. He divided all people into two categories—soldiers and civilians, into friends and enemies. He gloried in the dangers of struggle. There was nothing peaceful about this puffed-up bantam cock.

Most of all, the man was proud of his homosexuality. No judgment of his lifestyle is intended here. However, his preference had an important effect on his own destiny. He saw himself and his close homosexual friends as different from (and better than) the so-called normal "straights" of society. He was proud of his way of life. With Plato, he regarded homosexuality as practiced by superior beings because they were the most valiant of men. Had not the great Greek philosopher said: "After growing up, they, and they alone, are fit to rule the state"?

To all who would listen, Roehm preached that it was the misfortune of the current age that it was dominated by the feminine sex. Look to the past, he said—look at Caesar, Alexander the Great, Charles XII of Sweden, and Frederick the Great—conquerors, and homosexuals all. There must be no erotic sexual relations with women, which would ruin the nature of the true homosexual. Roehm denounced the political ideology of democracy on the ground that it gave women a high place in contemporary society. That was not satisfying for him nor, as he claimed, for Germany.

Roehm discussed his preference quite openly. He advocated homosexuality as the base for a new code of ethics. He projected a social order in which homosexuality would be regarded as a human behavior pattern of high repute. There would be no social pariahs in his new Germany. To give point to the argument, he flaunted his homosexuality in public and insisted that his cronies do the same.

What was needed, Roehm believed, was a proud, arrogant lot who could brawl, carouse, smash windows, kill and slaughter for the hell of it. Straights, in his eyes, were not as adept in such behavior as practicing homosexuals. No closets for them. Good citizenship in the bourgeois sense be damned—up with homosexuality.

Hitler was not one of them, despite attempts to read such a meaning into his relations with comrade Roehm. In the beginning, he saw friend Roehm as one of the most useful of his cohorts. Roehm was an efficient organizer. He was the best living trainer of militia. And Hitler needed paramilitary strength to throttle "subversive forces." He saw a place for such men who possessed instinctive ruthlessness without any compensatory moral qualms. In the early stages of the movement, Roehm and his followers, in Hitler's view, fitted with the special needs of the new Germany.

In the long run, Hitler found it necessary to eliminate Roehm and his homosexual clan. His excuse—by their political conduct they had become a threat to his leadership. The Blood Purge of 1934 solved many problems for the *Fuehrer*. It eliminated his fear of assassination by Roehm and friends. It allowed him to break away from the hateful father-image which Roehm at one time represented for him. And, most important of all, by entering the fray against homosexuals, Hitler could then pose before the German people as the true guardian of social purity, the champion of Nordic manhood and womanhood.

That was the end of the line for homosexuality in Hitler's Third Reich. Male worship for the male body had been common among officers of Wilhelminian Germany and even in the Weimar Republic. With The Night of Long Knives, Hitler could now present himself as the protector of normal heterosexual behavior.

The master had spoken. Homosexuals among Storm Troopers, black-shirted SS bodyguards, and *Wehrmacht* members began to fear for their lives. Some who challenged Hitler's authority over their sexual behavior ended up in concentration camps.

Ernst Roehm was born in Munich on November 28, 1887, to an old Bavarian family of civil servants. Attracted at an early age by the military, he became a professional soldier and was commissioned just prior to the outbreak of World War I. In combat he became known among his comrades as a fanatical, simple-minded swashbuckler who delighted in showing off his contempt for danger. In terms of war service, he was a good soldier. He took joy in the camaraderie of war and became a battle casualty in the process. Although thrice wounded, he insisted on being returned to the front each time ready for more combat. Half his nose was shot away and there was a bullet hole in his cheek. He thereafter faced the world as a disgruntled veteran ready for trouble wherever he could find it.

Like others who became leaders in the Nazi hierarchy, Roehm turned to the *Freikorps*, postwar freebooters who claimed they were working for the regeneration of Germany. The *Freikorps* became the training unit for those terrorists who played a significant role in German life in the immediate postwar years. Roehm also retained his post as captain in the *Reichswehr*, Group Headquarters A, in Munich. At the same time, he was prepared to support the freebooters and their polic, of evading limitations placed by the Treaty of Versailles on Germany's military strength. By backing the *Freikorps*, he saw the nucleus of a new army that would eventually avenge the humiliations forced on Germany by the postwar treaty.

The tough little freebooter was attracted by the great arsenal left behind by the defeated Germany Army. These arms were supposed to be destroyed by order of the peace treaty. Captain Roehm was able to persuade the Allied Control Commission that old armored cars and rusty machine guns were of no use in serious warfare, but they could be used effectively to prevent the spread of Bolshevism to the West. It was an effective argument.

Roehm and his henchmen went into action against those Germans inclined to report the existence of secret arsenals to the Allies. "We will transfer you," he warned, "from your rascally life to death." Roehm's bully boys of the streets became expert in "transforming" local enemies to death. In his mind, this was merely "soldierly self-defense." An illegal army appealed to his sense of proper conduct.

At the same time, Roehm turned his attention to war on the political front. He was interested in any party that could capture the working classes for a nationalist and militarist cause. The German Workers' Party had all the qualifications. At this time, Hitler was building up his movement and he needed the support of such tough veterans as Roehm. The thick-necked captain and his followers were just the right men to fight Communists in the battle of the streets. Roehm persuaded his colleagues to join the Nazi ranks. From these units came Hitler's first strong-arm squads, later to emerge as the notorious Storm Troopers.

Roehm did even more for Hitler. He persuaded his commanding officer, Maj. Gen. Franz Xavier Epp, a former *Freikorps* leader, to join the Nazis. Epp helped raise the sixty thousand marks needed to buy the *Völkischer Beobachter*, a weekly newspaper, for the Party. Politician Hitler appreciated this boost for his own career.

Meanwhile, a strong friendship developed between Hitler and Roehm. The two used the familiar *"Du"* ("thou") in conversation. From the beginning, Hitler was aware of Roehm's sexual preference but he decided at the time to pay little attention to it. The man was too valuable. He was indispensable in obtaining the protection of the army as well as the Bavarian government. Throughout his early career the budding young politician needed the tolerance of the army for his own campaign of violence and intimidation. Moreover, Hitler felt that Roehm and his bully boys, who took pleasure in smashing skulls, were absolutely essential in the Nazi drive for power.

In August 1921 the Weimar government, under pressure from the Allies, ordered the dissolution of the *Freikorps* and other nationalist organizations. To keep his disbanded forces together Roehm organized a "Gymnastic and Sports Division" inside the Party. Its membership was the same as the freebooter units dedicated to winning the battle of the streets against the Communists. Later that year, in October, its name was changed to *Sturmabteilung* (the *SA*, or Storm Section). In December 1922 Hermann Goering, who had won a reputation as flying ace in World War I, was made commander of the brown-shirted Storm Troopers.

Hitler now had his private army and he was grateful to Roehm for its personnel and arms. The NSDAP, the National Socialist German Workers' Party, could muster a strong force to embody and propagate the military idea. The new *SA* was pledged to cultivate loyalty between comrades, and "joyful obedience to the Leader."

In late September 1923 Roehm decided to resign from the *Reichswehr*. His reasons were not altogether clear. It was rumored at the time that he was the target of government investigations about armament swindling. In any event, his role as a liaison between Hitler and the army was at an end. He chose now to turn all his efforts to supporting a National Socialist revolution under the leadership of Hitler.

Roehm played a role in the bizarre Munich Beer-Hall *Putsch* of November 8–9, 1923. The entire idea brought him into a state of euphoria. This was the kind of action the swashbuckler craved. He appeared on the scene with a fully packed soldier's kit as if prepared for a week's stay in the trenches. There was something pitiful about this schoolboyish desire for action.

Together with a small band of followers, Roehm occupied army headquarters during the night of November 8, when Hitler was leading his dramatic coup at the Beer Hall, the *Bürgerbräu Keller*. At dawn Hitler returned to the hall, leaving Roehm to hold out at his assigned post.

Meanwhile, troops of the regular army surrounded Roehm and his men. Both sides were reluctant to open fire. Many lower echelon officers of the army sympathized with Roehm and his battle against the Treaty of Versailles. The trapped Nazis sat back to await events.

When the Munich police fired on the Nazi parade, leaving sixteen Nazis dead in the streets, the intended coup was smashed. Two hours later, Roehm was persuaded to capitulate at Army headquarters and was taken into custody. Roehm was one of the nine in addition to Hitler who were accused of treason. Although found guilty, Roehm was discharged on the day sentence was pronounced.

While Hitler was serving his sentence at Landsberg Prison, Roehm set about the task of rebuilding the movement. An able organizer, he began to reconstruct what he now called the *Kampfbund* (Militant League). He journeyed from one end of Germany to the other, proposing, arguing, demanding. He even went to Austria to bolster his rebuilding campaign. Within a short time, he had some thirty thousand men enrolled in his *Kampfbund*.

Meanwhile, Hitler in his cell at Landsberg was having some doubts about his swashbuckling friend. Above all, the *Fuehrer* wanted no powerful challenge to his own leadership. In common with gangsters everywhere and at any time, as top man he maintained a divide-and-rule policy which would have his henchmen at each other's throats. This was the instinctive Machiavellianism which he regarded as absolutely necessary for his cause.

The more successful Roehm was in his campaign of reconstruction, the more uneasy Hitler became. The Bavarian government arrested several *Kampfbund* leaders and even delayed Hitler's parole because of their activities. Roehm later wrote that Hitler felt that his approaching release was endangered and laid the blame, not on the enemy, but on the friends who were fighting for him.

Moreover, Hitler was annoyed by Roehm's creation of the *Kampfbund* as successor to the *SA*. He was not pleased by Roehm's initiative. In his eyes the *SA* was designed merely as a political front for the Party and must always remain subordinate to it. Roehm disagreed. He saw his Storm Troopers as a military movement and made the demand that they be given appropriate representation in the parliamentary group "and that they should not be hindered in their special work."

It was a serious crack in the Nazi structure.

The issue came to a head in April 1924. In a meeting with Roehm on April 16, Hitler told Roehm bluntly that the *Kampfbund* must go and that the *SA* must be reconstructed from the ground up. He, the *Fuehrer*, would not accept Roehm's claim that the political and military movements were entirely independent of each other.

The next day an angered Roehm wrote to Hitler resigning from leadership of both Kampfbund and *SA*. "I take this opportunity, in memory of the great but difficult hours we have had together, to thank you for your comradeship. I urge you not to exclude me from your personal friendship."

There was no reply. When, on February 27, 1925, Hitler called a mass meeting at the Bürgerbräu Keller, Roehm was pointedly absent.

Craving action in the old style, Roehm went off to Bolivia to serve in its army. Like other German officers who were without work, he moved to South America to enjoy a steady income in a post for which he felt himself to be professionally qualified. He remained in Bolivia for more than five years.

In 1930 Hitler was having trouble with his revived Storm Trooper organization. Prior to the elections of September 1930, the Berlin *SA* mutinied and destroyed the Nazi Party's headquarters. Storm Troopers claimed that they were not getting the pay promised them. In addition, there was strong discontent with leadership. Hitler tried to correct the situation by levying a special tax on all Party members for the benefit of his Storm Troopers. In hectic meeting with the rank-and-file, he finally managed to bring his dissidents around by promising better pay and more effective leadership.

Even though his Party went on to electoral successes, Hitler did not forget his troubles with the *SA*. He got in touch with Roehm, urging him to forget the past and return to Germany to take over his post as Chief of Staff. He needed a tough-minded taskmaster who could keep the *SA* in hand. On his part, Roehm regarded his recall as fully justified. Had he not, along with Goering and Goebbels, been at Hitler's side during the two years before the Nazis took power?

Roehm was now operating at a high level. In the fall of 1931 he arranged a meeting with Hitler and General Kurt von Schleicher. He was present during subsequent conferences with Schleicher and Chancellor Heinrich Bruening. The cocky little man was rising in the Nazi world.

But a gap was widening between the two comrades. There were two issues at stake: Roehm's desire to incorporate his *SA* into the regular army, and his leaning toward a Second Revolution, the proposed socialist side of National Socialism. In both cases irreconcilable differences rose between the two former comrades-in-arms.

Hitler remained loyal to his compact with the generals. He told his *SA* chieftains that they formed "an army of political soldiers" who had won the German Revolution for him. True, they had defeated the Communists in the streets, but now that National Socialism had emerged victorious, the Party had no further use for them. He, Hitler, had to compromise with existing institutions, especially the *Wehrmacht*, and he intended to remain loyal to the "glorious old Army."

Angry repercussions from Roehm. His Brown Shirts had won the revolution for Hitler. They had committed excesses in the process, he admitted, but this was no time to cast aside the faithful troopers who had boosted Nazism to power. In a speech delivered in November 1933 before top officers of the *SA*, he bitterly attacked "reactionaries," businessmen, and army officers, all of whom Hitler now relied upon for help. The *SA*, he said, had not lost its reason for existence. If necessary, he would see to it that "these gentlemen will be changed in a gentle, or if necessary, an ungentle manner." His brawling street fighters knew exactly what he meant.

Added to the army question was the considerably more important issue of the so-called Second Revolution. Since the early days of the Party, Roehm, along with Gregor Strasser and others, formed a left-wing branch that leaned toward the socialist side of the National Socialist movement. Hitler had won his way to power by emphasizing a nationalist ideology, by utilizing the help of the army, industrialists, and bureaucracy. Roehm and others began to call for an extension of the Party's socialist aims. "The National Socialist struggle," he said, "has been a Socialist revolution. It has been a revolution of the workers' movement. Those who made this revolution must speak for it." The implication was that the *SA* would see to it that the revolution would not slow down.

Dismaying dilemma for the *Fuehrer*. He wanted to retain Roehm as a good Party comrade, but he also needed the support of both army and industrialists. And those two interested parties had only contempt for Roehm and his aggregation of roughnecks and misfits. Hitler felt that he had no choice in the matter. The regular army refused to take in the Storm Troopers, and the financial interests were utterly opposed to the idea of a Second Revolution.

Trying to reason with Roehm, Hitler sent for him on June 4, 1934, and in a five-hour meeting literally begged his old comrade to conform. "Forget the idea of a Second Revolution. Believe in me. Don't cause any trouble." The *Fuehrer* promised that he would not disband the *SA*, to which he owed so much. But the matter was becoming critical. He ordered the Brown Shirts to go on leave for a month, during which time no uniforms were to be worn. Another meeting with Roehm was arranged for July 1 at Bad Wiessee.

The close friendship between Hitler and Roehm came to a tragic end during the Blood Purge of 1934, also called The Night of Long Knives. The *Fuehrer* decided to unleash an "educational campaign" against the growing power of the *SA*. In the process, seventy-seven leading Nazis were to lose their lives, including Ernst Roehm. There were, in addition, many other victims of the purge.

On the morning of June 29 Hitler, at the time staying at a hotel in Bad Godesberg overlooking the Rhine, summoned Viktor Lutze, *SA-Obergruppenfuehrer* (general) of Hanover and informed him that he was to succeed Roehm as *Stabschef* (Chief of Staff) of the *SA*. Astonished, Lutze accepted at once. Meanwhile, Goebbels flew in from Berlin to be at the *Fuehrer's* side. He told Hitler that Karl Ernst, *SA* chief in Berlin, was at that moment alerting Storm Troopers "certainly for some ill purpose.'' It was a calculated lie: Ernst, who had just been married, with Roehm and Goering in attendance, was on his way to Bremen with his bride and was about to board a passenger ship for a honeymoon in Madeira.

At one o'clock on the morning of June 30, Hitler received urgent messages from Goering and Himmler to the effect that an *SA* uprising was being synchronized in Berlin and Munich for the following day. Both Goering and Himmler knew that Hitler was supposed to meet his old comrade Roehm within the next few hours. Soon the entire *SA* was supposed to go on leave. The two plotters knew that few would believe the tale of a massive *SA* conspiracy.

Hitler was stirred into action. This was to be the Second Revolution and he would stifle it at its proposed birth. He made the drastic decision to purge the traitors. He ordered Goering to take care of the situation in Berlin, and that two companies of his personal *SS* bodyguard, under command of Sepp Dietrich, be sent from Berlin to Munich.

Hitler, accompanied by Goebbels and Lutze, flew from an airport near Bonn southward across Germany. His plane landed at Munich at 4 A.M. At the Ministry of the Interior two chiefs of the Bavarian *SA* saluted the *Fuehrer*, only to be greeted with an outburst of hysterical rage. Hitler tore off the insignia of rank from the shoulders of the astonished officers and screamed abuse at them. He drew his revolver, but before he could use it, one of his bodyguards shot the men at close range. Hitler kicked one of the corpses and remarked: ''These men were not the most guilty.''

Gathering together his *SS* guards, Hitler set off at the head of a cavalcade of cars for Bad Wiessee. His goal was to deal personally with Roehm, who was staying with several associates at a private hotel. Roehm lay in bed, fast asleep.

The vengeful band raced to Roehm's hotel. An *SS* detachment kicked open the door of *Obergruppenfuehrer* Edmund Heines, who was in bed with his young chauffeur. Both were shot dead.

Hitler raced toward Roehm's own room and banged loudly on the door.

''Who is there?'' Roehm called sleepily.

''It is I, Hitler. Open up!''

Roehm unbolted the door, saying: ''Already. I wasn't expecting you until tomorrow.''

"Arrest him!" Hitler shouted to his aides.

Roehm stared dumbfounded at the open doorway crowded with Hitler's band. Together with other prisoners he was hustled into a car and taken at great speed to Munich.

Meanwhile, Goering and Himmler in Berlin went ahead with their part of the blood bath. Top *SA* leaders suspected of disloyalty to Hitler were arrested and placed in a coal cellar at the Lichterfelde Cadet School barracks. Most had no idea why they were being shot. Some went to their death shouting *"Heil Hitler!"*

In Munich, Rudolf Hess turned the Brown House there into a trap for *SA* officers. As Storm Troopers arrived, they were taken prisoner by an *SS* cordon. One after another the bewildered men were taken to Stadelheim Prison and executed.

Hitler arrived at the prison to meet the sullen Roehm. Defiantly, Roehm demanded to see his friend, Adolf, the man he had launched on his career. Surely Adolf would understand his loyalty. But now Hitler wanted no meeting. Instead, he snapped a new order: "Shoot his chauffeur Max. And tell him what you have done. Lock him in his cell and await my orders."

Hitler then demanded that a revolver be left in Roehm's cell so that he could take the "honorable" way out.

Roehm refused to use it: "If I am to be killed, let Adolf do it himself."

On July 2, two *SS* officers, acting on the order of Sepp Dietrich, entered Roehm's cell. Stripped to the waist, Roehm was about to say something but he was told coldly to shut up. The *SS* men emptied their revolvers into him at point-blank range. With an expression of contempt on his face, Roehm slumped to the ground.

The deadly relationship between Hitler and Roehm reflected the true nature of the Nazi regime with its plethora of thugs and cutthroats. The close relationship between comrades-in-arms, the surge to political power, the struggle for supremacy, the resort to execution by the stronger—all this is familiar stuff from the underworld of Sicily to Al Capone's Chicago. The parallel with gangsterism is there—despite the *Fuehrer's* shrill claim of political legality.

5

RUDOLF HESS:
PALADIN
EXTRAORDINARY

Hitler is pure reason incarnate.

—*Rudolf Hess*

Sportpalast, Berlin a huge crowd hums with expectancy. The public awaits its hero. The audience is composed of a cross section of the German people—workers with gnarled hands, beer bellies, and egg-like heads, smug white-collar workers, excited women, giggling girls, and self-satisfied students.

Suddenly there is silence as the hall darkens. To the blare of trumpets a solitary figure, covered with a moving spotlight, makes his way down the aisle. Adolf Hitler mounts the podium.

To the side of the speaker's platform stands a tall, beetle-browed man in Nazi uniform. His eyes are fixed on the *Fuehrer* in euphoric adoration.

Rudolf Hess shouts at the top of his voice: "The *Fuehrer*! *Sieg Heil*!" ("The Leader! Hail Victory!").

The transfixed audience in a mighty roar repeats the slogan. A second *"Sieg Heil!"* and a third.

Bowing and smiling, Hitler stands proudly before the waiting crowd. He raises his hand and the thunderous noise stops as if by magic.

The fanatical Nazi at the side of the speaker's platform is deputy to the *Fuehrer* and at one time Hitler's appointed successor after Hermann Goering. Instantly recognizable because of his deep-set eyes in a square-cut face, he is known because of his absolute, doglike devotion to Hitler.

Richard Rudolf Hess was born on April 26, 1894, in Alexandria, Egypt, the son of a German wholesale importer. His relationship with his parents, who were widely respected in the large German community, was always good. At the age of twelve he was sent to Germany to attend the *Evangelisches Pedagogium* school at Godesberg-am-Rhein. At seventeen he enrolled in a business school in Switzerland. He then went to Hamburg to join an export house and began to serve his apprenticeship as a third-generation member in the family business.

Unhappy in the business world, young Hess in 1914, when war broke out, volunteered and was accepted by the 1st Bavarian Regiment. Serving on the Western Front as a shock-troop leader, he was commissioned as a lieutenant. Later he was transferred to the Air Corps where he had his first taste of flying. He was wounded three times but never seriously.

Like millions of other German veterans returning home after the conflict, the twenty-four-year-old Hess was in a quandary. He abandoned all thoughts of a commercial career. He had gone to war in an outburst of enthusiasm, but now the supposedly invincible German war machine was no more and the country had turned to the unwanted and unloved Weimar Republic. He joined the *Thule Gesellschaft*, a paramilitary unit of the *Freikorps*, composed of former officers, demobilized soldiers, nationalists, and unemployed youths. These rightist freebooters attributed Germany's misfortunes to Social Democrats and Jews, who had "stabbed Germany in the back." They demanded elimination of all "traitors to the Fatherland." Hess's unit was commanded by Major General Franz Xavier von Epp, later a leading National Socialist.

At the same time, Hess enrolled at the University of Munich to study history, economics, political science, and geopolitics— the latter a subject that was to have a critical influence on him for the rest of his life. He began to attend the classes of Dr. Karl Haushofer, professor of geography and founder of the Institute of Politics. Professor and student became close friends. Haushofer, who had been a general in the war, had a profound influence on young Hess.

From his persuasive teacher, Hess absorbed the theory of geopolitics, a concept that called for a fusion of geography and politics. Haushofer believed that the British Empire, a naval power, was in decline, and that it was the turn of a continental state to take over world leadership. Otherwise, living space would be controlled by Eurasians. Germany, which needed *Lebensraum* (living space), had to expand, especially to the east, where the agricultural Ukraine should be appended to the industrial German *Herzland* (heartland).

Later, when he flew to Scotland on his peace mission in May 1941, Hess carried with him the visiting cards of Professor Haushofer and son Albrecht. He would claim that the idea of flying to Scotland came to him from the elder Haushofer. The professor and his son, strong Anglophiles, believed that the two countries—Germany and Britain—had so much in common that it was senseless for them to be at war with one another.

While at Munich University, Hess took part in the usual student brawls in beer halls. He also kept himself busy distributing anti-Semitic pamphlets. Attending a meeting of the new Nazi Party in 1920, he was captivated by Hitler, the shouting, gesticulating politician. Like Hermann Goering and others who later became Nazi leaders, Hess was so impressed that he joined the movement.

In an essay for a university thesis, Hess wrote about the man who would lead Germany back to its former great status. His country needed a strong man:

When all authority has vanished, only a man of the people can establish authority. The more the dictator is originally rooted in the broad masses, the better he understands how to treat them psychologically.

He, himself, has nothing in common with the masses. Like every great man he is all personality.

When it is necessary, he does not shrink from bloodshed. Great questions of the day will always be settled by blood and iron.

To reach his goal, he is prepared to demolish even his closest friends.

The lawgiver proceeds with terrible hardness.

As the need arises, he can trample with the boots of a grenadier.

When politician Hitler was shown a copy of Hess's essay, he was delighted. He had little use for the university crowd, but he felt that this student knew what he was talking about. He, Hitler, fitted the description perfectly of Hess's proposed authoritarian leader.

Hess, too, was pleased by Hitler's reaction. This was the ruthless politician who could implement the ideas the student believed were necessary for Germany's future. From then on, Hess was faithful to Hitler and followed him with utter devotion.

Hess had his first chance to show his loyalty when he was at Hitler's side at the Munich Beer-Hall *Putsch* of November 8–9, 1923. He was with Hitler at the Odeonplatz near the Feldherrn Halle when a thousand Munich police faced three thousand Nazi marchers and killed sixteen of them after a fateful fusillade. Hess managed to escape to the Haushofer home in the Bavarian Alps, but was arrested and sentenced to eighteen months in Landsberg-am-Lech Prison. Hitler was given a jail term of five years.

The Nazi prisoners at Landsberg were pampered. They read voraciously, entertained visitors, and regarded their detention as no more than a comfortable interruption in their lives. It was considered an easy vacation. A close friendship developed between Hitler and the adoring Hess. For Hitler, Hess was different from the intellectuals he both feared and loathed. The energetic young man, with his deep sense of loyalty, was special. He rose steadily in Hitler's estimation.

Hitler was anxious to show that he, despite his meager education, had formed a political philosophy. He would write a book. He called on fellow prisoners Hess and Emil Maurice to help him get his ideas into manuscript form. At first he titled his work *Four and a Half Years of Struggle Against Lies, Stupidities, and Cowardice*. Later, before the book went to press, his enterprising publisher, Max Amann, dissatisfied with the long title, shortened it to *Mein Kampf (My Struggle)*.

Hitler's plea for *Lebensraum* was probably absorbed from Hess, who was said to have passed along to him Professor Haushofer's geopolitical ideas. Later, when in Spandau Prison, Hess said that he did not remember whether he did this or not.

From the beginning of his relations with Hitler, Hess subjugated himself completely to his master. He literally worshipped the man who was to lift him from obscurity as a purposeless student to posts of high authority in the Third Reich. Introverted, without the ability to hold an audience, Hess knew only unconditional faith in Hitler: "With pride," he said, "we see that one man remains beyond all criticism. This is because everyone feels and knows that Hitler is always right, and that he will always be right." When he was later placed on trial at Nuremberg, Hess insisted that he had never lost faith: "It was granted me for many years to live and work under the greatest son whom my nation has brought forth in the thousand years of its history."

That kind of devotion proved rewarding for Hess. Because of it, he became Hitler's closest confidant, a relationship that lasted until some time before his flight to the British Isles in 1941. On April 21, 1933, he was appointed deputy to the *Fuehrer*, and the following December he was made "Reich Minister Without Portfolio." In early 1938 he was appointed a member of the Secret Cabinet Council, in late August 1939 he was given a seat on the Ministerial Council, and in September 1939 the important post as successor-designate after Hermann Goering. It was a dizzying round of promotions for the somewhat shy and introverted paladin.

As deputy *Fuehrer*, Hess was the top Nazi for handling all Party matters. He had the authority to make decisions in Hitler's name in matters of lower-level leadership. As Reich Minister Without Portfolio, he could approve any legislation proposed by various Reich officials before it could be enacted into law.

Hitler used Hess in his preparations for war. Hess's signature appeared on the law of March 10, 1935, establishing compulsory military service. In his speeches he supported the policy of vigorous rearmament. He was careful to echo Hermann Goering's aphorism: "Guns instead of butter."

Hess was in the midst of Hitler's aggressions against Austria, Czechoslovakia, and Poland. From the time of the murder of Austrian Chancellor Engelbert Dollfuss to the *Anschluss* (union) between Germany and Austria, Hess was in close touch with the illegal Nazi Party in Austria. He was in Vienna on March 12, 1936, when German troops moved in. On March 13, 1938, he signed the law for *Anschluss*. His participation in the administration of Austria was provided for in a law promulgated on June 10, 1939.

Hess was also involved in the Czechoslovak crisis. For some time he had retained close relations with Konrad Henlein, chief of the Sudeten German Party in Czechoslovakia. In late September 1938, at the time of the Munich crisis, Hess arranged with General Wilhelm Keitel to carry out Hitler's instructions to make the machinery of the Nazi Party available for secret mobilization. On April 14, 1939, he signed a decree setting up the government of the Sudetenland as an integral part of the Third Reich. The following June he issued an edict for his own participation in the administration of the Sudetenland.

On August 27, 1939, when Hitler's proposed attack on Poland was temporarily postponed in an effort to induce Great Britain to abandon its guarantee to Poland, Hess publicly praised the *Fuehrer*'s "magnanimous offer to Poland." At the same time, he attacked Poland for "war agitation" and Britain as responsible for Poland's attitude. After the invasion of Poland, Hess signed decrees incorporating Danzig and certain Polish territories into the Reich and setting up the *General Gouvernement* of Poland.

All these steps, outlined by the prosecution at the Nuremberg Trials, revealed Hess's role in Hitler's plans for aggressive warfare. They were responsible eventually for his sentence to life imprisonment.

Hess's highest honor from the *Fuehrer* came on the day (April 21, 1933) when Hitler proclaimed: "I hereby name to be my deputy, the leader of the central political commission, Party Member Rudolf Hess, and give him all the powers of attorney in all questions of decision of Party leadership to be decided in my name— Adolf Hitler."

With that decree, beetle-browed Hess was to dominate universities, schools, and religious societies. He was active in organizing the Labor Front. In 1935 he appended his name to the anti-Jewish legislation of the Nazi dictatorship. Clearly, he had won his way to the top of the Nazi hierarchy.

During the first nine months of World War II, Hitler surged ahead with his extraordinary conquests—Poland, then Belgium, Holland, and France. He expected that intelligent Britons would see that the odds against them were hopeless and that they would make peace. He was astonished when they turned down his offer. The British were not cowed by Nazi *Blitzkrieg* techniques.

Meanwhile, Hess was beginning to have doubts. The best Germany could hope for, he felt, was a draw. Moreover, he was becoming more and more depressed. Although he held high offices in the Third Reich, he was not a happy man. He sensed that he was being pushed gradually into the background by other Nazis. The situation was by no means an isolated one in the strange milieu of the Third Reich. There was bitter competition in the immediate retinue of Hitler for his attention. The *Fuehrer* was the omniscient man-god in the topsy-turvy world of Nazism. His colleagues in the inner circle fought savagely for advantageous spots. Goering and Goebbels detested one another; Ribbentrop was criticized by other Nazis as a weakling; most Nazis scorned Streicher as a voluptuary and pornographer. Each one in his own way tried to outmaneuver the others. Hess began to feel that he was being left behind in the unending struggle for the *Fuehrer's* attention. He fretted and fumed about his bad luck. He had to do something to win back the good will and esteem of his beloved master. He must do something dramatic and altogether unexpected.

During the campaign in France, Hess expressed the opinion to Hitler that in the event of peace being concluded with Britain, it should, at least, cover what Germany had been deprived of by the Treaty of Versailles. Hitler contradicted him. He did not want, he said, a peace treaty comparable to that of Versailles, which would bring new wars in its wake. He said that he always aimed at an understanding with England. As far back as 1924, when he was imprisoned in Landsberg, he had declared that this was the main pillar of his foreign policy. All he wanted from the British could be summarized in two demands: (1) fixing of mutual spheres of interest; and (2) return of the German colonies.

Hess remembered. The idea came to him first like a blinking light and then—with sudden vividness. As a member of the inner circle he knew that the ten-year Nonaggression Pact between the Third Reich and the Soviet Union was in Hitler's mind only a temporary ploy. As soon as practical the *Fuehrer* intended to turn on his Russian partner, win a dramatic victory, and then offer peace on his own terms to the West. The time was approaching for that deadly switch.

Hess's mind was operating in high gear. Here was a glorious opportunity to win back the good favor of his *Fuehrer* by a magnificent act of sacrifice. It was a tragedy, he thought, for Germans and Britons, Aryan blood brothers all, to be fighting each other. The real enemy was the Soviet Union, bastion of global Communism.

He, Rudolf Hess, would fly to England, drop on the country by parachute, be received by top British officialdom, and present his case for Anglo-German cooperation against the hated Bolsheviks. How could the intelligent British not see the justice of his cause? A successful mission—and once again he would be in the good graces of his master and the envy of his outmaneuvered colleagues.

Hess already had a modicum of flying experience in the German air force during World War I. Through friend Willy Messerschmitt, noted designer of *Luftwaffe* aircraft, he had been able to gain access to the new warplanes. Using varied excuses, he got some rudimentary training in piloting and navigation with accent on navigation. He was a good pupil.

His plan was simple. During the Olympic Games held in Berlin in 1936, he heard about a British aristocrat who later became the Duke of Hamilton. Premier peer of Scotland, and 14th Duke in his line, Hamilton was head of Clan Douglas, which had provided Scotland with leaders for some 700 years. At the Olympic Games, Hamilton met Anglophile Albrecht Haushofer, son of the distinguished Professor Karl Haushofer, theoretician of geopolitics, with whom Hess had studied at the University of Munich. Albrecht spoke to Hess in glowing terms about the gracious British nobleman.

In 1940 Hess asked Albrecht Haushofer to write to Hamilton proposing a meeting in Portugal to discuss possible peace negotiations. Young Haushofer was to tell his Scotsman friend that

Germany and England, "the two master Aryan races," should on no account be at war with one another.

Hamilton consulted British Intelligence, which urged him not to reply for the time being. A response was being prepared at the precise moment when Hess suddenly flew to Scotland. Hess just could not wait. He felt certain that he would be warmly received. He would tell the duke: "Hitler is willing to meet with Britain to stop this war with honor." As Lord Steward of the Royal family, Hamilton would, of course, lead his visitor directly to the king, who would help him on his mission of peace.

On May 10, 1941, Hess borrowed a leather flying suit which he put over his officer's uniform without badge or rank. He appeared at flight-control at Augsburg and signed under his wife's maiden name for a flight to Stavanger in Norway.

Take-off. Unobserved, without fuel for a return trip, Hess lifted his *Messerschmitt-110* and headed for the North Sea and Scotland. He carried a map on which he had penciled his course. Later he described his flight in a letter to his wife from his prison cell at Nuremberg on June 21, 1947:

I flew direct except for the diversions I made in order to fool our friends the British.

It was impressive to be flying alone over the North Sea in magically beautiful evening light, strongly affected by the Northern latitudes in which I found myself. . . .

For some moments I thought of turning back. Then I said to myself, however, 'Night landing with this machine is a tricky business.'

And even if nothing happened to me, the *Messerschmitt* machine was bound to be damaged, possibly beyond repair, and that would be the end. . . .

I said to myself: 'Stick it out. Come what may.' . . .

I flew at full throttle for a thousand meters toward the coast and attained a terrific speed. That saved me from being overtaken and shot down by the *Spitfire* which was coming in behind me. . . . I could not see behind me because I was too confined in my seat and the cockpit window reflected the light too much.

I greeted England with a wild scream of my engines, flying a few meters above the rooftops of a small township on the coast, my speed being about 730 kms/hr. I was then out of sight of my pursuer since I was certainly invisible from above. . . .

I came down still lower to a height of perhaps five meters over the treetops, rooftops, cattle and people (the British airmen call it 'hedgehopping'). . . .

I thus arrived, pretty much according to program, almost touching the tops of a medium range of mountains as I flew past, until I reached the west coast and then on to the estate of my unsuspecting host.

It was, indeed, a fantastic 800-mile flight. Hess's navigation was remarkable. When he reached the vicinity of the Hamilton estate, he could not find a suitable spot for landing. Bailing out of his plane at a height of 2,000 meters, he came down with his parachute ten meters in front of the door of the only farmhouse in the vicinity. An injured leg prevented him from walking. A farmer armed only with a pitchfork awaited him.

"Take me to the Duke of Hamilton," he told the excited farmer. Instead, he was removed to a Glasgow hospital.

At first, Hess gave the name of "Captain Horn," but he soon admitted who he was. He had brought along photographs taken at various years of his life to establish his identity if questioned. He told his captors that his trip was not a one-man offensive but a one-way flight. His *Messerschmitt's* guns, he said, were empty.

The magnitude of Hess's determination was indicated by the fact that he had left behind his wife, whom he had married in 1927, and his three-year-old son. He was certain that eventually the Russians would fall on his country's back when Germany was engaged in a war with the Western powers. "Only by the destruction of National Socialist Germany," Hess wrote later, "would the way be paved for the old goal of spreading the world revolution westward. The right moment would appear to be when Germany's army—after landing in England—was tied down in great numbers on the other side of the channel. I would, therefore, steal a march on the Russian's surely planned attack. Attack is the best form of defense. It turned out that the *Fuehrer* had already decided this course himself.''

British authorities, as well as the British public, were astonished by Hess's flight. On Saturday night, May 10, a British patrol reported that a *Messerschmitt-110* had crossed the coast of Scotland and was flying in the direction of Glasgow. Because a German plane of that type could not possibly have enough fuel to return to Germany, the news was at first disbelieved.

But here he was. Rudolf Hess, indeed, had landed in Scotland.

Bustling activity in Whitehall. An officer of the Foreign Service, who had known Hess before the war, was hastily sent by plane to see him in the hospital. Hess optimistically gave the visitor his personal message. If the British would only halt hostilities, they could join their German brothers in a crusade against Bolshevism. The magnanimous *Fuehrer* would agree to give the British a free hand in their empire, while Germany would retain control of the European continent. There were some conditions: Germany's colonies, stolen from her by the Treaty of Versailles, must be returned. Iraq must be evacuated. The British must conclude an armistice with Mussolini.

That, Hess said, was the price of peace.

But there was another important provision, said the uninvited guest. The British must know that the *Fuehrer* would not negotiate with Prime Minister Winston Churchill. (Hitler had once said: ''I never met an Englishman who didn't say Churchill was off his head.'' Hess was careful not to mention that estimate.) The British, Hess warned, must see to it that Churchill should resign his office as Prime Minister.

It was a classic piece of foolish effrontery. With this demand, Hess revealed his total ignorance of the British character. He had little understanding of the way British democracy worked.

There was some skepticism in London, but the man was Rudolf Hess all right. The British Minister of Information declared that the visitor had been identified ''beyond all possible doubt.''

Hess was shocked when he was told that high British officials, at a loss as to what to make of his extraordinary flight, refused to talk to him. Here he, the *Fuehrer's* deputy, was giving them the opportunity of a lifetime to withdraw honorably from the war and they were failing to react to his offer. He was bewildered by their reaction.

Prime Minister Churchill declined to see Hess. Later he said: "Whatever is the moral guilt of a German who stood near to Hitler, Hess has, in my view, atoned for this by his devoted and frantic deed of lunatic benevolence. He came to us of his own free will and, though without authority, has something of the quality of an envoy. He was a medical and not a criminal case and should be so regarded."

The befuddled prisoner was moved to the Tower of London.

When he took off on his flight to Scotland that Saturday evening, Hess left two letters behind. One was to his wife. He placed the envelope among his son's toys, so that it would be found but not so quickly that the alarm would be raised to prevent his takeoff. The second sealed letter he gave to a trusted subordinate with instruction as to the exact time it was to be delivered to Hitler.

Sensation in Germany.

The *Fuehrer* had taken the letter and, thinking it was some unimportant memorandum, placed it aside untouched. When he slit open the envelope and saw the message he could scarcely believe what he was reading. The individual in whom he placed his complete trust, the man—after Hermann Goering—he had designated as his choice in the line of succession for the Third Reich, had made an inexcusable blunder. "My action," Hess wrote, "must not be interpreted as a sign of German weakness. On the contrary, I shall lay stress on the military invincibility of my country and point out that Germany did not have to ask for peace."

Hitler was furious. The blasted *Dummkopf*, the dummy! Without consultation, the blockhead had taken German foreign policy into his own hands and had placed the Third Reich in an impossible position.

What to do? Hitler summoned Goering and Air-General Ernst Udet to the Berghof and discussed with them the chances of Hess making it in the *Messerschmitt*. The angered *Fuehrer* sent Foreign Minister Joachim von Ribbentrop off to Rome to inform Mussolini of the shock "departure" of numskull Hess.

The German press had already reported that Hess had taken a plane in Augsburg for an unknown destination in violation of the *Fuehrer*'s order prohibiting him from flying "because of a physical ailment.'' Newspapers were now silent for forty-eight hours.

Panicky consultation with Propaganda Minister Goebbels. As always, the little mouse-general was ready. The public should be advised that Hess had gone crazy.

Jawohl! Just right! Hitler agreed. Then came an official governmental communique:

Rudolf Hess has met with an accident.

Party Comrade Hess, who because of a disease that for a year has progressively worsened, had been categorically forbidden by the *Fuehrer* to continue his flying activities, recently found means in violation of this command to come into possession of an airplane.

On Saturday, May 10, about 6 P.M., Party Comrade Hess took off from Augsburg for a flight from which until today he has not yet returned.

The *Fuehrer* immediately ordered the arrest of the adjutants of Party Comrade Hess who alone knew of these flights and knowing of their prohibition by the *Fuehrer* did not prevent or immediately report them.

Under the circumstances the National Socialist movement must regretfully assume that Comrade Hess has crashed or met with an accident somewhere on his flight, that he left behind unfortunately indicated by his incoherence, symptoms of a mental derangement that permits the inference that Comrade Hess became the victim of hallucinations.

That was it. The German propaganda machine informed the world that Hess was, in fact, mad.

Hess was stunned by his reception in Britain. He was merely a patriot who loved his country and Hitler passionately—and here he was cooped up in the Tower of London like a common criminal. The British kept him there until October 6, 1945, when he was removed to a cell in Nuremberg.

In the dock at the Nuremberg Trials, Hess sat on the front row next to Hermann Goering. He was a changed man. The former strapping, ramrod straight Nazi with the confident air of a bold Teutonic warrior had turned into an emaciated shadow of himself, with sunken cheeks and stooped gait. Most of the time he stared straight ahead as if oblivious as to what was going on around him.

Throughout the proceedings, Hess remained in a condition of shock or feigned amnesia. Psychiatrists did not agree on the state of his mental health. Some suspected that he was pretending to be insane as a means of escaping punishment. Others judged the broken man staring vacantly into space as more than slightly neurotic but knowing exactly what he was doing. Hess, indeed, made it a practice to confuse his captors. On one occasion, he declared proudly that he was feigning insanity all along.

When the indictment was read to the defendants each replied when asked to state his plea: "I hereby declare myself in the sense of the indictment as innocent," or a simple "Innocent!". Hess shouted *"Nein!"* ("No!"). Most of his co-defendants treated him as if he was not present or was suffering from some form of insanity.

The fall from Hitler's grace had been too much for Hess to bear. He had been catapulted to eminence in the Third Reich at the side of the one man on earth he loved and admired, a man to whom he had given his soul. And then in a simple act dedicated to peace he had flown to Scotland to help his master, who at long last was turning on the Bolsheviks. For his trouble he was labeled "crazy" by the one human being on earth he respected.

The sensitive Hess had cracked under the strain. And here he was at Nuremberg on trial for his life.

In his cell at Nuremberg Prison, Hess presented a thin and puzzled appearance. His face and body were now bony, his eyes haunted and angry. He began to complain about everything—from dental records to chocolates, which he charged were poisoned by the British. An entry in his diary:

17 Oct. Great excitement because I made a fuss because I had not received the things I'd asked for from my luggage. Afterward I was told that I could make a complaint to the Commandant but that I must not shout at people. American doctor prescribed white bread for my stomach. The promised injection to restore my memory is said to have not yet been administered because judges do not consider it important for *me*. The doctor said he would do what he could about this.

On August 31, 1946, when closing statements were to be made by the defendants, Hess before the session informed Goering that he would not speak. When Goering finished his own statement, he passed the microphone across Hess to Ribbentrop. Both Goering and the court were astonished when Hess intercepted it.

Hess asked the court if he could make a statement. After his request was granted, he launched into a long, incoherent speech. These were, he said, the last words he would speak publicly. He said that he had predicted before the trial that people would make false statements under oath and that some of the defendants would act strangely. He spoke of evil influences—"the secret force that made men act and speak according to the orders given them."

Hess rambled on incoherently for some twenty minutes. The president of the court finally interrupted him to say that the defendants could not be allowed to make lengthy speeches at that stage of the proceedings. He urged Hess to conclude his statement.

Hess ended with a tribute to his master. It was on this occasion that he called Hitler the greatest son Germany had produced in its history. "Even if I could, I would not want to erase this period of time from my existence."

And a final touch: "No matter what human beings do I shall some day stand before the judgment seat of the Eternal. I shall answer to Him, and I know he will judge me innocent."

The Nuremberg Tribunal did not agree. It found Hess guilty on Count 1: Conspiracy to Prepare Aggressive War, and Count 2: Crimes Against the Peace. It stated that his relationship with Hitler was such that he must have known of the *Fuehrer's* aggressive plans when they came into existence.

At the same time the court found Hess not guilty on Count 3: War Crimes; and Count 4: Crimes Against Humanity:

There is evidence showing that the participation of the Party Chancellery, under Hess, in the distribution of orders connected with the commission of War Crimes; that Hess may have had knowledge of, even if he did not participate in, the crimes that were being committed in the East, and proposed laws discriminating against Jews and Poles; and that he signed decrees forcing certain groups of Poles to accept German citizenship. The Tribunal, however, does not find that the evidence sufficiently connects Hess with these crimes to sustain a finding of guilt.

The Tribunal recommended that a full medical examination be made as well as a report on the defendant's mental condition. ''That Hess acts in an abnormal manner, suffers from loss of memory, and has mentally deteriorated during his trial may be true. But there is nothing to show that he does not realize the nature of the charges against him, or is incapable of defending himself. He was ably represented at the trial by counsel appointed for that purpose by the Tribunal.''

Verdict: life imprisonment.

Hess's counsel appealed the verdict against him. During his final days at Nuremberg, he planned for the future. He would walk away from his captors as an innocent man and take over control of shattered Germany. He would be the new *Fuehrer* as planned all along by Hitler. He felt that there was a great mission for him of which he had much evidence. ''To doubt that would be the same as to doubt that tomorrow the sun will rise.'' He even set to work drawing up bulletins that were to be published in the press under his direction. He issued decrees about labor, food distribution, liaison with the occupying powers in Germany. He ordered a new uniform for himself—the new *Fuehrer*. The clothing must have adjustable seams ''because I will probably gain weight when I am released.''

Hess carefully drew up a list of people he wanted freed at once from camps where they were being held by the Allied powers, so that they could help him govern his ''Fourth Reich.'' He decided that Munich was to be the seat of the new government and the capital of Germany.

In a lengthy decree, Hess prepared an oath his followers were to swear when taking office: ''By God the Almighty, I swear to be faithful and obedient to Rudolf Hess, to perform the duties of the National Socialist *Reichsrat* [Council of the Reich] to the best of my ability. And especially to be absolutely silent about any matter to be spoken here.''

He would deliver a long address to his new *Reichstag*, including a tribute to Hitler: "Cruel fate has decreed that the Founder of the National Socialist Reich had to die, faced by the apparent certainty that his creation was destroyed forever. The *Fuehrer* died a voluntary death. He took it upon himself to die because he had no choice. He could not expose himself to undignified treatment.''

Hess added a statement excoriating Bolshevism and the Jews: "Behind hunger, cold, murder and despair, Bolshevism rears its ugly head. It is only with the Bolshevization of Europe that the objective would be reached, which was the purpose of the war. The rule of Bolshevism is the rule of the Jew.''

Here he was about to go to prison for life, and Hess was playing the same old weary Nazi record. He apparently had little understanding of his dilemma. He was living in a curious dream world. Far from becoming the *Fuehrer* of the Fourth Reich, he was forced to serve his sentence.

Hess was sent to Spandau Prison, a fortress in West Berlin at the mouth of the Spree River. Here he became Prisoner No. 7, joining six others found guilty at Nuremberg: Grand Admiral Karl Doenitz (ten years); Constantin Freiherr von Neurath (fifteen years); Baldur von Schirach (twenty years); Albert Speer (twenty years); Grand Admiral Erich Raeder (life); and Walther Funk (life).

The entire prison complex at Spandau was set aside for the exclusive retention of the Nazi prisoners. Four Allied powers kept them in confinement, each for a month: France in January, Great Britain in February, the USSR in March, and the United States in April. The cycle was repeated in May and September. Each country provided a prison commandant to serve in rotation, two doctors, cooks, and other personnel. Costs were met by the city of Berlin and the federal government in Bonn.

Hess was a grumbling and protesting prisoner. Cantankerous and difficult to manage, he was an enigma to his warders. His eyes were sunk deeply into his head and he wore a puzzled smile. His whole presence showed withdrawal and suspicion. He abhorred exercise, studiously avoided work, and for periods refused any meals. For years he suffered from intense abdominal pains. His loud howls of agony reverberating through the stone walls of the prison disturbed the other inmates.

Lieutenant Colonel Eugene K. Bird, U.S. commandant, described Hess in confinement: "He strode along the garden path, leaning forward, almost running; his hands behind his back, overcoat flowing behind him, Groucho Marx style." The warder was told how Hess was repeatedly examined by the doctors who could find no medical reason for his pains and cramps.

By 1966, one by one, six of the seven prisoners at Spandau were released. Except for a four-month interval at a British hospital nearby for treatment of a ruptured ulcer, Hess remained in solitary confinement. It was an extraordinary situation, the strangest in history: nearly two hundred men rotating from four different countries had the responsibility of guarding one old man. Two dozen cooks, waitresses, and cleaners were kept employed for the incarceration of a single prisoner.

Hess constantly bemoaned his fate. "I am an innocent man," he complained. "I see no reason why I should not be turned loose. Even if I were guilty—which I am not—no other prisoner has been sentenced to life or even death for his war crimes and still remains in jail. I am the only one who has not been freed. It is all wrong."

Behind the scene the governments of the United States, Britain, and France, seeing no point in holding the aged prisoner any longer, repeatedly urged his release. But the Russians, unmoved by other governmental or public protests, vetoed each request. For them, life imprisonment in Hess's case meant exactly imprisonment until death. Although the Russians had agreed to the release of Raeder and Funk, both serving life sentences, they refused similar treatment for Hess. One of the Soviet warders told Colonel Bird: "You Americans look on war as a game of 'cowboys and Indians.' You do not know the horrors of war. Our country was devastated, and that devastation was caused by a Nazi hierarchy of which Hess was a vital part. I do not believe that my country will ever agree to the release of Rudolf Hess."

The case of Rudolf Hess is a special one. He was chosen for high office primarily because of his infantile sense of flattery. One observer put it bluntly: "Hess hangs with the eyes of a credulous child on the mouth of the deified leader." He was actually of limited intelligence though he saw himself as an intellectual. Prison psychologist G. N. Gilbert at Nuremberg estimated, on the basis of a retest after recovery, that Hess's IQ was 120, the fourth lowest among the twenty-one defendants.

Hess was originally a purer type than the scoundrels fighting for Hitler's attention. But he succumbed to the Nazi way of life and decided to make his way in its society. Along the road he lost whatever human instincts he may have had in his earlier years. He accepted the principle of violence because the *Fuehrer*—his god-man—advocated it. He longed to become Hitler's alter ego and work in the shadow of the man he regarded as his country's savior. He accepted disgraceful, inhuman behavior simply because his beloved *Fuehrer* condoned it. He saw his own conduct as dictated by loyalty and patriotism. His flight to Scotland, he said, was in the interest of peace: "My earnest desire was to stop the war, not to continue it. At the same time I wanted to warn about the coming danger of the Bolshevists, of communism. The world cannot say I did not warn of this."

Hess's mind eventually broke under the strain. It could have been overwork, amnesia, insanity, or nervous collapse—or a combination of them. Over the years some two hundred psychiatrists examined the sole prisoner at Spandau and there was little agreement among them.

What started out as a carefree student longing for a magnificent career turned into a sleazy organizer of Nazi savagery. Hess never understood the implications: "The reason that the Russians won't let me go is that they think I knew a great deal more than I did, and that I had a great deal more influence than I did have. That is why I am still in Spandau."

Late bulletin:

Berlin (Associated Press). Feb. 15, 1984:

An elevator is being built at a cost of $47,000 at Spandau Prison for it sole inmate, former Hitler deputy Rudolf Hess, 90.

Informed sources said yesterday the elevator is needed because the feeble Hess is unable to navigate the narrow iron stairway from his cellblock to the visiting room, and he cannot legally be deprived of the one-hour monthly visit by his family.

The United States, France and Great Britain have indicated that they are willing to free Hess on humanitarian grounds, but the Soviet Union has refused to go along. Unanimous agreement is needed.

On Monday, August 17, 1987, the world media reported that the 93-year-old inmate at Spandau was found with an electric cord around his neck and that he had hanged himself. A week later British authorities in Berlin issued another statement: "All available evidence—including results of a full autopsy and investigations by the special investigation branch of the Royal Military Police—indicates that Hess used an electrical extension cord to hang himself and that the cause of death was asphyxiation."

Close-out. With the last relic of the infamous Third Reich dead, Spandau was razed to frustrate attempts by neo-Nazis to turn the prison into a shrine.

6

JOSEPH GOEBBELS: HITLER'S LITTLE MOUSE-GENERAL

The Jew has destroyed our race! He has rotted our morals, sapped our tradition, and broken our power.
                                    —Joseph Goebbels

He was a short, thin bantam of a man, with hatchet face and a crippled leg. His colleagues at the summit of the Nazi jungle snubbed him as "the little mouse-general" and accused him of being overambitious, overpowerful, and oversexed. Aware of his closeness to Hitler, they ridiculed him but only behind his back. Nazi specialists in Aryan ethnology justified his un-Aryan appearance by according him a special classification—*Nachgedunkelnter Schrimpfgermane*, a "dwarflike German who grew dark."

Nor did he, as Hermann Goering, win the amused tolerance of the German public. He craved popularity but his fellow citizens—always in private—called him "the malicious dwarf" and "the latest reincarnation of the devil." They gave him such names as "Wotan's Mickey Mouse," "Mahatma Propaganda," and "the hegoat of Babelsberg."

Yet, with his cold and calculating mind, Joseph Goebbels was a decided asset to Hitler. The leading propagandist of the Third Reich, he eventually became dictator over German cultural life. It was largely due to his ritualistic pen that the German people followed the *Fuehrer* into the pit of destruction before they knew what they were doing. For one day—April 30, 1945—this little bundle of energy served as Chancellor of the Third Reich, appointed to that top post by Hitler in his underground Berlin bunker to the tune of exploding Red artillery shells and loud Wagnerian music. For a single day he was a successor to great Chancellor Otto von Bismarck.

Throughout his life Goebbels suffered from the stigma of being unable to serve his country in World War I. A crippled leg left him with a permanent limp. Despite his piercing intelligence, cynicism, and guile, he always resented the stares and suspected comments of onlookers. It was a painful task for him to preach the virtues of tall, healthy, blue-eyed Nordics while he was described even by colleagues because of his slight frame and black hair as "a half-Frenchman—and a pupil of the Jesuits."

The little mouse-general moved awkwardly among his well-built feeble-brained colleagues, who contemptuously dismissed him as a climbing cripple. An intellectual among thugs, he was motivated, like Rudolf Hess, by one consuming characteristic—absolute loyalty to Adolf Hitler. That led him to suicide along with this chieftain in a thunderous *Götterdämmerung*.

It is useless to apply ordinary standards of morality to this atavistic type. Goebbels had no sense of decency either in his personal or public life. Like other Nazis, he was blinded by ambition as he clawed his way to the top of Hitler's world. Oblivious to principles of right or wrong, contemptuous of ethical conduct, he was the embodiment of Nazi evil.

The little man was filled with venom. "Hatred, that's my trade," he admitted. "It takes you a long way farther than any other emotion."

To win the eternal gratitude of Hitler, he expressed his feelings about Jews in language he knew would give satisfaction to his master: "A Jew is for me an object of disgust. I feel like vomiting when I see one. Christ could not possibly have been a Jew. It is not necessary to prove that scientifically—it is a fact. I treasure an ordinary prostitute above a married Jewess."

This was the nihilist appointed as guardian of German *Kultur*.

Biographer Curt Riess gave this estimate: "There can be no doubt that Goebbels did not belong in the category of the crazed, chauvinistic petty bourgeoisie as Hitler and Himmler, or the great gangsters as Goering or the little gangsters as Sauckel *[Fritz Sauckel, chief of slave labor recruitment]*. In terms of the law he was neither a criminal such as Streicher, nor mad as Hess, nor perverse and oversexed as Roehm and Heines *[Edmund Heines, SA general, intimate of Roehm]*. He *[Goebbels]* was in a class by himself." Former French Ambassador in Berlin André François-Poncet declared, with some justification, that Goebbels was "the most dangerous man of the Hitler regime."

Paul Joseph Goebbels was born on October 29, 1897, in the industrial town of Rheydt in the Lower Rhineland of some 30,000 inhabitants. His father Fritz, of peasant stock, was a factory clerk, farmer, and teacher, who later became manager of a textile plant. His mother, Maria Katherina, was the daughter of a blacksmith. The parents were pious Catholics, who raised all three sons in that faith. Though not poverty-stricken, the family was in relatively modest circumstances.

During the first seven years of his life, when he attended the Catholic *Volkschule* (elementary, or primary school) at Rheydt, the thin little boy with the too large head seemed normal enough, though shy and withdrawn. Then came what for him was the tragedy of his life. He fell ill with osteomyelitis, inflammation of the bone marrow. The distraught parents agreed to an operation. The result was that his left leg became four inches shorter than his right, and remained scrawny and without strength. He was left with a permanent limp and had to wear special shoes and braces.

Later, because of the partially disabled leg and his uneven gait, the legend arose that Goebbels was born with a clubfoot. The enemies who hated him, and there were many, charged that he had Jewish blood in his veins and cited his "clubfoot" as evidence. Before he became a man of power in the Nazi realm he was often referred to as Mephistopheles, the devil, who was pictured with a horse's hoof. One newspaper article compared Goebbels with Talleyrand, the clubfooted French statesman in the Napoleonic era. Like Talleyrand, it was said, Goebbels was a man of "racially conditioned mental and physical disharmony."

The operation on his leg and its aftermath were of enormous

significance in molding the character of the young boy. Unable to participate in games with other children, he became a loner. He would show them by his intellect that he was superior to them. He developed a sharp and cynical tongue, which gave him the reputation of being belligerent and hostile. Those characteristics, a mixture of cynicism and cunning, were to remain with him for the rest of his life. Much of his later behavior can be explained by that unfortunate incident in his early days.

When World War I began on August 4, 1914, all Germany seemed to explode in an outburst of patriotic euphoria. Troop trains that passed through Rheydt were decorated with chalked slogans: "On to Paris by Christmas!" Youngsters not yet seventeen surged to recruiting centers. Exultant Goebbels limped along with them. He was pronounced unfit for military duty, another crushing blow scorching his psyche. He went home and wept. Later, during his university days, he attributed his limp to a wound received in combat. And still later, when a powerful man in the Third Reich, he wore the Nazi uniform as often as possible.

After attendance at *Gymnasium* (grammar school) young Goebbels, as was the custom of the day, wandered from university to university, studying history, philology, and the history of art and literature at Würzburg, Bonn, Frieburg, Heidelberg, Cologne, Frankfurt-am-Main, Berlin, and then back to Heidelberg. He was helped by Catholic scholarships. At Heidelberg he studied Goethe and Shakespeare with famed Jewish Professor Freidrich Gundolf (born Gundolfinger). A few years later Goebbels was writing: "We must fight against the withering poison of the international-Jewish spirit."

The slim young man with the large dark eyes took his doctorate with a dissertation on the German Romantics. At once he insisted on being called "Dr. Goebbels" and retained the habit for the rest of his life. Any other form of address triggered a withering glance.

Shut out from physical activity, Goebbels decided to become a great writer. His first published book, *Michael*, an autobiographical novel written when he was twenty-four, was partly in free verse. It was an ignominious failure. Two plays, also in free verse, were rejected by Berlin producers. Goebbels applied to the *Berliner Tageblatt* as a reporter but he was turned down. He denounced the editor and owner of the paper as Jews. Once again he was humiliated.

Meanwhile in 1922, purely by chance, Goebbels entered a meeting hall in Munich and heard Hitler speak. Until then he was not interested in politics, but there was something about the nervous Austrian that affected him deeply. There was a community of interest: both had come from poor families and both had been failures in their attempted start in life. Goebbels began to copy Hitler in manner, speech, and ideology.

Hitler had found a willing and able disciple.

Goebbels decided to penetrate Hitler's inner circle. He began a shrewd campaign of flattery and affected eagerness, which he knew would impress the Austrian with the colossal vanity.

Unlike Goering, Roehm, Streicher, and Hess, who had already ingratiated themselves with Hitler, Goebbels did not share the experience of taking part in the unsuccessful Beer-Hall *Putsch* of November 8-9, 1923. But his opportunity to reach the ear of the Nazi leader came with the subsequent trial for treason. He recognized as a masterpiece of propaganda Hitler's feat in turning the trial into a one-man show. Goebbels dashed off a glowing letter: "Like a rising star you have appeared before our wondering eyes. You performed miracles to clear our minds and, in a world of skepticism and desperation, you have given us faith. You towered above the masses. For the first time we were able to see with shining eyes a man who tore off the mask from faces distorted by greed. What you said are the greatest words spoken in Germany since Bismarck. You expressed the need of an entire generation. What you said is the catechism of a new political belief, born out of the despair of a collapsing Godless world. We thank you. One day Germany will thank you."

The ardent young flatterer's campaign was going well. In him the Nazi leader found one who could listen for days to his long-winded speeches. "The man burns like a flame," Hitler said. Others could denounce Goebbels as "the Mephisto of the Party" or "the scheming dwarf," but Hitler was satisfied with his admirer and took steps to promote him.

By this time Goebbels had decided on a career in journalism. He moved to the Ruhr district in 1924 and became editor of the *Völkische Freiheit (People's Freedom)* in Elberfeld. The next year he became business manager of the Rhineland-North *Gau* (district) of the NSDAP, the Nazi Party. At the same time he was named editor for Gregor Strasser's *NS-Briefe (National Socialist Letters)*.

While working with Gregor Strasser and his brother Otto, Goebbels became embroiled in a controversy between Hitler and the Strassers on the extent of socialism in the National Socialist movement. For a time Goebbels took the Strasser side and made his famous demand that "the bourgeois Adolf Hitler should be expelled from the National Socialist Party." But in 1926 Goebbels suddenly made an about-face and deserted the Strassers. Once again he began his campaign of flattery. He spoke of Hitler as "either Christ or St. John." "Adolf Hitler, I love you!" he wrote in his diary.

Hitler was willing to forgive the man who, after all, had betrayed the Strassers. He appointed Goebbels *Gauleiter* (district leader) for Berlin, "responsible to me alone." Thus began a career in Nazi officialdom which was to have enormous consequences for Germany as well as for the entire world.

The nervous young Rhinelander soon began to make an impression both inside and outside the party circles. He seemed to be a born master of agitation and propaganda. He edited a newspaper, *Der Angriff (Attack)*, which he dedicated to the spread of National Socialism. So reckless was he in assaults on individuals that at one time there were many libel suits pending against him.

In Berlin, Goebbels emerged as an expert in slander and intrigue. He knew how to circulate false rumors, exploit people, and build himself up as a champion of Nazism. In the battle of the streets against Communists, he had Storm Troopers wear around their heads large white bandages covered with a red liquid so that they could be regarded as heroes by the Berlin public. Limping from his "war wounds," he marched at their head. He published articles, always in the third person, describing "Doctor Goebbels's extraordinary courage." He discovered a political martyr in Horst Wessel, a Nazi who had been killed by Communists in a brawl. He promoted Wessel's doggerel verse as the official party song, and later gave it the status of a national anthem. He had millions of swastika leaflets distributed on the streets of Berlin.

Most of all, Goebbels, after Hitler, was the most effective orator of the Nazi movement. Eyewitnesses described how the diminutive Goebbels, with his flat brow, protruding ears, and cadaverous face, limped into meetings surrounded by bodyguards. On the podium he was a wizard of eloquence. He used his loud, penetrating voice and cynical intelligence to denounce real or fancied enemies. His thin arms beat the air with a sense of finality. Bossman Hitler was delighted with his drum-thumping little mouse-general. The man was promoting Nazism in Berlin and was making it a stronghold next to Munich. He was a "thinking tool." In 1928 the "leader" had Goebbels elevated to *Reichstag* membership.

Later that same year, Hitler appointed Goebbels Reich Propaganda Leader for the Nazi Party. After the Nazi assumption of power in 1933, Goebbels was made Minister for Public Enlightenment and Propaganda. He was now in an executive position of great power in a post in which he, as Hitler's mouthpiece, could implement national socialist ideology.

Soon after he became Propaganda Minister, Goebbels took part in one of the most shameful episodes in German history, a spectacle that revealed much about his character. A somewhat similar incident had taken place a century earlier. Since the Middle Ages, German students had been known for their rollicking, carefree lifestyles suffused with emotional romanticism. There was an unforgettable episode in the early nineteenth century. On October 18, 1817, at Würzburg near Eisenach, on the 300th anniversary of Martin Luther's revolt starting the Protestant Reformation, some five hundred students, many intoxicated, decided to light a huge bonfire. In imitation of Luther they consigned to the flames symbols of what they despised, including a corporal's cane, a Prussian military manual, and stacks of conservative pamphlets. Students and professors from nearby Jena made speeches praising "Freedom and Fatherland."

On May 10, 1933, university students in Berlin, inspired by Nazi propaganda, invaded public and private libraries, collecting books by Jewish, Marxist, Bolshevist, and other "disruptive" authors, and consigned the volumes to a huge bonfire. The books included those by both living and deceased authors, classics as well as pornographic trash. The works of Karl Marx, Sigmund Freud, Thomas Mann, Maxim Gorky, Henri Barbusse, Lion Feuchtwanger, Walther Rathenau, Heinrich Heine, and many others were thrown into the flames. More than 20,000 books were burned.

Faculty members from the University of Berlin presided enthusiastically over the proceedings. Professor Alfred Baumler marched at the head of students wearing brown shirts and carrying torches. Among the books burned were those by several of his colleagues.

The little Propaganda Minister, sensing a good story, deemed it essential that he join the proceedings. Wearing as usual his too-big trench coat, he appeared at the bonfire. Amid Nazi salutes and protected by uniformed bodyguards, he mounted a swastika-draped platform and spoke in his booming, mellifluous voice: "Jewish intellectualism is dead. National Socialism has hewn the way. The German folk soul can again express itself. These flames do not merely illuminate the final end of the old era, they also light up the new. Never before have the young men had so good a right to clean up the debris of the past. If the old men do not understand what is going on, let them grasp that we young men have gone and done it. The old goes up in flames, the new shall be fashioned from the flame in our hearts."

Goebbels told the students that as they had the right to destroy the books, they also had the duty to support the government. The fire would signal to the entire world that the enemies of Germany had sunk into the earth and a new spirit had risen.

There were similar bonfires throughout Germany—in Munich, Frankfurt-am-Main, Breslau, and Kiel. In Frankfurt, books went into the flames to the strains of Chopin's *Funeral March* as thousands of students in full fraternity regalia stood at attention.

Goebbels expected the whole world to see the bonfires as the signal of a new spirit. He was partly right—the world reacted in disgust. The next day he had some uncomfortable second thoughts. He instructed all German newspapers to play down the burning of the books. The day before he had proclaimed: "Students are thriving, spirits awakening. Oh century, it is a joy to live!" Now he was concerned by the backlash.

What psychological motivation impelled Goebbels the intellectual to take part in so degrading a spectacle? There is a clue in the very word "intellectual" as he envisioned it. He, himself, was of university background, a representative of the intelligentsia that Hitler despised. And it was always necessary to appease the *Fuehrer*.

Goebbels was well-aware that in *Mein Kampf* Hitler had shown his contempt for intellectuals. Hitler wrote about "the pitiful cowardice of our so-called intelligentsia" which, he charged, lacked "necessary will power." Professors and their books,

Thomas Mann and all the rest, with their inane intellectualism, were leading Germans away from their good Aryan-Nordic heritage.

That was enough for the toadying Propaganda Minister. The master had spoken and it was Goebbels's duty to implement his slightest desire. If Hitler hated intellectuals, then Goebbels must desert their ranks and hate them, too. Whatever the *Fuehrer* believed was holy writ for the willing servant.

Goebbels would use the students to promote National Socialism and with it his own budding career. The students, frustrated by their country's political and economic woes, had found in the Nazi movement an ideal means of discharging their hostility. He, Goebbels, would use them to promote the Nazi way of life, with its romantic accent on the irrational.

Goebbels's ministry was officially set up on June 30, 1933, with a decree making him "responsible for all factors influencing the mental life of the nation, for winning allegiance to the State, its culture and its economy, for the conduct of internal and external publicity, and for the administration of all institutions contributing to these ends." Goebbels now had a post of tremendous power, by which he became the *de facto* ruler of press, radio, cinema, theater, and virtually all cultural, scientific, and musical activities. There were clashes with jealous rivals, with Goering over control of the Prussian theater and with Rosenberg over authority in art. But the mouse-general had the ear of the *Fuehrer* and that was vital—he eventually was victorious in the battle for leadership of Nazi *Kultur*.

Goebbels became president of the Reich Culture Chamber. He managed May Day, harvest festivals and the winter relief campaign. New laws concerning press and cinema gave him even greater power. He was also awarded a huge propaganda fund for influencing the foreign press.

In directing Nazi propaganda, Goebbels was careful to pay close attention to Hitler's advice that the greater the lie the more people would believe it. The Propaganda Minister had a working theory: "You can make a man believe anything if you tell it to him in the proper way."

Even more important from his own viewpoint was the necessity of glorifying the *Fuehrer* in speech and print. Six months after the advent of the Nazi regime and immediately after his appointment as Minister for Public Enlightenment and Propaganda, Goebbels delivered a speech praising Hitler's accomplishments. Again the fawning flattery. There were some unteachable individuals, he said, who actually believed that little had been accomplished, but these know-it-alls would be punished. There had been breath-taking accomplishments. "It is the strong central authority, which is centered in the person of Hitler. He and his colleagues will carry out the most difficult historical tasks ever placed before our times and our generation." Hitler had been able to overcome the multiple party system and unify the whole German people into one will and readiness for common action—a great historical accomplishment.

"The entire nation gives Hitler its confidence. At no time in German history has a government been able to represent its people as that led by him. When necessary it may proceed harshly against our opponents in order to demonstrate to them the principles we represent. It foregoes tenderness and magnanimity when it becomes absolutely necessary to bring back again to the great German people's community those who have been corrupted or still doubt."

"It foregoes tenderness and magnanimity." Here the reader may well find a clue for the later Nazi descent into barbarism and mass murder.

Goebbels's propaganda style took into account his earlier words that "the only instrument with which one can conduct foreign policy is alone and exclusively the sword." His glorification of war, often expressed in almost hysterical terms, won instant approval from the *Fuehrer*. Goebbels called for all-out battle against democracy, liberalism, plutocracy, capitalism, Bolshevism, and above all, against Judaism. Later he would turn on the Allies and Soviet Russia.

Always the Jews! Earlier in his career, while writing pamphlets for the budding National Socialist Party, Goebbels expressed a kind of intellectual anti-Semitism, a somewhat restrained attitude of annoyance. "Don't be an anti-Semitic knave," he had written in his Ten Commandments for National Socialists. "But be careful of the *Berliner Tageblatt*."

That early benign conception of Jews and Jewry changed drastically when Goebbels realized the extent of Hitler's hatred. To please his master, the Propaganda Minister devoted all his talents to the task of arousing contempt for Jews and their role in German national life. Soon the pamphlets flowing from his pen excoriated Jews in language highly pleasing to the *Fuehrer*. The style of writing was influenced by editorials in the American Hearst press, which made heavy use of capitalization, question marks, and exclamation points. Goebbels's strictures set a standard for the compounding Nazi anti-Semitic campaign, which culminated in the horrors of the Final Solution:

Why are we enemies of the Jews?

We are enemies of the Jews because we are warriors for the freedom of the German people. THE JEW IS THE CAUSE AND THE BENEFICIARY OF OUR SLAVERY. He has used the social troubles of our broad masses in order to widen the split between right and left among our people. He has made TWO HALVES OF GERMANY. Here is the real reason for the loss of the World War on one side and for the betrayal of the revolution on the other side. . . . The Jew has no interest in the solution of the questions of German fate. He CAN'T have an interest because he wants it to remain unsolved. . . . He has a better trump in his hand when a nation lives in slavery than when it is free, busy, self-conscious and self-contained.

THE JEW HAS CAUSED OUR MISERY, AND TODAY HE LIVES ON OUR TROUBLES!

That is the reason why AS NATIONALISTS AND AS SOCIALISTS we are enemies of the Jew. HE HAS RUINED OUR RACE, ROTTED OUR MORALS, CORRUPTED OUR TRADITIONS, AND BROKEN OUR POWER. We can thank him for being the goats of the world today. As long as we were Germans, he was a leper among us. Since we have forgotten our German character, he has triumphed over us and our future.

THE JEW IS THE PLASTIC DEMON OF THE FALL OF MANKIND. Where he scents rubbish and putrefaction, there he appears and begins a criminal game of chess with other people. He takes on the mask of those whom he wants to deceive, pretends to be the friend of his victim, and before the unfortunate one knows it, he has his neck broken. . . .

WE ARE JEW-HATERS BECAUSE WE ADMIT THAT WE ARE GERMANS. THE JEW IS OUR GREATEST CALAMITY.

It isn't true that we eat a Jew with every breakfast.

But it is true THAT HE IS EATING US UP SLOWLY BUT SURELY, TOGETHER WITH ALL OUR POSSESSIONS.

THAT IS GOING TO CHANGE, AS SURELY AS WE ARE GERMANS!

When, on November 7, 1938, Herschel Grynszpan, a Polish citizen of Jewish origin, broke into the German Embassy in Paris and shot Ernst vom Rath, just a minor secretary, Goebbels reacted violently. "There can be no doubt," he thundered, "that Grynszpan was hidden by a Jewish organization and systematically prepared to execute this cynical crime." He attacked the "parasitical race" of Jews in Germany as well as Jews all over the world. It was not one Jew, he charged, but Jewry as such.

Goebbels's drumfire provoked a "spontaneous" reaction against the assassination. All over Germany synagogues were burned down, Jewish stores were looted and destroyed, and Jews were beaten and taken to concentration camps. The little mouse-general, directing the campaign behind the scenes, spoke with satisfaction: "The outburst of indignation among the people shows that their patience is completely exhausted."

Psychohistorians and other specialists in abnormal psychology agree that Goebbels's behavior in high office was based partly on his deep-rooted desire to compensate for what he regarded as gnawing failures. He gave highly emotional responses to both mental and physical problems.

Goebbels's mental reaction was closely associated with his lack of success as a playwright in his early years. The rejection by Berlin directors and producers tore at his soul and left him in despair. A product of a small Rhineland village, he would show those city slickers what he could do. He would strike back at Berlin Jews who had monopolized German *Kultur* and had flung back his own bid for early recognition.

For the little man it was historical justice. In the battle for control of the German mind, he, the unproduced and unpublished playwright, had conquered the *Schweinehunde* (pig-dogs, or filthy fellows) and had become master of national propaganda. He, not the pestilential Jews of Berlin, would dictate "public enlightenment."

In his drive as cultural dictator, Goebbels had one enormously effective weapon. His body was diminutive and his leg crippled, but his voice was powerful, honeyed, hypnotizing. On the speakers' platform he could turn into a raging Demosthenes as he pronounced damnation on Jews and enemies of Aryan domination. He could rise to lyrical heights in glorification of the beaming *Fuehrer*. His oratory rivaled that of Hitler himself. In one respect he was even more impressive: where the *Fuehrer's* voice had a kind of Austrian Cockney accent, Goebbels could soar to heights of ecstasy in impeccable German with a slight Rhineland regional twist.

Goebbels's second response to his handicaps was geared to his physical appearance. The runty little body, the thin, sharp face, that damned crippled foot which caused his rejection for military service, these gave him much pain and embarrassment. It was an ironic and unkind fate that made him short, dark, and ugly, instead of tall, blond, and handsome in the preferred Nordic fashion. To critics who said he was tainted by bad blood, he replied with acid vituperation. "Utter nonsense!" he said.

How could the little man compensate for his flawed looks? Again he would show them! The unprepossessing Goebbels emerged as Nazi Germany's outstanding superstud.

Goebbels's attention to various prominent German and Austrian actresses became the subject of scandal throughout the Reich. Stories of his romantic peccadillos began to appear in gossip sheets. Young would-be-stars of stage, screen, and radio were attracted to the all-powerful Propaganda Minister. The body was blemished but the power was magnetic. Moreover, there was a put-on charm and a studied aloofness that drew the attention and admiration of scores of young German beauties. They accepted his invitations with pleasure and willingly went to his private office at the Propaganda Ministry or to his estate in Lanke, given to him by the city of Berlin. Just as some of Hollywood's beauteous starlets stormed the couches of producers and directors, so did their German counterparts seek access to the lecherous Propaganda Minister.

For Goebbels it was a comfortable situation and one that he felt he had earned as a power broker. That he was in the process of producing six children by wife, Magda, meant little difference to him. Besides, he was having marital difficulties. His promiscuous sex life conducted in the broad daylight of public opinion was causing strains in his marriage. Wife Magda (Ritschel) Quandt, whom he married in 1931, had previously been the spouse of one of the country's most prominent industrialists. She was more than twenty-five years younger than her first husband. As Goebbels's wife, she called herself the First Lady of the Reich. A strong character, she was not inclined to accept her spouse's wanderings gracefully.

The suspicious Magda soon learned that her husband was deceiving her and that all Berlin seemed to know about it. Offended and angry, she reproached him for his affairs with giggling young actresses. He, in turn, struck back and reminded her that he had never promised to be faithful. She had to understand, he told her, that he was a normal German male. Was she not aware that he had performed his marital duties successfully? Had he not given her six children—Helge, Hilde, Helmut, Holde, Hedda, and Heide—all names beginning with "H"? The one boy, Helmut, admittedly was shy and not too bright, a disappointment the father curiously attributed to Magda. Were not the children the favorites of Uncle Adolf? What he did outside his marriage, Goebbels insisted, was in his view none of his wife's business.

The marriage was already on shaky ground when Goebbels met famous Czech actress Lida Baarova. The young motion-picture star, though not a classic beauty, was small and thin, with attractive dark eyes, and glowing personality. She was living with a handsome actor in the summer of 1937 when she met Goebbels. For the Propaganda Minister it was love at first sight. For the ambitious Czech actress it was a golden opportunity to further her career.

For a time the affair went smoothly. Then one night the actress's boyfriend discovered Goebbels and Lida in what is usually described as a compromising situation. In the German press it was "reliably reported" that the aggrieved actor had beaten Goebbels within an inch of his life. Public contempt for the

Propaganda Minister was so great that for a time the enraged actor became a popular hero.

Infuriated, Magda Goebbels broke with her husband and demanded that he live separately from her and the children. There was a complicating factor. Karl Hanke, young and awkward secretary to Goebbels, had fallen in love with Magda and wanted to marry her. Magda resisted for a while but then, apparently to punish her unfaithful husband, decided to accept the proposal after she had gotten a divorce.

Scandal in the *Fuehrer's* entourage. Hanke sent a petition to Hitler for approval of his marriage to Magda, but the *Fuehrer* categorically refused to permit a divorce "for reasons of state." Hitler called Goebbels and his wife to be with him at a Wagnerian festival. Albert Speer reported the depressed and drawn Magda as saying: "It was frightful the way my husband threatened me. I was just beginning to recuperate at Gastein when he showed up at the hotel. For three days he argued with me incessantly, until I could no longer stand it. He used the children to blackmail me; he threatened to take them away from me. What could I do?" Sitting in the big central box at the theater, Magda cried incessantly, silently, and uncontrollably throughout the performance of the Wagnerian opera, *Tristan and Isolde*.

The next day Hitler sent for Goebbels and gruffly informed him that it would be better for him if he left Bayreuth immediately with his wife. Allowing no reply, he refused to shake hands. He was cold to his minister and said to Speer: "With women, Goebbels is a cynic."

The misanthropic Goebbels, like a small boy spanked by his father, went sheepishly back to his marriage. Later, photographs in newspapers throughout the Reich showed Hitler with the smiling couple.

The unrepentant propaganda expert soon resumed his extramarital affairs. So much for love among Nazi troglodytes.

The opening campaigns of World War II were for Goebbels a time of unrestrained joy. In the war of nerves before 1939 he filled the German press and radio with stories of Polish atrocities. He celebrated one Nazi victory after another with encomiums for "the greatest military genius in our history." Typical boast: "The Western offensive has descended upon the plutocracies." He described the utter confusion and panic of the enemy when face to face with Nazi *Panzer* divisions and the

screaming dive-bombing *Stukas*. Fanfares played by brass bands
greeted reports of new triumphs. The more German victories,
the louder the tone of Goebbels's propaganda drums.

In the spring of 1941, Goebbels concentrated the venom of his
hatred on Winston Churchill, in whom he saw the most powerful
and relentless of his enemies. In a stream of sarcastic articles,
he attacked "the drunk who is responsible for this war. To satisfy his blind and ruthless vanity, he will walk over dead bodies.
He does not seduce children but nations. If the time comes to
write the history of the collapse of the British Isles, its most
decisive chapter will be titled 'Churchill.' "

And then came the invasion of the Soviet Union, war with the
United States, and the subsequent battle of Stalingrad. The long-
dreaded Second Front was there. Goebbels's propaganda machine went into action against the Jews. World Jewry was the
real enemy—Bolshevist, plutocratic, democratic, imperialistic,
capitalistic—and Jewish. The Goebbels dictum—the United
States had entered the war in service of Judaism.

All to no avail. The Propaganda Minister was faced with a
serious dilemma. At a time when most German cities were being
blasted to rubble, he was trying to improve the morale of a
miserable and now bewildered people. The days of triumph by
the great *Fuehrer* were past. All the old strategems and tricks were
ineffective on a people now consumed with doubt. The loss of
manpower was staggering. It would become necessary eventually
to recruit old men and young boys to replace the vanished legions.

In early 1945 Hitler appointed his Propaganda Minister "De-
fender of Berlin." Unwilling to trust the generals he held responsible for the July 1944 attempt on his life at Rastenburg, the
Fuehrer needed someone on whom he could rely unconditionally. At long last the little mouse-general had a top military
command he always wanted. But it was too late—Germany was
on the verge of defeat.

Goebbels still put on a show of confidence. He was certain
that somehow Providence would grant a miracle to Germany.
Then on April 12 came the great news that Roosevelt "has just
died." "This is the miracle we have waited for." Goebbels
rushed to the telephone: "My *Fuehrer*, I congratulate you. It
was written in the stars that the turning point would come in the
second half of April. This is the turning point." Goebbels was
exultant. Among his favorite stories was Frederick the Great's

desperate situation in the Seven Years' War. The depressed king had decided to take poison when his fiercest enemy, the Czarina, died unexpectedly. Prussia was saved by a miracle, and now, "Franklin D. Rosenfeldt," the man "who had criminally misjudged the general world situation," had died at precisely the right moment.

Goebbels was whistling in the dark of impending defeat. Nothing could save the Third Reich from collapse.

In mid-April Hitler left the Chancellery and moved down into his specially built concrete bunker under the garden. Here, in twelve small cubicles and eighteen tiny rooms, "the greatest German in history" spent his last days in what has been called the *Götterdämmerung*, the Twilight of the Gods, to the tune of Richard Wagner's crashing cymbals. Others described the scene as "that cloud-cuckoo land of the bunker." The increasingly hysterical *Fuehrer* staged daily fits of rage. He screamed that he was betrayed on all sides by traitors in the army, by Himmler and Goering, by the German people. Germany was not worthy of him and deserved to be destroyed. The Third Reich was finished. He would stay in his bunker and die a hero's death. Meanwhile, with trembling arms he placed colored pins on large war maps to move phantom divisions for a last-minute victory.

Goebbels, too, decided on suicide. He, the noble knight, would stay at the side of his *Fuehrer* and choose death rather than the disgrace of capture. He brought Magda and the six children to the bunker with the intention of ending their lives as part of his own suicide.

Always the propagandist. Although there is no way of knowing, it is probable that Goebbels convinced his master of the need for dying. One must think of posterity. The Propaganda Minister had built Hitler into a figure of global importance and it was now necessary to maintain the legend. One day the German people would see what they had lost in the demise of their magnificent Siegfried. With his death he would become deified in German annals. Let him die in an aura of mystery and thereby enhance a legend for all time.

If Hitler, the god of nihilism, should take his life in this fantastic atmosphere, should not his loyal junior die along with the master? Survival would be illogical. He, the faithful servant, would stay and die with the *Fuehrer*.

At four o'clock on the morning of April 29, 1945, a distraught

Hitler signed his personal will, witnessed by Goebbels, Martin Bormann, and Colonel Nicholas von Below, and his Political Testament, witnessed by Goebbels, Bormann, Wilhelm Burgdorf, and Hans Krebs. In the second part of his Political Testament, Hitler appointed Goebbels to the post of Reich Chancellor, an office Goebbels was to hold for just one day.

After signing these two papers, Goebbels withdrew to his own small apartment in the bunker and there wrote an "Appendix to the *Fuehrer*'s Political Testament," in the form of a personal apologia. He denounced the defection of Goering and Himmler as a "delirium of treachery," and pronounced himself as unconditionally loyal to the *Fuehrer* until his death. He was doing this, he wrote, as the best service he could do to the future of the German people. Men would always be found to lead the nation to freedom *[sic!]*:

> The *Fuehrer* has ordered me, should the defense of the Reich capital collapse, to leave Berlin, and to take part as the leading member of the government appointed by him.

> For the first time in my life I must categorically refuse to obey an order of the *Fuehrer*. Otherwise—quite apart from the fact that feelings of humanity and loyalty forbid us to abandon the *Fuehrer* in his hour of greatest need—I should appear for the rest of my life as a dishonorable traitor and common scoundrel, and should lose all my self-respect together with the respect of my fellow citizens; a respect I should need in any future attempt to shape the future of the German Nation and State. . . .

> For this reason, together with my wife, and on behalf of my children, who are too young to speak for themselves, but who would unreservedly agree with this decision if they were old enough, I express my unalterable resolution not to leave the Reich capital, even if it falls, but rather, at the side of the *Fuehrer*, to end a life which will have no further value to me if I cannot spend it in the service of the *Fuehrer* and by his side.

When General Hans Krebs offered Goebbels and his family an armored car to escape from the bunker, the Propaganda Minister, assuming the pose of a man of honor, indignantly refused. "No, thank you. I am no longer interested in life."

At 8:30 P.M. on May 1, Goebbels and Magda, after poisoning their six children ("They must not grow up in a non-National Socialist Germany!"), walked up the stairs of the bunker into the garden. Immediately a shot was heard. Both were found lying dead on the ground. Goebbels had shot himself and Magda had taken poison. And *SS* guard fired twice into the bodies to make sure they were dead.

Then orderlies poured four cans of petrol over the corpses, threw on a match, and withdrew. The Russians later found the bodies.

There was no doubt about it. The sharp, hatchet face was that of Goebbels. Rumors started at once. Goebbels had fled in a submarine to Argentina. The body was that of a double. The clever Propaganda Minister had erased his identity by fleeing to a monastery. The champion myth-maker of Germany, after a bungled cremation, became the object of another legend. He would have enjoyed the macabre mysticism surrounding his suicide.

What are we to make of this extraordinary character, this intellectual (one of the rare Nazis of this breed), this clever wordsmith who kept a nation in bondage? His justification for his life was in the power he wielded, power such as few men have enjoyed. An ambitious demagogue used his Jesuitical training and ease of argument that made him more successful as a propagandist than any other blowhards of Hitler's entourage. This little man with the booming voice could persuade Germans that their defeats were victories, that the Allies were paper tigers, and that new weapons were coming to wipe the enemy from the face of the earth. The lie was his contribution to "public enlightenment."

Here was the quintessential champion of nihilism, a voice of destruction that held that all social, political, and economic institutions must be destroyed completely in order to make way for new institutions. He was responsible for the original slogans of revolutionary Nazism, by which the *déclassés*, human outcasts, would take their places at the head of a new society.

Goebbels was precise in defining his goals. "If we want to keep the Party intact, we must appeal to the primitive mass instinct—to the instincts of the stupid, lazy, cowardly." For him the horrors of war were necessary evils of "sanitary destruction." "The bomb terror," he said, "spares the dwellings of neither the rich nor the poor. In the process of ruination, the past has gone and everything old and outward has gone." The mouse-general gloried in his theory of permanent revolution.

This kind of amoral nihilism, if confined to the armchair, would merit only a footnote in the book of history. But Goebbels was propelled to a position of power where he became one of the most important figures of the twentieth century. Without the magic of his propaganda it is doubtful if Hitler could have become the world menace he turned out to be. Millions of his countrymen became victims of this little man and succumbed to his time-bomb propaganda separated from all moral considerations.

200 200 200 200

XL BONUS POINTS PROGRAM

Ed Withall

0144902

Redeemable in merchandise only.

"XL BONUS POINTS" have no cash value.

7

BROWN EMINENCE: MARTIN BORMANN

The war against the Soviets is a partisan war. It enables us to eradicate everyone who opposes us.

—Martin Bormann

Historians agree that Nazi Germany was a swampland of intrigues and struggles for power. In this environment, with its gangster-like rivalries, jackbooted brutality, and simple-minded vulgarity, there was one sure road to success—the good will of the mustachioed Siegfried in Berchtesgaden. Hitler's favor meant promotion, glory, prestige, and money in the land of the swastika.

One winner in the sweepstakes for Hitler's grace was an energetic little Saxon in a badly fitted civil service uniform. He was known as "the Brown Eminence," "the man in the shadows," "Machiavelli behind on office desk," and "Hitler's Mephistopheles." He brings to mind Grey Eminence Friedrich von Holstein, the man of mystery in the German Cabinets of the Wilhelminian era.

Hitler's factotum was short and thick-set, with balding head,

shifty eyes, bull neck, and pugnacious shoulders. With his protruding beer belly and stooping gait, he looked for all the world
like a shuffling pugilist past his prime on the way to oblivion.
But there was an aura of danger about this man.

This was Martin Bormann, intimate secretary, handyman, and
Hitler's selected eyes and ears until the dictator's suicide. Among
the most bloodthirsty of advisers, Bormann was one of the most
influential men in the Third Reich. He made it a point to work
behind the scenes. William L. Shirer described him as "a mole-
like man who preferred to burrow in the dark recesses of Party
life to further his intrigues." He made a religion of National
Socialism. Through Hitler he was able to make a mark on history. The *Fuehrer's alter ego*, a trusted comrade who carried out
the master's slightest wish, he could make or break a man in the
flash of an instant. This amoral human being was a powerful
iron fist among Nazi thugs.

Bormann's task, with a team of like-minded fanatics, was to
implement Hitler's ideology. The domestic scene in Germany
was to be cleansed in an all-out *Gleichschaltung*, a policy of
coordination by which the nation's political, economic, social,
and cultural life was to be brought into the Nazi mold. Courts,
bureaucracy, education, entertainment—all aspects of national
life—were to be remodeled on the basis of *Mein Kampf*, Hitler's
autobiographical blueprint. The National Socialist German
Workers' Party, the NSDAP, was to control the State, not vice
versa, and the designated controller of the Party was Martin
Bormann. The onetime Saxon farmer would use every weapon
in the lexicon of armed might to transform the defeated Fatherland into the strongest power on earth.

The loyal henchman worked with furious energy. He studied
the moods of his irascible master and did everything possible to
carry out his slightest wish. He kept precise records of everything Hitler said in his official capacity, as well as private table
talks. He gave top priority to the important business of keeping
rivals away from the man-god. He watched them all and schemed
day and night to hold them from "The Presence." At the
slightest mistake on their part, he would move in for the kill.
Jealous competitors were always aware of what pudgy little bureaucrat M. B. was doing. Sworn enemy Hermann Goering summarized their feelings: "I hope he rots in hell."

Like the diminutive Dr. Goebbels, Bormann remained with

Hitler to the end while assuring his boss of undying loyalty. But, unlike the Propaganda Minister, he had no intention of sacrificing his life for the cause. On the night of May 1–2, 1945, he left the besieged bunker, determined to make his way to safety through the battle-scarred streets of Berlin. Whether or not he made it remains one of the unsolved mysteries of the twentieth century. The fat little Saxon with his unmanageable paunch, who always preferred to operate his intrigues in the dark, disappeared into the shadows of history. A search by trackers, one of the greatest manhunts in history, failed to find any trace of Martin Bormann.

He was born on June 17, 1900, in Halberstadt in Central Germany, the son of a cavalry sergeant, a trumpeter who later became a civil servant. His father died when Martin was two, after which his mother married a bank director. His early life, like that of other Nazi ruffians, was normal enough. He attended *Realgymnasium* (semiclassical secondary school) for several years but dropped out to work on an estate in Mecklenburg. Called up for army service in the last months of the war of 1914–1918, he was assigned as a canoneer in Field Artillery Regiment 55. The young gunner never saw any combat action.

After the war Martin returned to a defeated Germany, where jobs were scarce and there was little to do for young men like himself without a profession and no job training. Deciding to try farming again, he took a post as trainee manager and inspector of an 800-acre farmland owned by the Treuenfels family at Gut Herzberg. His employer was Hermann von Treuenfels, a former officer and fanatical right-wing nobleman.

Working with Bormann on the Treuenfels farm were a half dozen ex-soldiers, whose main task was to keep an eye on left-wing agitators then active in postwar Germany. These tough men were all veterans of the Rossbach unit, an illegal paramilitary organization dedicated to "liberation from traitors." The group placed its members on such farms as that owned by the Treuenfels family.

This was Bormann's first contact with politics and he found it to his liking. Elected treasurer of the Rossbach *Freikorps*, he soon got himself into deep trouble. Walter Kadow, a former schoolteacher and fellow Rossbacher, borrowed thirty thousand marks from treasurer Bormann (in inflation-ridden Germany this amounted to all of five dollars). A short time later Bormann had to fire Kadow from his job in the farm's brickyard with his debt still unpaid.

There was a dangerous complication. Word got around that Kadow had allegedly betrayed to the French his comrade Albert Leo Schlageter, who was to become one of the greatest Nazi folk heroes. Schlageter was executed as a saboteur during the French occupation of the Ruhr. Rossbachers learned that Kadow was boasting at a local tavern about a visit he had made to Moscow. Bormann, recommending that a good beating was in order, lent his angered comrades a small horse and cart to fetch Kadow and work him over, "but take it easy with the beating."

Convinced that they were dealing with a traitor who had denounced a comrade, furious Rossbachers snatched the drunken Kadow and beat him to death, despite his pleas of innocence. Among the executioners was Rudolf Franz Hoess, brutal ex-machine-gunner who later would achieve global notoriety as commandant of Auschwitz death camp, a post for which he was sponsored by pal Bormann.

Hoess was sentenced to ten years for the assassination. Convicted as a collaborator for the crime, Bormann spent a miserable year in a Leipzig prison. The earnest young Saxon was shocked by his prosecution as a dangerous criminal. He had merely advised a "good beating," and here he was being punished as an accessory to murder. He, Martin Bormann, had come from a fine middle-class family with impeccable reputation, and he was being jailed for something he had not done. He complained of a terrible miscarriage of justice.

Later, when Rossbachers became folk heroes because of their disposal of Kadow, Bormann graciously accepted the Blood Order decoration from Hitler for his participation in the Kadow affair. Anything for the noble cause.

Jail at Leipzig meant transformation of Bormann's personality. Here he was introduced to the violent world of political criminals, hardened veterans prepared to kill. He lost his belief, instilled in him by pious Lutheran parents, in a merciful God. Angered by the *"Diktat"* of the Treaty of Versailles, he was filled with hatred for the establishment, the bourgeois Weimar Republic. He would strike back at the despicable system that had enslaved him. "The punishment," he wrote later, "did not break us. Indeed, it hardened us. It strengthened our hatred against all those who had abused these people. One day before I was released the judge told me to keep away from the Nationalists. It would be better, he said, for me to think of my future and my career. One day after my release I was back in the ranks of my old comrades.''

Freed from prison in March 1925, Bormann tried for a time to take up his old job at the Treuenfels farm. But he soon came to resent the noble Treuenfels family which he now regarded as just as money-mad as the contemptible bourgeoisie. He joined the *Frontbann*, another paramilitary organization of rightist inclinations.

The obscure young farmer was curious about another political party, the National Socialists, then coming into prominence under the leadership of a loquacious and eccentric Austrian. On February 17, 1927, Bormann became member No. 60,598 of the NSDAP. He was not one of the Old Boys, but within a decade he was to become one of the most powerful men in the Nazi world.

Bormann's rise in party circles was steady if unspectacular. From the beginning he was careful to avoid publicity for himself, and refused to allow photographs to be taken of him. He would work in the background, a preference that remained with him for the rest of his career. For a time he worked for National Socialist newspapers in Thuringia. In 1928, after only a year in the Party, he was promoted to the staff of the supreme command of the *SA*. He served as assistant to Captain von Pfeiffer, a hardboiled former regular soldier who headed the brown-shirted Storm Troopers in Munich.

Then came an important break for the shy bureaucrat. In Munich he met twenty-two-year-old Gerda Buch, daughter of Major Walter Buch, a former soldier in the armed forces and longtime friend of Hitler. Father and daughter were fanatical National Socialists. In true Nazi fashion they denounced the Treaty of Versailles, the November traitors who had stabbed Germany in the back, Jews, and Catholics.

The affair between the undersized Saxon farmer and the Nazi-minded young Munich girl was encouraged by her father. They were married on November 2, 1929. There were two important witnesses—Adolf Hitler and beetle-browed Rudolf Hess.

Their first child was born within a year and named Adolf after his godfather. In all, Gerda Bormann bore her husband ten children. But the marriage was a strange one with an unhappy family life. Martin turned out to be a crude philanderer with a roving eye. Albert Speer recorded that at the Berghof, Bormann often disappeared into the rooms of young stenographers, thereby eliciting spiteful remarks from Eva Braun, Hitler's mistress. He even had his movie-actress woman visit him at Obersalzberg,and actually stay at his home in the midst of his family. Incomprehensively, Frau Bormann accepted the situation. She even suggested that he have a child by his actress friend, and that she and the actress take turns each year in becoming pregnant. In her eyes clouded by love for the *Fuehrer*, the man-god would thus be presented with the wonderful gift of good Aryan children. Furthermore, she said, it was a pity that the good actress had been denied offspring. There is no record of Bormann's response to this somewhat odd recommendation.

Promotion was in the air. After the birth of his first child, Bormann was appointed head of the NSDAP *Hilfskasse*, the Party's Aid Fund, which assisted Nazis injured in street battles against Communists. His tireless work in this capacity brought him into contact with hundreds of future Nazi officials. At the same time he was able to provide Hitler with money when funds needed for Party work were scarce.

Wife Gerda smoothed the way for her ambitious husband. He began to rise in Party circles because of his ability to make himself indispensable. He carefully made alliances with those in authority. He made certain that news of his work reached the *Fuehrer*. Slowly he built his private empire; he was indefatigable in enlarging his claims. In time he became one of the great feudatories of the Nazi court.

Six months after he became Chancellor in early 1933, Hitler approved Rudolf Hess's choice of the thirty-three-year-old Bormann as a *Reichsleiter*, a member of a small group that had direct access to the *Fuehrer* and responsibility to him. He was also chosen to serve as a National Socialist deputy in the *Reichstag*.

Bormann was rising rapidly and his *modus operandi* was paying dividends in power. He worked quietly behind the scenes. No publicity, no interviews, no photographs. Contemptuous of the outer trappings of power, what he wanted was real inside control. He placed his own men in key posts. He made it clear to comrades that Party appointments and promotions lay in his own hands.

Bormann was subservient to boss Hess, but he shrewdly manipulated his superior officer. Hess, given to mysticism, intent on his astrological charts, and worried about his health, had no interest in administration. That was just what Bormann wanted. He took over and became an important link in the decision-making process. One after another the *Gauleiters*, district leaders, came under his control. The man had a flair for the type of organization that promoted his own standing.

The field was wide open for Bormann. He lurked in the background of every major political decision. For future use he collected damaging information about bully boy Ernst Roehm and his *SA* comrades. To him they were an obnoxious ''gang of fairies'' and he did what he could to destroy them. He gave his material to Hess knowing that it would be passed on to Hitler. The idea was to raise the *Fuehrer's* anger against rival Roehm and his male harem.

The ploy was successful. The Blood Purge of 1934 eliminated Roehm and his comrades and extinguished the call for a Second Revolution toward socialism. Another important competitor of Bormann had been wiped from the slate.

By the mid-1930s Bormann was engaged in a flurry of activities, ranging from the building of Hitler's Obersalzberg complex to measures for improving the *Fuehrer's* personal finances. Convinced that he had found a reliable and able servant, Hitler, who had little understanding of the depth of Bormann's ambition, placed his complete trust in his anonymity-seeking aid.

Then came the opening for which he was waiting. When in May 1941 Hess made his dramatic flight to Scotland and was pronounced crazy by Dr. Goebbels, the distraught *Fuehrer* shouted: ''Bormann at once! Where is Bormann?'' The sickened dictator issued a new order: ''The Office of the Deputy under the *Fuehrer* will now be called Party Chancellery. It will come under my direct control. Its leader will be, as up to now, Party Member Martin Bormann.''

Success at last! The erstwhile farm manager now saw his personal status extended to a dizzying height. It was to become even more powerful during the course of the war, until he had virtually complete control of the Third Reich. Now he was director of the Party Chancellery, Reich Minister, and member of the Minister's Council for Defense. From now on he sat in on all war conferences and stayed at the *Fuehrer's* field headquarters. By 1942 he obtained a directive giving him authority to handle the Party's share in all legislation, appointment of civil servants, and contacts between war ministries and the Party. Hermann Goering, who had hoped to succeed Hess, was devastated. From then on, the fat *Luftwaffe* commander looked upon Martin Bormann as his deadly enemy.

In April 1943 Bormann was appointed official secretary to the *Fuehrer*. For years he had yearned for that post and now he had it. This was the fulcrum of power in the Third Reich. The secretary's overriding task was to make himself indispensable to his master. In constant attendance, he drew all threads of administration into his own hands. He knew everything the *Fuehrer* read or said. He always carried little white cards in his jacket pocket to take down Hitler's words and to save them for posterity. His ministerial skill consisted of shrewdness in knowing the most favorable hour or minute for Hitler to make a decision.

The servant adjusted his way of life to that of the master. He made it a point to rise at midday and go to bed at the same time as his boss. He was always a member of the private circle and seldom missed a meal with the *Fuehrer*. In intimate conversations he did his best to radicalize his patron. Both were trapped in the fever swamp of Nazi ideology. Both were narcissists, who believed that the *Fuehrer's* remarks at table were pure wisdom to be preserved for all time. Both were unaware of their enormous distortions of judgment.

Hitler was grateful for the skill and organizational ability of his faithful assistant. Like Hess, the *Fuehrer* had always detested administrative duties, and was delighted that he was being relieved of a thousand minor details. Moreover, he admired Bormann's ability in handling money affairs—unlike the spendthrift Goering. Most of all, he was sure of his aide's absolute loyalty. Let the other *Dummkopfs* (blockheads) complain: they were a jealous lot of slobs whose value to him was nothing compared to that of his handy factotum.

Bormann was aware that his position among the brass in Naziland was precarious. He had mounted a slippery ladder and he intended to stay at the top. His built-in mechanism for intrigue was more than equal to the task of outwitting his rivals for the *Fuehrer's* favor.

Bormann and *Reichsfuehrer-SS* Heinrich Himmler became for a time twin wielders of power in the Third Reich. Both used the familiar *Du* in addressing each other. Both put on a careful show of friendship, but actually there was little respect between them. Bormann held a nominal commission in Himmler's *SS*. Their wives saw one another when their husbands were away, and Himmler was godfather to Bormann's fourth son. But there was little love between the former chicken farmer and the erstwhile inspector of farmlands—now lords of the realm in Hitler's Third Reich.

Between Bormann and Hermann Goering, *Luftwaffe* chief and discredited economics expert, there was venomous antipathy. They were bitter enemies. Bormann had only contempt for Goering's Falstaffian image and his eccentric posturing. The day would come when Hitler's secretary would demand Goering's death for treason.

Party autocrat Bormann and Propaganda Minister Goebbels maintained a shaky truce. Both were intelligent men who respected each other as masters of intrigue and who deemed it judicious to steer clear of the other's territorial imperative. Each one silently condemned the other as an "arse-crawler," and each worked energetically to prove to the master that he was a loyal executor of orders from the holy heights.

There were clashes between Bormann and Goebbels. Bormann suspected the little mouse-doctor of promoting a movie based on Kleist's *The Broken Jug*, in which star Emil Jannings gave a satirical portrayal of a village magistrate. Bormann, convinced that the part was a caricature of himself, held up release of the picture for a time.

There was a nasty confrontation between the two in early 1944. Goebbels drew up a 40-page memorandum in which he stated that victory was no longer possible. Agreement with Roosevelt and Churchill could not be made, hence the *Fuehrer* must come to terms with Stalin, who was anti-American and anti-British. It was feasible, Goebbels believed, to combine forces with the Russians against the West. Foreign Minister Ribbentrop was not the man for the job. He, Goebbels, was prepared to take the assignment—with a vial of poison hidden in his mouth.

Goebbels waited patiently for Hitler's reply. No word. He was stunned when he learned that his message was never received. The wily Bormann had killed the memorandum because he believed the war situation did not warrant such desperate measures. Chalk up another victory for the Guardian of The Presence.

Albert Speer, Hitler's architect and member of the intimate circle, reported in his memoirs that among many ruthless men Bormann stood out for his brutality and coarseness. He was "a man without culture, a subordinate by nature who treated his own subordinates as if he were dealing with cows and oxen." At the same time, from his own vantage point, Speer gave this account of Bormann's status:

With his typical perseverance, from 1934 on Bormann followed the simple principle of always remaining in closest proximity to the source of all grace and favor. He accompanied Hitler to the Berghof and on trips, and in the Chancellery never left his side until Hitler went to bed in the early morning hours. In this way Bormann became Hitler's hardworking, reliable, and ultimately indispensable secretary. He pretended to be obliging to everyone, and almost everyone availed himself of Bormann's services—all the more so since he obviously served Hitler with utter selflessness.

A major source of Bormann's power was his ability to handle finances. In the chaotic atmosphere of the Nazi aristocracy, there was a mad scramble for floating money. "What's in it for me?" became the prevailing philosophy.

Hitler saw Bormann as Herr Moneybags, the financial genius who was able not only to draw vast sums into the party's coffers but also to multiply the master's personal fortune. He praised the financial skill of his assistant. He boasted of Bormann's success in introducing compulsory accident insurance for all Party members. The income from that fund exceeded expenditures. The Party was able to use the money for other purposes.

Together with court photographer Heinrich Hoffmann, Bormann conceived of a plan to enrich his patron. The two arranged through Minister of Posts Wilhelm Ohnesorge to give the *Fuehrer* rights to his photograph, which appeared on all postage stamps. The percentage was infinitesimal, but the profits were enormous.

Bormann found a second profitable source for money in his Adolf Hitler Endowment for German Industry. He urged or, more properly, demanded that entrepreneurs profiting from the economic boom concurrent with rearmament show their appreciation by "voluntary" contributions to the fund. Other Party leaders had the same idea, but Bormann won a monopoly on such contributions. He was careful to return some of the money to officials "on behalf of the Party." It was another way to extend his power in Party circles.

With access to huge sums of money, Bormann prepared the way for Hitler's luxurious living quarters. He became the real builder at Berchtesgaden. He expropriated century-old farms from their owners in the vicinity, tore down buildings and even chapels (to the dismay of parishioners), confiscated state forests, and laid out networks of roads on the landscape. He built a huge complex, including a manor house, a hotel for guests, and barracks for security troops. At the summit of Hitler's private mountain, Bormann constructed a house for the *Fuehrer* in somewhat tasteless ocean-liner style. The retreat was reached by a precipitous road ending at an elevator. Bormann spent more than 20 million marks on this access road.

Bormann devoted similar efforts to building the Berghof, the *Fuehrer*'s chalet in a secluded valley. After the outbreak of World War II, Bormann turned energy and money to constructing underground quarters for the leader and his entourage.

Hitler accepted all this without criticism. He liked to pretend that he was a modest man-of-the-people, content to live without luxury. But he quietly accepted Bormann's grandiloquent plans. "It's all Bormann's doing. I don't want to interfere."

Bormann's attitude to Jews parroted the monamania of his *Fuehrer*. Early in life he developed a contempt for Jews and Judaism. In 1920, after his discharge from the army, he joined the anti-Semitic "Society Against the Presumptuousness of Jewry." Like other right-wing *Freikorps* members, he was convinced that Germany had lost the war only because she was stabbed in the back by the November criminals—Social Democrats and Jews in Berlin. The Jews, he believed, were behind the iniquitous Treaty of Versailles. Moreover, he regarded left-wing agitators and Communists as primarily Jewish.

Like Goebbels and other Nazis, Bormann at first regarded his anti-Semitism as mere antipathy. But his attitude changed sharply when he realized the extent of Hitler's hatred for Jews. Important discovery and the way to the *Fuehrer*'s heart! He would fight harder than anyone else against "the Jewish conspiracy." The great leader would appreciate his energy in the struggle.

Wife Gerda, convinced that Germany could be saved only by a right-wing party such as the National Socialists, encouraged her husband's rising sense of anti-Semitism. Later in the war she was to write him: "My Dearest Heart: Every single child must realize that the Jew is the Absolute Evil in the world, and that he must be fought by every means wherever he appears." It was not necessary to remind the hardened husband, who wrote in the margin: "Quite true!"

Bormann was eager to act as transmission belt for measures taken against the Jews. On November 12, 1938, three days after *Kristallnacht*, the pogrom called Night of Broken Glass, he sent a letter to Goering containing an urgent order from the *Fuehrer*. In compliance, Goering called a meeting of the Council of Ministers and passed the word: "Today's meeting is of decisive importance. I have received a letter from Bormann sent to me by order of the *Fuehrer*, asking that the Jewish question be now, once and for all, treated in its entirety and settled in some way." That way eventually led to the Final Solution.

Bormann had a hand in most of the several hundred anti-Jewish laws and decrees. He insisted that *"Yid"* be made compulsory as the middle name for all Jews, and only reluctantly accepted the compromise of "Israel" for males and "Sarah" for females. He ordered that Jews lose the right to institute civil suits and that they could not challenge a judge on the ground of partiality. He dropped the hint that the euthanasia program should not be limited merely to mental defectives, the feeble-minded, or the incurably ill. His representative was present at the Wannsee Conference on January 20, 1942, at which plans were made for the Final Solution. Again and again he spoke to the *Gauleiters* (district leaders) about the necessity for extermination of Jews.

Motivated by Hitler's attitude as well as by that of wife Gerda, once pious Lutheran Bormann turned against Christianity. Both Gerda and he detested Christianity, whether Protestant, Catholic, or Jehovah's Witnesses. They might accept a "Positive Christianity," based on old Nordic pagan mythology, and reject Christ's "weak" turn-the-other-cheek philosophy.

Bormann was not averse to making his views on religion known publicly. "National Socialism and Christianity," he said in 1941, "are irreconcilable." There must be a continuous struggle against the churches, one which would serve to reactivate National Socialist ideology. At Hitler's round table Bormann noted that the *Fuehrer* was a bit hesitant in pursuing the campaign against the churches and felt that it was necessary to await a more favorable time. Not Bormann. He spoke up against any prudent pragmatic program. The reckoning, he said, must not be postponed.

But Bormann shrewdly moved slowly with his anti-Christian maneuvers. No subject could be raised at Hitler's table that might possibly spoil his humor. The scheming handyman would goad one of the dinner guests to tell how this or that pastor or bishop had uttered seditious lines in his sermons. Hitler would suddenly become interested and demand details. Bormann would reply offhand that it was unpleasant, unimportant, and one must not bother the *Fuehrer* with it. Immediate attention! By this time the infuriated man-god would refuse to eat and would demand immediate punishment for traitorous preachers. Success! The pudgy little expert at methodical deceit had scored again.

Hitler was ambivalent on the matter of religion, but Bormann was brutally direct. In May 1941 he warned *Gauleiters* not to be misled by the tactics of the Catholic Church, which was exploiting the facts that many priests had been awarded medals for bravery in action and that others had been killed in combat zones. When on July 30, 1941, Hitler ordered that seizure of monasteries or other church property be halted without obtaining his permission first, Bormann only reluctantly passed the order on to the *Gauleiters* under his jurisdiction.

Bormann continued his anti-clerical campaign but with care not to endanger his standing with the *Fuehrer*. In January 1942, in concurrence with Party philosopher Alfred Rosenberg, he forbade any further discussion of religious questions in the Party's work of ideological indoctrination. Sensing Hitler's unwillingness to pursue anti-religious actions, Bormann issued orders to ignore the churches as much as possible. If he could not destroy them, he could at least demand that his subordinates pay little attention to clerical matters.

As the war went on and Hitler became increasingly occupied with military affairs, he began to allow the internal management of the Reich to slip more and more into the hands of his major-domo. Bormann not only ran the Hitler household, but also by this time he had become, along with Himmler, a most powerful potentate in Naziland next to the *Fuehrer* himself.

For years Bormann had been little more than his master's shadow. He had never dared to take a lengthy trip or a vacation for fear that his influence might diminish. After becoming official secretary in April 1943, he alone was responsible for drawing up Hitler's appointments calendar and deciding which ministers, *Gauleiters*, or civilians could see the *Fuehrer*. He could make scores of decisions—and Hitler would automatically agree.

With his new extraordinary powers, Bormann began to speak up and present ideas of his own. He announced a postwar policy of double marriage for decorated veterans, a program of selective polygamy to redress the drop in birth rate and stimulate a race of Aryan supermen. He denounced Allied pilots as "Anglo-American murderers," and urged that they be lynched when caught. He recommended that prisoners of war be treated with unmerciful harshness.

Bormann was highly pleased by his promotion on September 26, 1944, to head the *Volkssturm*, last-ditch units composed of men between the ages of 16 and 60 to compensate for the terrible loss of German manpower. He had to share command with Himmler, but he saw it as his own army and he was proud of it.

In the late days of the war, when Nazi Germany was in the process of decay, Bormann became the loudest advocate of a scorched-earth policy. Hitler, frantically denouncing Germans as not worthy of him, demanded destruction of what was left of the country. Ecstatic approval from Bormann. Smash everything—power plants, water supplies, food, clothing! The damnable Allies and subhuman Russians must find nothing of value in conquered Germany.

Bormann was in the Berlin bunker during the final days. While Hitler roamed around his underground fortress like a half-demented zombie calling nonexisting regiments into action, his faithful yes-man became, in effect, the ruler of the Third Reich. The busy, peripatetic Bormann was now the stage manager of the Wagnerian *Götterdämmerung*, the last rites of a smashed regime. For two months, March and April 1945, between collapses into drunken stupor, he issued orders to the surviving colony of trapped Nazis.

An eyewitness described Bormann's days in the bunker:

Bormann moved about very little and kept close to his writing desk. He was recording 'the momentous events' in the bunker for posterity. Every word, every action went down on his paper. Often he would visit this person or that demanding scowlingly what exact remark had been made by the *Fuehrer*. This document was to be spirited out of the bunker at the last moment. It would, according to Bormann, 'take its place among the greatest chapters in German history.'

Hitler wanted to die, but Bormann planned to survive. While assuring his master of eternal loyalty, the faithful paladin spent much of his energy plotting how he could escape before the end, how he might ally himself with whoever would inherit power in defeated Germany. When Hitler ordered Field Marshal Wilhelm Keitel, General Alfred Jodl, and Bormann to fly to Berchtesgaden, all three indignantly refused.

Like his crushed boss, Bormann put on a show of tough retaliation against the onrushing Allies. In March 1945 he encouraged Hitler to issue an order that all Allied bomber crews captured in the future by the *Luftwaffe* were to be turned over to the *SD*, the security service, for liquidation.

On April 23 came a great moment for Bormann. His despised enemy Goering had made a stupid mistake. He was the first to see Goering's telegram and with great excitement he brought it to Hitler. "Goering is engaged in treason!" he said triumphantly. "He is already sending telegrams to members of the government announcing that on the basis of his powers, he will assume your office at 10 o'clock tonight, *mein Fuehrer*."

Unerringly, Bormann directed Hitler's attention to the deadline for reply. "This is an ultimatum!"

Pandemonium in the bunker. Outraged, Hitler told Bormann to draft a telegram dismissing Goering from all his offices and from his rights of succession. Bormann wrote the proposed text and Hitler authorized it. It informed the *Luftwaffe* chief that he had committed high treason, that the penalty was death, but that he would be excused this extreme step in view of his earlier services to the Party.

This was sweet revenge—but still not enough for Bormann. On his own he sent an additional telegram to his subordinates at Obersalzberg; "The situation in Berlin is most tense. If Berlin and we should fall, the traitors of April 23 must be exterminated. Men, do your duty! Your life and honor depend upon it!'' The telegram was delivered to the commandant of the fortress where Goering was imprisoned, but the officer refused to recognize Bormann's authority. Goering was spared.

Along with Goebbels, Bormann was present at the wedding of Hitler and Eva Braun in the map room in a private section of the bunker. Both declared that they were of pure Aryan descent and free from hereditary disease. Bormann signed the marriage certificate:

> Reichs Leader Martin Bormann
> born 17 June 1900
> resident in Obersalzberg
> identified by: [illegible]

At 4 A.M. on the morning of April 29 Bormann signed his name as witness to two documents—Hitler's Last Will and his Political Testament. In his private will Hitler wrote:

> As executor of this will, I appoint my most faithful Party comrade, Martin Bormann. He is given full legal authority to make all decisions. He is permitted to take out for my brothers and sisters whatever has any value as a personal memento or is necessary to maintain a modest standard of living *[zur Erhaltung eines kleinen bürgerlichen Leben]*.

The doomed *Fuehrer* made Bormann a central figure in his Political Testament:

> A number of men such as Martin Bormann, Dr. Goebbels, and others, including their wives, have voluntarily joined me. They do not wish to leave the capital of the Reich under any circumstances; they are willing to die with me. Nevertheless, I must ask them to obey my request, and in this case to put the interests of the nation above their own feelings. By their work and loyalty as associates they will be just as close to me as I hope my spirit will be to them; may it linger among them and accompany them always. Let them be hard but never unjust; above all let them never allow fear to influence their actions, and let them put the honor of the

nation above all else on earth. Finally, let them be conscious
of the fact that our task for the coming centuries is the
continuing construction of the National Socialist state, and
this places every single person under an obligation always
to serve the common interest and to subordinate his own
advantages to this end.

This was the *Fuehrer*'s final appeal to posterity. In it he asked
his loyal retainers to put nation above their own feelings. There
was nothing romantic, however, about Bormann. He had already
chosen the path of survival and escape. He was interested in the
reality of power and he would once again offer his services to
any successor who would be willing to make use of his indispensable talents.

On Hitler's instructions, Bormann sent the Political Testament
to Grand Admiral Karl Doenitz, successor to the throne. Bormann's covering letter read: "Dear Admiral: Since none of the
expected relief divisions have arrived, and our position seems
hopeless, the *Fuehrer* last night dictated the enclosed Political
Testament. *Heil Hitler!*"

Bormann helped carry the body of Eva Braun to the Chancellery courtyard. He was one of the small group of mourners, who
gazed on in riveted attention as a rag dipped in petrol was cast
on the bodies of Hitler and his wife. The little group stood at
attention as Russian artillery thundered. They gave a final Hitler
salute and withdrew into the bunker.

Bormann and Goebbels made one final attempt to save the
situation. They contacted Russian headquarters by wireless
asking negotiations for an armistice or truce. The cold reply—
"Unconditional surrender!"

There was no alternative. There must be a mass escape.

What happened then dissolved into mystery. Hugh R. Trevor-
Roper, British Intelligence officer and Professor of History at
Oxford, in his classic *The Last Days of Hitler* (New York: Mac-
millan, 1947), accepted the claim of Artur Axmann, *Reichsju-
gendfuehrer* (Reich Youth Leader), who was among the small
group escaping from the bunker on May 1. According to Axmann, Bormann and Dr. Ludwig Stumpfegger, Hitler's surgeon,
were thrown to the ground by the violent explosion of a tank,
but escaped injury. The two walked eastward along the Invalidenstrasse toward the Stettiner Station. And then:

Axmann, coming upon a Russian patrol, turned back and followed the direction in which Bormann and Stumpfegger had gone. Before long he overtook them. Behind the bridge, where the Invalidenstrasse crosses the railway line, he found both of them lying outstretched on their backs with moonlight on their faces. Stopping for a moment, he saw both were dead, but Russian fire prevented closer examination. There were no obvious wounds, no signs of a shattering explosion. Presumably they were shot in the back.

Trevor-Roper admitted that the account of the death of Bormann rested on the evidence of Axmann only. "But since Axmann's account (apart from accidental error of time) has proved accurate in other particulars, it is probably correct here also, unless he is deliberately lying to protect Bormann."

Others were not satisfied with Trevor-Roper's conclusion. Gradually, the legend arose that Bormann was still alive. An extraordinary manhunt began for the missing Saxon. Intelligence agents, police, newspapermen, and private individuals from a dozen nations began to search from one end of the world to another.

Sensation followed sensation. Bormann was reported to have been seen as a monk in Italy or as a businessman hiding his identity in South American countries, favorite haunts of Nazi refugees. In 1973, ex-naval intelligence officer Hungarian-American Ladislas Farago claimed that he knew where Bormann was—that he was living as a millionaire in Northern Argentina near the border with Paraguay. Farago said that Bormann had fled Germany in a submarine, after being helped by the Vatican and had been protected by several prominent Latin American politicians, including dictator Juan Domingo Perón.

Nazi hunter Simon Wiesenthal was skeptical. He found the Farago disclosure a mixture of truth and fantasy. "There have been about twenty-five Bormanns since the war. There have been so many because the man has a common face. In Munich or Frankfurt you will find people on the street with his face."

In April 1973 a West German court formally pronounced Bormann dead on the evidence of a skeleton unearthed half a mile from the site of Hitler's bunker between the Weidenheimer Bridge and the Lehrter Station in Berlin. The court ordered all search warrants quashed and future reports of Bormann sightings to be ignored. Simon Wiesenthal voiced his dissent: "Some doubts must remain whether the bones found in Berlin are really those of Bormann."

Private investigator Charles Whiting examined every facet of the case and professed himself mystified in his book *The Hunt for Martin Bormann* (New York: Ballantine, 1973):

> Somewhere is Bormann; the "man in the shadows" to the very last. Perhaps buried in some forgotten Berlin backyard: a handful of black ashes in a grinning little white skull, showing no indication of its manner of death save for a few tiny pieces of glass way back in what—over a quarter of a century before—had once been a throat. Or perhaps some toothless old man, living in his memories, ensconced under some waving palm tree, swigging the local tipple of rotgut and coke and laughing at the foolish efforts of all those men—British, American, Russian, Israeli, Brazilian, German—who have sought him so unsuccessfully for so long. Who knows?

In 1946 Bormann was among the indicted at Nuremberg but he was not there to face trial. His lawyer's only defense was that his client was dead. The court of the International Military Tribunal found the absent accused guilty on Count 3: War Crimes, and Count 4: Crimes Against Humanity. He was sentenced *in absentia* to death.

How such a verdict would be carried out, should Bormann ever be found, is not altogether clear.

8

ALFRED ROSENBERG: PHILOSOPHER OF THE ABSURD

There is no German official who thinks less clearly or indulges in more bunk.

—Ambassador William E. Dodd

He was called Hitler's Father Confessor, the Grand Inquisitor of the Third Reich, the man behind the Nordic Faith Movement, the ideologist who had the greatest influence on the direction of Nazi Germany's foreign policy. But he saw himself as philosopher, as successor to Plato, Aristotle, and Socrates in the eternal search for wisdom and truth. He presented himself to the German people as practitioner of the universal science that aims at an explanation of all the phenomena of the universe by ultimate causes. This was the ''intellectual'' chosen by Hitler to create ''a religion of the Blood''—the official high priest and interpreter of the Nazi way of life, custodian of the Nazi *Weltanschauung*, its world-view.

Flawed reputation. Alfred Rosenberg was no respected scholar; if anything, he was a philosopher with a sour stomach. This garrulous lightweight produced what was required of him—

a wild complex of ideas that reached the high watermark of German irrationalism. An egomaniac, he was moody, retiring, maudlin, and glibly persuasive. Although of shallow mind, he saw himself as a towering intellect. His pseudo-scientific jargon impressed Hitler, who judged erudition by involved expression. It alienated many intelligent Germans.

Journalist Dorothy Thompson, keen observer, described Rosenberg as a man of intellect but also a complete fool.

This lonely man was said to have had only one friend in the Third Reich—Adolf Hitler. But that was enough to create a career in the Nazi scheme of things. Rosenberg became one of the *Fuehrer's* trusted apostles.

It was also enough to lead him to the gallows at Nuremberg. The once dandified and perfumed intellectual was reduced to a shaking hulk as he paid the extreme penalty for his crimes.

Alfred Rosenberg was born at Reval (Talinin) in Estonia on January 12, 1893, the same day as Hermann Goering's birth in Bavaria. His mother, Minna (Marcus) Rosenberg, was a Latvian and his father, Johann Rosenberg, was an Estonian. (Their background is not clear: Rudolf Olden described Rosenberg's mother as an Estonian and his father as a Lithuanian.) The elder Rosenberg was an official in a German trading firm and had a reputation of being loyal to German traditions. His son was raised in a household priding itself on its German attachments.

After attending grammar and high schools in Reval, Rosenberg in 1915 was sent to Riga and Moscow to continue his studies. Despite the dramatic events of World War I and its revolutionary aftermath, he was able to carry on his studies without interruption. He was not drafted. There was some mystery about his activities during the war. It is believed that, while studying at Riga in 1918, he went to Paris. Later he said that he was on a counter-revolutionary mission. His enemies charged that he made the trip on behalf of the Soviets. Others claimed that he worked for French Intelligence and left Paris only after he saw no chance for a career there. Hermann Goering, his special enemy in Nazi officialdom, later stated publicly: "I wonder what kind of job Rosenberg had when he was in Paris in 1918."

Rosenberg returned to Reval. When German troops took the city they were approached by Rosenberg, who identified himself as a German who wanted to volunteer to fight the Bolsheviks.

The German commandant, somewhat suspicious, rejected the offer. Rosenberg decided to earn a living as a high-school drawing instructor.

By this time, aiming to become an engineer, Rosenberg passed his first examination for an engineering diploma at the *Technische Hochschule* (Technical College) in Riga. In late 1918 he and his young bride, a poverty-stricken couple, moved to Munich. His wife became seriously ill with tuberculosis and died soon afterward.

In Munich, Rosenberg joined the National People's Party and became a German citizen. Here he worked with White Russian émigrés, all of whom were consumed with hatred for the Bolshevik regime. And here, too, he joined the company of the many cafe anti-Semites. Gifted with writing ability, he began to publish a series of pamphlets outlining his personal beliefs.

Rosenberg's writings brought him to the attention of Dietrich Eckart, Nazi poet and journalist. Despite his poverty, Rosenberg was always dressed well, perfumed, and marked with a certain supercilious air. Eckert was at first annoyed by the eccentric Rosenberg, but later he was impressed by the man's voluminous writings, his intellectual posture, and his emotional anti-Semitism. He put Rosenberg to work writing pamphlets for the nascent German Workers' Party, forerunner of the National Socialist German Workers' Party.

Together with Eckart, Rosenberg founded the Thule Society, devoted to the promotion of Aryan racial ideas and the creation of a Nordic religion. The two writers directed their scorn at the Treaty of Versailles. They denounced Jews as parasites and Communists as vermin.

It was not long before Rosenberg met Hitler at a small inn called "The German Reich." The two were brought together by Eckart in what turned out to be a fateful meeting of minds. Hitler, inclined to mysticism, was captivated by the young Balt and his vision of a victorious Germany whose blond Nordics would rule global society. Through long night sessions the leader was fascinated by Rosenberg's loquacity and seemingly vast fund of knowledge. Soon Rosenberg was named editor of the *Völkischer Beobachter*, the Nazi newspaper.

Rosenberg now had a job and a mission. From then on he was a devoted follower of Hitler and the Nazi movement.

In 1921, when there was a rebellion against Hitler's leadership,

Rosenberg was loyal to his leader. Hitler never forgot it. When the new National Socialist German Workers' Party was formed, he assigned Rosenberg to write its platform. Rosenberg's definition of a German became famous among Nazis: "He is a German citizen who is a fellow countryman. He is a fellow countryman who is of German blood. Therefore, no Jew can be a German."

Rosenberg now began to produce a voluminous amount of writing, mostly on Jewish and Marxian problems. His first pamphlet, *The Trace of Jews in the History of the World*, was written in the kind of pseudo-scientific verbiage that was to distinguish his masterpiece later. He re-issued the spurious *Protocols of the Elders of Zion*, which had long been exposed as a forgery. In July 1923 he published a pamphlet titled *The Protocols of the Elders of Zion and the Jewish World Problem*. This kind of writing brought him spiritual leadership of the up-and-coming National Socialist Party.

Rosenberg solidified his standing with Hitler by taking part in the unsuccessful Beer-Hall *Putsch* at Munich on November 8–9, 1923. He was at Hitler's side, brandishing a revolver, on the November 9 march. When the firing began, he lay on the ground near the front line. Behind him was another Nazi firing at the police. He found his comrade's bravery quite superfluous, and yelled at him, in the name of the devil, to stop. He finally crawled away from the line of fire and managed to avoid arrest.

During Hitler's imprisonment at Landsberg-am-Lech, Rosenberg visited him every day. Their talks on racial dogma found their way into Hitler's *Mein Kampf*. The *Völkischer Beobachter*, which Rosenberg was editing and which eventually became a daily newspaper, was suppressed during Hitler's term in jail. It reappeared in 1925 with Rosenberg as editor. In 1926 he founded the German People's Publishing House. In 1929 he organized the Fighting Alliance for German *Kultur*. He was making his way in the Nazi jungle.

When he was fifteen years old, Rosenberg had acquired a copy of Houston Steward Chamberlain's *Foundations of the Nineteenth Century*, in which the Germanized Englishman presented a racial interpretation of history. The Chamberlain work was to become the basis for Rosenberg's own *magnum opus, Mythus des XX. Jahrhunderts (The Myth of the Twentieth Century)*, which surely, along with Hitler's *Mein Kampf*, deserves a place on any list of the world's worst books.

Rosenberg conceived the idea in 1917 in the midst of World War I. He would produce a compendium of the ideas of Chamberlain plus those of Baron de Gobineau (Nordic supremacy), Oswald Spengler (voice of the blood and will of the race), Friedrich Wilhelm Nietzsche (the Superman), Freidrich von Bernhardi ("war is a biological necessity"), Heinrich von Treitschke ("war is elevating"), and Paul Anton de Largarde ("Jews are purveyors of decadence"). Rosenberg worked on his book for eight years. He submitted the manuscript to Hitler, who kept it for a full year. It was returned unread to the author with the comment that it was "well done."

The book was published in Munich in 1930 with the subtitle: *A Valuation of the Spiritual-Intellectual Conflicts of Our Times*. The jacket described the author as an inspired thinker and endowed seer: "This book is a fountainhead of fundamental precepts in the fields of human history, religion, and cultural philosophy, almost overwhelming in magnitude." "It teaches," read the blurb, "a new world history." And further: "The *Mythus* is the Myth of the Blood, which, under the sign of the Swastika, released the World Revolution. It is the Awakening of the Soul of the Race, which, after a period of long slumber, victoriously puts an end to racial chaos."

The *Mythus* deserves attention if only because of its importance in the history of the Third Reich. It was perfect for Nazi purposes—it attacked Jews, Catholics, Protestants, Free Masons, Bolsheviks, Social Democrats, and Liberals.

Rosenberg's first concern was to give a "scientific" justification for the prevailing Nazi blood myth. A nation, he wrote, is constituted by the definite character formed by its blood, as well as by language, geographical environment, and the sense of a united political destiny. But the decisive element is always the blood. Great poets and heroes testify to the eternal value of special blood soil. The profound significance of blood now mysteriously circles our planet, "irresistibly gripping one nation after another."

Each race, wrote Rosenberg, has its own soul and its own religion. The soul simply means race from the interior, and, inversely, race is the external aspect of soul. Race is the head of a hierarchy of values that embrace state, art, and religion. The so-called unity of races, Rosenberg went on, is an absurd hypothesis. Every race is distinguished by its own special character. The Nordic race is, of course, superior and creative. It came, he wrote, from a vanished continent to the north of Europe, where it took on spiritual qualities from the blue waters and gleaming ice of the Arctic. Nordic branches could be recognized in the Amorites of Egypt, the Aryans of India, the early Greeks, Romans, and finally in all Germanic peoples. This Germanic element ''brought order out of chaos in all the world.''

The spirit of the superior Nordic race, Rosenberg wrote, was personified in the god Wotan—honor and heroism, the art of song, the protection of right, and the eternal striving for wisdom. That spirit could be found only in such Nordics as Luther, Dante, Frederick the Great, Goethe, Bismarck, and Hitler.

What about Christianity, the Renaissance, and the Enlightenment? These were, according to Rosenberg's analysis, not movements of progress, but rather forces for disintegration of Nordic truth. Where Nordic blood intermingled with inferior stocks, there civilization deteriorated, as witnessed by the decline of the West, a certain product of ''criminal bastardization of races and denordicization. Today a new faith awakens the myth of the blood, the faith that by defending the blood we defend the divine nature of man. The faith, embodied in scientific clarity, that the Nordic blood represents that mystery which has replaced and conquered the ancient sacraments.''

Thus far Rosenberg's Blood Myth was little more than a rehash of Chamberlain's *Foundations* and Gobineau's *Essay on the Inequality of Human Races*. But both Chamberlain and Gobineau were impassioned Christians. Rosenberg, however, denounced Christianity as a poisonous product of the Semitic-Latin spirit, as a disintegrative Judaistic conception. Christian churches, especially the Roman Catholic, he wrote, are ''prodigious, conscious, and unconscious falsifications.''

Rosenberg demanded that the Old Testament be abolished as a book of religion. There must be an end of 1,500 years of this book trying to transform Germans mentally into Jews, ''an effort to which we owe our present Jewish domination.'' In place of the Old Testament cattle breeders and exploitation of prostitutes, Rosenberg recommended Nordic sagas and fairy tales. ''Not the dreams of hatred and murdering Messiahship, but the dream of honor and freedom must be kindled through the Nordic, German sagas.''

Who, asked Rosenberg, was the ''real Christ''? He charged that the true picture of Jesus had been distorted by fanatics like Matthew, by materialistic rabbis like Paul, by African jurists like Tertullian, and by mongrel half-breeds like St. Augustine. The real Christ, wrote Rosenberg, was an Amorite Nordic, aggressive, courageous, ''a man of true Nordic character,'' a revolutionary who opposed the Jewish and Roman systems with sword in hand, bringing not peace but war. Institutional Christianity, in Rosenberg's view, had been made unrecognizable by Popes and Jesuits.

Rosenberg poured his most venomous hatred on the Roman Catholic Church. That Church, he charged, had kept civilization in slavery, and to this day remained a pitiless force working against the Nordic ideal. Roman Catholics had always taken into the fold any human being regardless of racial origin, in Rosenberg's eyes a complete misunderstanding of the all-importance of racial purity. The Catholic doctrines of love and pity, he wrote, were directly contrary to the Germanic virtues of heroism and honesty. There were irreconcilable differences between Catholic and Germanic mentalities. Springing from the Orient, Catholicism was contrary to the spirit of Nordicism. The Pope, Rosenberg said, was merely a Roman medicine man; church history was a compendium of atrocities, swindles, and forgeries.

What could be done to rescue the white Nordic race from the disruptive Etruscan-Syrian-Judean-Asiatic-Catholic influence? Rosenberg recommended a solution. Away with the medicineman Pope and his voodoo practices, away with mongrelized Catholicism, away with attempts to transform good Germans into Jews, away with historic Christianity (Catholic, Lutheran, or Protestant), away with the decadent Sermon on the Mount, away with doctrines of sin and salvation and the cross! Substitute in their place the swastika as the ''living symbol'' of race and blood; revive the virtues of the early German barbarians. Christianity only leads to the internationalism of Marx. Abandon liberty, equality, and fraternity, those creations of Judaistic-Christian decadence, because they are ''idiotic principles designed to enslave the Nordic peoples.''

After this denunciation of Christianity, Rosenberg went on to say that he favored a ''positive Christianity,'' which would pu-

rify the Nordic race, re-establish the old pagan virtues, and substitute the fiery spirit of the hero for the crucifixion. Christianity
would be removed from all its traditions and become one with
the old Norse paganism to form a new German religion. Catholic
universalism would disappear in the fire of a healthy Nordicism.

Rosenberg was just as bitter in his denunciation of Jews. Both
his adversaries, he wrote, were Jewish in origin: Christianity
and humanism (in their modern political guise, liberalism and
Marxism). Jews were the opposite of Nordics. Where Nordics
were noble, creative, and constructive, Jews were ignoble, par-
asitic, and destructive. Rosenberg attributed every possible evil
to Jews. Only German Nordics have the happy faculty of understanding "the religion of blood," to which the entire future of
mankind belonged. It was the might of the Germanic soul that
had prevented the ultimate victory of Rome and Jerusalem.

The same for Free Masonry. Free Masons, Rosenberg warned,
attempted to fashion a religion of humanity and aspired to a
"humanization of mankind" that would fuse all racial and national ideas. Therefore, Germans must oppose Free Masonry as
running counter to the German spirit.

Equal contempt for Marxism. "Today," Rosenberg wrote,
"Marxism and liberalism are engaged in retreat skirmishes along
their entire front. For decades it was considered impressive to
talk about nothing but 'humanity,' to be a citizen of the world,
and to shrug off the racial question as reactionary. Now all these
basic delusions are not only done for politically but their entire
basic philosophy is decaying, so that it won't be long before they
will have collapsed completely in the souls of those who are at
least halfway decently led or misled." Germans must fight
against both the democratic shopkeeper ideal of the bourgeoisie
and the Marxist concept of the dictatorship of the proletariat.

Rosenberg's myth-of-the-blood, a compendium of insipid nonsense, marked the transition of German irrationalism to extreme
Nazi mysticism. In the hands of this "philosopher" what was
left of German humanism and rationalism was obscured in a
confused neo-romanticism, spurious and undignified.

When Rosenberg's *Mythus* was published, there was still freedom of speech in Weimar Germany. The book was greeted by a
storm of criticism. Reviewers ridiculed it as a projection of stale
Nazi claptrap. Churchmen, especially, were alienated by Rosenberg's attacks on Christianity. Ernest Boyd, an American re-

viewer, described the book as "a wild mumbo-jumbo of bad Nietzscheanism and stale ethnology out of Chamberlain, out of Gobineau, out of Spengler." Taken aback, Rosenberg immediately offered to quit as editor of the *Völkischer Beobachter*. Hitler wrote diagonally across Rosenberg's letter of resignation: "Doesn't enter my head. You stay."

With Hitler's dictum that Rosenberg's *Mythus* expressed National Socialist ideology perfectly, the book went on to become a national best-seller. By December 1936 a half million copies were sold. On January 12, 1943, Rosenberg's fiftieth birthday, it was announced that more than three quarters of a million copies had been bought, despite the fact that it had been translated into only one foreign language, Japanese. Nazi Party members distributed the book, along with *Mein Kempf*, on festive occasions. By 1944 a million copies had been sold in Germany.

Rosenberg's *Mythus* became a kind of National Socialist bible. The author was hailed as the great philosopher of Nazism. Pamphlets and books appeared in the hundreds to emphasize Rosenberg's philosophy: the race-individuality of the Nordic accounts for all great cultures of the past, notably the Greek and Roman; all decay and corruption were caused by the infusion through intermarriage of inferior blood strains; man's full potentialities could be achieved only by recapturing the Nordic racial purity of the ancient Germanic tribes.

Hitler had the ideological mouthpiece he needed and wanted.

During the struggle between national and socialist elements in the Nazi movement, which culminated in the blood purge of 1934, Rosenberg hewed strongly to the national line. Again he won Hitler's confidence. Deprived for a time of his editorship of the Party newspaper, he was restored to his post after the massacre of dissenters.

In 1930, the same year as publication of his *Mythus*, Rosenberg was elected to the *Reichstag*. From 1931 to 1935, during the years when the Nazis were striving for political power, Rosenberg worked in the diplomatic service. In 1933 he was sent on a good-will tour of England, an indication of the *Fuehrer*'s high regard for his Party ideologist.

Rosenberg's stay in England was a fiasco. On May 1, 1933, he came to London to explain to British leaders the peaceable, defensive nature of the Nazi movement. The sight of the cold, morose figure of this Nazi emissary did much to intensify British mistrust of the new Hitler regime. Rosenberg told his British hosts that Germans and Britons were destined to rule the world because they both had Nordic blood flowing in their veins.

The Nazi visitor then made a classic blunder. He placed a swastika wreath on the tomb of the Unknown Soldier. The response was instantaneous. One veteran grasped the wreath and threw it into the Thames. Workers demonstrated against the ambassador of good will. "Down with Rosenberg!" graffiti appeared on the walls of London. Rosenberg called a press conference to protest his treatment and then departed hurriedly for Germany.

An angered *Fuehrer* responded by appointing Rosenberg to the post of Director of the Foreign Policy of the National Socialist Party. The organization, controlling a network of societies with branches abroad, exerted an important influence on the German Academic Exchange Service. In this office Rosenberg drew up what was called the Rosenberg Plan, designed to lure Poland into an alliance against Soviet Russia. Poland would be promised a part of the Ukraine, but she would then be attacked as a "mongrel nation" unworthy of survival.

The Russo-German Non-Aggression Pact just before the outbreak of World War II nearly broke Rosenberg's heart. For the time being he had to stop his polemics against the Russians. Nevertheless, he continued to meet with White Russians and anti-Bolsheviks of every kind. He never ceased to hope that Hitler would eventually turn on the Russians. His goal was realized when, on April 2, 1941, he was called in by Hitler and informed of the coming attack on the Soviet Union. He was ecstatic. He promised to do all he could as "political advisor" in the struggle against the Soviet Union.

On July 17, 1941, Hitler appointed Rosenberg Reich Minister for the Eastern Occupied Territories and publicly charged him with responsibility for civil administration. In this post Rosenberg helped formulate the policies of Germanization, exploitation, forced labor, and extermination of Jews. He set up the administration that carried out these aims of Nazi policy. He did not know it at the time but his work in racial cleansing was to cost him his life.

William L. Shirer reported that at the Nuremberg Trials, Rosenberg was reduced to a shaking hulk: "He has lost weight, the puffiness on the sallow square face is gone. Dressed in a dark brown suit, this dull, confused but dangerous Balt who contributed so much to the Nazi race hatreds, who superintended the loot of objects from the conquered lands, and who finally helped direct the dreadful extermination of the Slav people in the conquered Russian territories, is nervous in the dock, lurching forward to catch every word, his hands shaking.''

Reacting to the indictment, Rosenberg declared his innocent intentions: ''I must reject an indictment for 'conspiracy.' The anti-Semitic movement was only positive.''

To prison psychologist G.M. Gilbert, Rosenberg professed himself flabbergasted by the whole business. ''Of course, it was terrible, incomprehensible. I would never have dreamed it would take such a turn. Terrible? Hitler must have given the orders, or Himmler did it with the *Fuehrer's* approval. . . . We didn't contemplate killing anybody in the beginning. I can assure that I always advocated a peaceful solution. . . . I had no idea it would lead to extermination in any literal sense. We just wanted to take the Jews out of German political life.''

Before his judges, Rosenberg started defending his philosophy with his usual abstruse philosophical rationalization. Interrupted by the court, and even by his own defense counsel, he was told to get down to cases. He testified that he always was in favor of a chivalrous solution to the Jewish question. He defended his activities as Commissioner for the Eastern Territories by insisting that he had disapproved atrocities but could not do much about it. He also did not defend the *Fuehrerprinzip* (leadership principle). It was all the fault, he charged, of unruly subordinates.

The Tribunal was not impressed. The Court's judgment:

Rosenberg had knowledge of the brutal treatment and terror to which the Eastern people were subjected. He directed that the Hague Rules of Land Warfare were not applicable to the Occupied Eastern Territories. He had knowledge of and took an active part in stripping the Eastern Territories of raw materials and foodstuffs, which were all sent to Germany. He stated that feeding the German people was first on the list of claims on the East, and the Soviet people would suffer thereby.

His directives provided for the segregation of Jews, ultimately in Ghettos. His subordinates engaged in mass killings of Jews, and his civil administrators considered the cleansing of the Eastern Occupied Territories of Jews as necessary. . . .

He gave his civil administrator quotas of laborers to be sent to the Reich, which had to be met by whatever means necessary. His signature of approval appears on the order of June 14, 1941, in the *Heu Aktion*, the apprehension of 40,000 to 50,000 youths, aged 10–14, for shipment to the Reich.

Verdict: guilty on all four counts.
Sentence: death by hanging.

On the morning of October 16, 1946, at about 1:44 A.M., just after the execution of Field Marshal Wilhelm Keitel, the scaffold at Nuremberg was made ready for Alfred Rosenberg.

Dull, his cheeks sunken, Hitler's ideologist was brought into the execution hall. His complexion was pasty brown. He walked with steady steps to the gallows. He gave his name and replied "No" to a question as to whether he had anything to say. He was accompanied by a Protestant chaplain who followed him and stood praying at his side.

The condemned man looked at the chaplain but said nothing. Ninety seconds after entering the execution hall he was swinging from the end of the hangman's rope. It was the swiftest execution of any of the condemned men at Nuremburg.

In a sane society a perverse character such as Alfred Rosenberg would have been relegated to a back table at a cafe in Vienna together with other crackpots of his persuasion. But in the topsy-turvy world of the swastika, where simple decency was seldom understood, Rosenberg, along with other charlatans, was promoted by the master of Berchtesgaden to a position of power and prestige.

The career of this Germanized Balt accurately mirrors the nature of the Nazi regime. The ideologist, with his pseudo-scientific racial nonsense and spurious theories, came to Hitler displaying his irrationalism and found a perfect partner for revolutionary nihilism. The lackey, spitting out his poisonous drivel, was rewarded with high office in the Nazi wonderland.

Losers in the process were the German people, those who had won a global reputation for their magnificent contributions to civilization. The mystery remains as to how so many Germans could accept the idiotic twaddle of this lightweight Balt who dared to call himself a philosopher, a seeker of truth.

9

CHAMPAGNE SALESMAN
RIBBENTROP

Ugh! Such a washout for a Foreign Minister! Such a good-for-nothing, stupid weakling! That Ribbentrop—he wasn't even good enough to be a bootblack.
— *Dr. Hjalmar Horace Greeley Schacht,*
at Nuremberg

In today's vivid vernacular the odious scoundrels in the company of Hitler hated one another's guts. It was common for each one to denigrate sarcastically any other Nazi who stood in the way of access to the holy land around the *Fuehrer*. The idea was to denounce the personality, character, and career of any rival for the leader's attention. This was standard operating procedure in any gangster milieu.

Thus the acid comment of Propaganda Minister Joseph Goebbels: "Von Ribbentrop bought his name, he married his money, and he swindled his way to office." Other jealous higher-ups, including Hermann Goering, Rudolf Hess, and Alfred Rosenberg, nicknamed him "Iago," because he had won Hitler's favor by "poisoning his ear." Others took pleasure in calling Ribbentrop "the wild man of the Reich."

English aristocrats, amused by Ribbentrop's British butler and valet and his hint of an English accent in his German, gave him the name of "Ribbensnob." After Ribbentrop attended the court of George VI in 1936 and greeted the new and astonished king with a Nazi salute and a *"Heil Hitler!"* repeated three times, London's press conferred upon him the nickname of "Brickendrop." For Londoners, the Berliner peacock was their favorite "Ugly German."

This man, who despite his efforts merited little respect anywhere, became the Foreign Minister of the Third Reich, programmed by Hitler to exist for a thousand years. Ribbentrop, himself, lasted for seven and a half years as Reich Minister for Foreign Affairs.

It was a strange career, one that merits the attention of behavioral scientists. He was at various times draftsman, assistant engineer, bank clerk, railroad worker, playboy among the idle rich, and champagne salesman. The unexpected surge of the Nazis to power brought him opportunity for political advancement and he was quick to take advantage of it. It brought him to the side of Hitler—and eventually to the gallows at Nuremberg.

Joachim Ribbentrop was born on April 30, 1893, at Wesel on the Rhine, the son of Sophie (Hertwig) and Richard Ribbentrop, a retired army officer. He attended school at Metz and the Imperial Lyceum there. Although his family was of modest means, he was sent to Grenoble in France by a wealthy aunt by marriage who had taken a liking to him. After schooling there, he went to London, where he worked for a time as a clerk for a German importing firm. He moved to Switzerland and then in 1910 set out for the United States.

Young Ribbentrop spent several months in New York and Boston, earning a part of his living as a free-lance journalist. For the next several years he went from job to job to make a living, including stints as railroad worker, wine salesman, and commercial representative. When war broke out in August 1914, he decided as a patriotic young German to get back to the Fatherland as soon as possible. How he accomplished this is not altogether certain, but it is believed that he managed to hide on a Dutch steamer and was able to elude a search while on the Atlantic.

At first Ribbentrop served on the Eastern Front. According to later critics, he won his Iron Cross (First Class) not for bravery in action but as a retroactive result of his own petition to the military authorities. This devious conduct was said to be typical of the man.

Because of his knowledge of English and his earlier sojourn in America, Ribbentrop in 1915 was given a special post in the German military mission in New York working under Franz von Papen. There von Papen, who became notorious for his clumsy secret-service activities, was expelled as *persona non grata*. Shortly after von Papen left, Ribbentrop, too, returned home. By early 1918 he was with von Papen again, this time in Turkey as adjutant to the Plenipotentiary of the War Office.

Once again, von Papen's mission failed. There was a rumor to the effect that young Ribbentrop had saved him from being captured by the British. But as with so many other purported events in Ribbentrop's career, there is no hard evidence to prove the rescue of his superior officer.

In 1919, after the war, Ribbentrop was named adjutant to the defeated German delegation, which had been called to Versailles to sign the peace treaty at Allied command. With his knowledge of both French and English, he waged a one-man campaign among Allied delegates, informing one and all who would listen that Germany remained a valuable buffer state against the new Bolshevik regime, and that she must never be weakened on that account. He was totally unsuccessful. The Treaty of Versailles was a hard peace. Like millions of other Germans, he resented what he called the *Versailles-Diktat*. He pledged himself to work against it to the best of his ability.

When he returned home after Versailles, Ribbentrop found that there was no place for him in the political structure of the new Weimar Republic. Meanwhile, he had insinuated himself into the lower ranks of Berlin cafe society. His travels had convinced him that his place was with the moneyed aristocracy. He knew and liked their way of life. But the all-important matter for him became the acquisition of money in order to keep up with the fast lifestyle of those he envied.

There were many ways of making money in the chaotic days of the French occupation of the Rhineland. Ribbentrop speculated in inflated marks. By slipping bribes to customs agents, he managed to import French wines duty-free and sold them to eager buyers. His success with wines won him a job with the prominent French firm of Pommery and Greno. So productive was Ribbentrop as traveling salesman for French sponsors that he was offered a position with the German champagne firm of Henckel-Trocken. It was a good break for the up-and-coming salesman. There was further opportunism in the availability of Henckel's daughter Annaliese. The brash young salesman married her and was taken into his father-in-law's firm as a partner.

Fast-talking Ribbentrop had come a long way. Until his marriage and the tremendous boost in his financial situation, he had had socialist inclinations. For a time he believed that the future of Germany was in that direction. But with a rich wife and new status as co-owner of the valuable Henckel cellars, he found that capitalism after all had most attractive features. His urge for socialism vanished.

Ribbentrop no longer lived in modest circumstances. He moved into a beautiful country house in the suburbs near Berlin. He was voted membership in the *Herrenklub* (Gentleman's Club), which brought him into contact with an aristocratic crowd of noble lineage, industrialists, and bankers. He was the kind of eager young man who attracted attention because of his ability to speak foreign languages as well as make friends among important people.

In his new status at the upper level of German society, Ribbentrop became intimate with prominent Jewish banking families. He often visited their salons. He claimed to enjoy the attention of Madame Rothschild, at whose home he played the part of a gentleman in English society comedies. Later, Ribbentrop would be accused of taking a real-life role in the grotesque extermination of German Jews, a charge he indignantly denied.

One thing was missing in Ribbentrop's new aristocratic life—he lacked the German nobility title of "von." Nearly everywhere he went he found aristocrats in the new democracy making careful use of their "von" title. He resolved the problem in a typical way—in 1926 he added "von" to his name by the expediency of getting himself adopted by the same favorite aunt who had been so helpful to him in his youth. From then on, he made full use of his secondhand acquisition of the noble title. Germans, including former Austrian Hitler, were impressed.

Ribbentrop met Hitler for the first time in the fall of 1929. It was said at the time that he was introduced to Hitler as "the man who gets as big a price for German champagne as others get for French champagne." There was mutual attraction between the two. Hitler was interested in Ribbentrop's suave manners and dashing behavior. Besides, friendship with the obviously wealthy man might give the ambitious politician entrée into the wealth and influence of the *Herrenklub*.

In January 1933, at the critical moment when Hitler was on the verge of becoming Chancellor, Ribbentrop was influential in staging a meeting between Hitler and von Papen at the home of banker von Schroeder. At this conference Hitler found what he desperately needed—access to big money. He never forgot Ribbentrop's role at that important stage of his political career.

When Hitler came to power he made Ribbentrop his foreign policy adviser and in the same year representative of the Nazi Party on foreign policy. In 1934 Ribbentrop was appointed delegate for disarmament questions, and in 1935 Minister Plenipotentiary-at-large. In this post he negotiated the Anglo-German Naval Agreement in 1935 and the Anti-Comintern Pact in 1936.

Ribbentrop's career in the higher circles of Nazidom was well under way. On August 11, 1936, he was appointed ambassador to England. In London he was considerably less of a success than he expected. He made it a point to be seen with the Cliveden set, the Marquess of Londonderry, King Edward VIII, and Mrs. Simpson, and several of their friends. Despite his affected British manners, despite his tennis and bridge activities, he was unable to get into exclusive English clubs. It was rumored at the time that his son was turned down by Eton, a refusal that angered him beyond words. The German ambassador with his Nazi salutes did not enjoy the popularity he craved in London.

On February 4, 1938, Ribbentrop succeeded Constantin von Neurath as Reich Minister for Foreign Affairs, as part of the general reshuffling that went along with the dismissal of Generals Werner von Fritsch and Werner von Blomberg. Hitler wanted his own followers in high office, and Ribbentrop was his man. Von Neurath's reaction: "May God have mercy on the Reich!" Later, in prison at Nuremberg, von Neurath elaborated on his estimate of the champagne salesman: "You will not find another official who is held in lower esteem than that man Ribbentrop. Some of the people in the dock are surprised by the extent of his stupidity and the shallowness he is showing in court, but to me it is an old story. I had to put up with that nonsense for years—just a lot of gab and no sense. He actually did more harm than good with his stupid meddling."

Hitler, however, was satisfied with his Foreign Minister—and Hitler's word was law in the Third Reich. The *Fuehrer* was partial to a diplomat who would carry out his slightest desire without question. In Ribbentrop he had the ideal yes-man. Critics be damned!

On January 2, 1938, while still ambassador to Britain, Ribbentrop sent a memorandum to Hitler presenting his opinion that a change in the *status quo* in the East in the German sense could be carried out only by force, and suggested methods to prevent England and France from interceding in a European war fought to bring about such a change. Ribbentrop, in his dim-witted way, did not realize it, but in sending this memorandum he was, in effect, signing his own death warrant.

When Ribbentrop became Foreign Minister, he was informed by Hitler that Germany still had four problems to solve: Austria, Sudetenland, Memel, and Danzig, and mentioned the possibility of "some sort of showdown" or "military settlement" of their solution.

Eight days after he became Foreign Minister, Ribbentrop attended the meeting between Hitler and Austrian Chancellor Kurt von Schuschnigg, at which the *Fuehrer*, by clear threats of invasion, forced Schuschnigg to grant a series of abject concessions, including Nazi control over the Austrian police. Ribbentrop blandly informed the British that Germany had intervened in Austria only to prevent civil war. On March 13, 1938, he signed the law incorporating Austria into the German Reich in Hitler's hotly desired *Anschluss* (union).

The Foreign Minister, in his obtuse way, had little understanding that he was cooperating with his *Fuehrer* in a program of aggression. He took a leading role in Hitler's plans directed against Czechoslovakia. Working closely with the Sudeten German Party in Czechoslovakia, he urged its members to keep alive the issue that might serve as an excuse for the assault that Hitler expected to make on Czechoslovakia. The Munich Pact of September 1938, by which Britain and France deserted their Czechoslovak ally "to maintain peace in our time," was the result and triumph of Ribbentrop's diplomacy-for-Hitler.

Meanwhile, Ribbentrop was feeding Hitler dangerous misinformation about the English. Still angry about the lack of success of his London mission, he persistently told the *Fuehrer* that Britons were so lethargic and paralyzed that they would accept without complaint any aggressive moves by the Third Reich. Hitler, he said, need not fear any effective British support for Poland. Under no circumstances, he advised, would the British fight. Hitler accepted the word of his Foreign Minister because that was precisely what he wanted to believe.

Again, Ribbentrop was behind the diplomatic activities that led to the attack on Poland. At a conference held on August 12, 1939, dedicated to obtaining Italian support in the event of a general European war, Ribbentrop admitted that he had tried to deceive the British ambassador into believing that Germany had no intention of attacking Poland when he knew otherwise. There was no good faith here.

On August 23, 1939, Ribbentrop went to Moscow to sign with Soviet Foreign Minister Vyacheslav M. Molotov the nonaggression agreement containing a secret clause providing for the partition of Poland. The pact opened the way for Hitler's attack on Poland and the subsequent outbreak of World War II. On September 28, 1939, Ribbentrop signed a second German-Soviet treaty readjusting the partition. All the while he piously denied any efforts at "aggression."

When Hitler sent his armies crashing into Norway, Denmark, and the Low Countries in 1940, Ribbentrop prepared the official Foreign Office memoranda justifying the attacks. Aggression? Not in Ribbentrop's mind. These were merely defensive moves forward. For Hitler's Foreign Minister, all German attacks were defensive steps designed to thwart enemy plans. At a conference held on January 20, 1941, at which Hitler and Mussolini discussed a proposed attack on Greece, Ribbentrop was there to enunciate and support this "defensive action." The following March he assured Yugoslav officials that Germany would respect their country's sovereignty and territorial integrity—at a time when Hitler was actually planning to attack it.

Ribbentrop's one outstanding characteristic was his sense of loyalty to Hitler. He remained absolutely subservient to his chief and became the *Fuehrer's* shadow. To him, foreign policy meant simply anything that was approved by Hitler. He was careful to learn beforehand exactly what was on Hitler's mind when he approached him with any problem or recommendation. To him, the *Fuehrer's* word was law. Even in prison he retained his sense of complete loyalty. "Even with all I know, if in this cell Hitler should come to me and say: 'Do this!' I would still do it." His desire to please the *Fuehrer*, like others in the entourage, was matched only by his ambition, Yet, even many of his subordinates had only contempt for him as a fawning flatterer.

Ribbentrop was one of the loyal clan who remained with Hitler in his Berlin bunker almost to the end. The arrogant architect of the *Fuehrer's* disastrous foreign policy joined his chief in denouncing the generals whom they accused of betraying Germany to England. In the bunker an optimistic Ribbentrop continued to remind Hitler that there would be an inevitable split between the Western Allies and the Soviet Union. This was a point of view the depressed *Fuehrer* was anxious to hear.

Virtually all the top Nazis in the underground shelter with Hitler—Goebbels, Himmler, Bormann—lined up against Ribbentrop and agreed he must go. Goebbels, especially, even at this late date, had his eyes on Ribbentrop's post as Foreign Minister. The camarilla, notably Goering, who hated Ribbentrop, worked assiduously without success for his dismissal. But Hitler, as in the past, always replied that they misjudged Ribbentrop, who was "a second Bismarck" and could not be spared from his position. Again, delusions of grandeur—"the second Bismarck" did only what Hitler told him to do. The *Fuehrer's* "intuition" led him to appoint Ribbentrop in the first place and one did not challenge his reasoning.

Ribbentrop continued to insist that all would be well, but Hitler at long last lost patience with his Foreign Minister. In his Political Testament dated April 29, 1945, in which he gave his apologia and his "last warning" against international Jewry, the *Fuehrer* named Grand Admiral Karl Doenitz as Reich President and Goebbels as Reich Chancellor. There was no room for his "second Bismarck": he appointed Artur Seyss-Inquart, the Austrian Quisling and oppressor of Holland, as Foreign Minister.

Dejected, Ribbentrop had no desire to remain in the bunker and—like fanatic Goebbels—die a Wagnerian death in its ruins. The last time he saw Hitler was on April 23, 1945. By then he was quite sure that the *Fuehrer* intended to take his own life. Later he said: "Hitler did not actually say so, but it was obvious. That was the first time he had ever mentioned defeat." Ribbentrop rightly guessed that this, indeed, was the end.

In his *Nuremberg Diary*, psychologist G.M. Gilbert painted

an extraordinary picture of Ribbentrop in confinement. The prisoner begged the American to believe him. He complained bitterly that he was in no way responsible for what happened in the Third Reich. He only did what he was supposed to do for his adored *Fuehrer*, who was a political genius. Why hold him responsible for the sins of others and of which the great man was totally unaware?

"Tell me frankly," Ribbentrop asked Gilbert, "do any of us look like murderers? I can't conceive of Hitler ordering such things. I can't believe that he knew about it. He had a hard side, I know, but I believed in him with all my heart. He could really be so tender. I was willing to do anything for him. Himmler must have ordered those things."

To follow-the-leader Ribbentrop, Hitler "could really be so tender." "Of course, I was one of his faithful followers. That is something hard for you to understand. The *Fuehrer* had a terrifically magnetic personality. You can't understand it unless you have experienced it. Do you know even now, six months after his death, I can't completely shake off his influence. Everybody was fascinated by him. Even if great intellects came together for a discussion, why in a few minutes they just ceased to exist and the brilliance of his personality shone over all."

Ribbentrop was certain that any atrocities should be attributed to Himmler, who must have ordered those things. "I doubt if Himmler was a real German. He had a peculiar face. We couldn't get along." And again: "Hitler was hard but not cruel. Himmler was the cruel one. He must have gone insane. I believe he must have talked Hitler into it. He had the cruelty of a schoolmaster— a man who made up his mind pedantically and cannot be swayed by any human considerations."

It was, of course, all the fault of the dead Himmler. Ribbentrop in his cell at Nuremberg at last began to talk of "human considerations."

Before the Nuremberg Tribunal, Ribbentrop vehemently denied any wrongdoing as Foreign Minister. But the bill of particulars against him was damning. Nuremberg prosecutors accused him of participating in a meeting held on June 6, 1944, at which it was agreed to start a program under which the Allied aviators carrying out machine-gun attacks should be lynched. In December 1944, the prosecution charged, Ribbentrop was informed of plans to murder one of the French generals held as a prisoner of

Hermann Goering

Heinrich Himmler

Julius Streicher

Ernst Roehm

Rudolf Hess

Joseph Goebbels

Martin Bormann

Alfred Rosenberg

Joachim von Ribbentrop

Baldur von Schirach

Reinhard Heydrich

Ernst Kaltenbrunner

Adolf Eichmann

Rudolf Hoess

Josef Kramer

Ilse Koch

Josef Mengele

Theodor Morell

Otto Skorzeny

war. He directed his subordinates to see that the details were
worked out in such a way as to prevent any detection.

Ribbentrop was also accused of War Crimes and Crimes
Against Humanity in his activities in occupied countries and in
Axis satellites. His representatives serving in both Denmark and
Vichy France put into effect his general economic and political
policies. According to the prosecution, Ribbentrop urged Ital-
ians to adopt a ruthless occupation policy in Yugoslavia and
Greece.

Aggression? Who, me? Germany, said the former Foreign
Minister, had been in a desperate situation since World War I.
So much misery and unemployment. Germany needed *Lebensraum*, living space. "If you had given us a single colony, you
would never have heard of Hitler." The insolent Poles had started
the war. What about the Gleiwitz incident? (On September 1,
1939, there was an assault by "Polish" troops on a small German radio station at Gleiwitz, one mile inside the German border. The next day, in a high state of excitement, Hitler informed
the German people that they were at war with Poland. The "Polish" troops were actually Germans in Polish uniforms, a fact
Ribbentrop found it convenient to overlook.)

And what about the Jews? Ribbentrop informed prison psychologist Gilbert that he was never anti-Semitic. "This accusation is absolutely against my nature." The persecution and
atrocities were revolting. "Nobody used up so much nervous
energy in trying to dissuade Hitler from persecution of Jews. I
had five very severe clashes with Hitler on the subject. There
was simply nothing you could do."

Ribbentrop claimed that he had dealings with Jewish businessmen all the time. He said that he had even introduced foreign Jews to Hitler in the early years. "I myself always thought
the anti-Semitic policy was madness. Naturally, in the public I
had to support Hitler in every way. It was a mass psychosis—
everybody suffered from it."

Prosecutors at Nuremberg, however, accused Ribbentrop of
playing an important role in Hitler's Final Solution of the Jewish
problem. There were specific charges. In September 1942 he
ordered German diplomatic representatives accredited to various
Axis satellites to hasten the deportation of Jews to the East. In
June 1942 the German ambassador to Vichy France apparently
on Ribbentrop's solicitation, requested Premier Laval to turn over

50,000 Jews for deportation to the East. On February 25, 1943, Ribbentrop protested to Mussolini against Italian slowness in deporting Jews from the Italian occupation zone of France. On April 17, 1943, he took part in a conference between Hitler and Horthy on the removal of Jews from Hungary, and informed Horthy explicitly that "Jews must either be exterminated or taken to concentration camps."

All this was attributed to the Foreign Minister who claimed he knew nothing about extermination of Jews and who insisted that "some of my best friends were Jews." He pointed to his earlier days when he was intimate with prominent Jewish bankers and frequented their salons. Was he not an honored guest at the home of Madame Rothschild?

Everyone should know, Ribbentrop told Gilbert, that he was not an ideological fanatic, like Rosenberg or Streicher or Goebbels. He was merely an international businessman who wanted to have industrial problems solved and national wealth properly preserved and used. What he resented most of all, he said, was that his integrity was being maligned by the prosecution, which had made an issue of the six houses he owned. "Is it a crime for statesmen to have money and property? Don't your statesmen have money and property, too? Didn't Roosevelt live in a big White House. It's the same with me. The *Fuehrer* wanted it that way, and so did the people."

Ribbentrop made his defense before the Tribunal on March 26, 1946. His performance in the courtroom was pathetic. Pale, stooped, and beaten, he sobbed his innocence. On direct examination he gave a weak recital of pre-war conditions, the Party's rise to power, the difficulties of the Versailles Treaty, the rearmament question, the anti-Comintern Pact, and the Munich Pact. He contributed little, if anything, to what was already known.

His fellow-prisoners were appalled by Ribbentrop's performance on the stand. Dr. Hjalmar Schacht: "Hitler and Goering were brutal criminals—all right, that is something. But that Ribbentrop—he wasn't even good enough to be a bootblack." Franz von Papen: "*Ach*, there's no use letting that man talk any more—he had convicted himself already. Just imagine the casual way he passed off such a catastrophic event as the declaration of war against the United States—('Well, they are already shooting at our U-boats, so we might as well declare war.' '' The man, said von Papen, was a fool and a stupid amateur.

Nothing could help Ribbentrop, now reduced to a hulking wreck. He was convinced that he was paying the penalty for being on the losing side in the war. Power was in the hands of his accusers. They would never grant that he was merely a patriotic German working for his beloved Fatherland. It was criminal, he believed, to accuse him of being a criminal.

The verdict:

> Ribbentrop's defense against the charges made against him is that Hitler made all the important decisions, and that he was such a great admirer and faithful follower of Hitler that he never questioned Hitler's repeated assertions that he wanted peace or the truth of the reasons that Hitler gave in explaining aggressive action. The Tribunal does not consider this explanation to be true. Ribbentrop participated in all of the Nazi aggressions from the occupation of Austria to the invasion of the Soviet Union. Although he was personally concerned with the diplomatic rather than the military aspect of these actions, his diplomatic efforts were so closely connected with war that he could not have remained unaware of the aggressive nature of Hitler's actions. In the administration of territories over which Germany acquired control by illegal invasion, Ribbentrop also assisted in carrying out criminal policies, particularly those involving the extermination of the Jews. There is abundant evidence, moreover, that Ribbentrop was in complete sympathy with all the main tenets of the National Socialist creed, and that his collaboration with Hitler and with other defendants in the commission of Crimes against Peace, War Crimes and Crimes against Humanity was wholehearted. It was because Hitler's policy and plans coincided with his own ideas that Ribbentrop served him so willingly to the end.

The Tribunal found Ribbentrop guilty on all four Counts: (1) Conspiracy to Prepare Aggressive War; (2) Crimes Against Peace; (3) War Crimes; and (4) Crimes Against Humanity.

The punishment: death.

A short time before he was scheduled to lead ten other condemned members of the Nazi hierarchy to the gallows on the morning of October 16, 1946, former *Reichsmarschall* Hermann Goering cheated the gallows by committing suicide. The crown prince of Nazidom managed to hide in his mouth, chew, and swallow a vial of cyanide.

This gave the gallows place of dishonor to Ribbentrop. The former Foreign Minister was the first to mount the scaffold in the electrically lighted barn-like interior of the small gymnasium at Nuremberg city jail.

The once arrogant Ribbentrop entered the execution hall at 1:11 A.M.

While waiting for the black hood to be placed over his head, he said loudly in a firm tone: "May God save Germany!" He then asked: "May I say something else?" The interpreter nodded. The former diplomat then said: "My last wish is that Germany realize its entity and that an understanding be reached between East and West. I wish peace to the world."

The trap was sprung at 1:16 A.M. Ribbentrop was pronounced dead at 1:30.

A confirmed Nazi had faced the retribution of an outraged world. Here was another gangster-minded rascal who placed power, prestige, and wealth above any consideration of simple decency. Some characters with Ribbentrop's ambition, notably Martin Bormann, had managed to escape the hangman's noose. But Hitler's diplomat was not so fortunate. With his smooth salesman's delivery he had sold case after case of Rhenish champagne. As Foreign Minister he could present a defense of Hitler's aggressions. But he had no luck in swaying his accusers.

He had had his little triumphs. He failed in his ultimate test— and succumbed to the judgment of Nuremberg.

10

BALDUR VON SCHIRACH: MISLEADER OF GERMAN YOUTH

"Heil Hitler!" This genius grazing the stars.
—Baldur von Schirach

Scoundrels and rogues come in all age groups and have no common social status. In the bizarre Nazi environment there was an oversupply of such villains. Included among them was an aristocratic misleader of the young.

Adolf Hitler boasted that his Third Reich would last for a thousand years. To attain that goal the Nazi regime needed the support of German youth and the generations succeeding it. The process is a familiar one in all dictatorships. Italy's Sawdust Caesar had his young Italians in hilarious goose-step while jutting out their jaws in approved Mussolini style. Indoctrination of the young in Marxist-Leninist principles is given top priority in Communist countries. Hitler, too, saw the winning of youth to his cause as an absolute necessity for the continued existence of National Socialism.

The *Fuehrer* knew what he wanted. "A violently active, dom-

inating brutal youth—that is what I am after. I will have no
intellectual training. Knowledge is ruin to my young men.''
Whoever has the youth, Hitler said, has the future. ''I begin
with the young. We older ones are used up. We are rotten to the
marrow. But my magnificent youngsters! Are there any finer
ones in the world? Look at these young men and boys! What
material! With them, I can make a new world. This is the heroic
stage of youth. Out of it will come the creative man, the man-
god.''

To lead his magnificent youth, Hitler chose a foppish aristocrat, who at Nuremberg admitted that he had misled a generation
of German youth. Vain, dandified, affected, narrow-minded, he
was a romantic who considered himself to be a heroic nationalist. Somewhat effeminate in manner (he was proud of his all-
white bedroom), he was addicted to poetry and saw himself as
a noble esthete. He wrote tearfully sentimental verses in praise
of Hitler. At Nuremberg, Hermann Goering dismissed him as a
weakling.

This was Baldur von Schirach, youth leader of the German
Reich, whose task it was to re-educate young Germans in the
spirit of National Socialism. There was intelligence here (psychologists at Nuremberg rated his IQ at 130, which placed him
at the upper level of the accused). There was organizing ability,
which enabled him to bring most young German boys and girls
to Hitler's side. But there was also a driving force influenced by
Alfred Rosenberg's weird paganism and Julius Streicher's special
brand of anti-Semitism.

Moreover, the Nazi aristocrat had a shrewd sense of what was
good for his own advancement. Studying Hitler's personality, he
found an inviting chink in the *Fuehrer*'s armor. What he learned
was enough to bring him into the circle of Nazi leadership and
keep him there. Schirach discovered the extent of Hitler's sus-
ceptibility to flattery. The *Fuehrer* was pleased to have himself
described as greater than Bismarck, as, indeed, ''the greatest
German of all time.'' He poured through the pages of Streicher's
pornographic *Der Stürmer* and Goebbels's vitriolic *Der Angriff*,
eagerly absorbing the glowing tributes to himself. Because most
Nazis of his court knew this well, they took pains to have their
praise reach the ears of the leader.

Among competitors for the *Fuehrer*'s favor, Schirach easily
walked off with the brown ribbon of success. His servility was

classic in its intensity. When the vacuous Rudolf Hess at the podium of the *Sportpalast* in Berlin fixed his eyes on his adored *Fuehrer* and broke into hysterical *"Heil Hitlers!"*—that was to be expected. But Schirach was someone special for Hitler—an aristocrat who could spout both socialism and racialism, an organizer who could thrust National Socialism into the future, but especially a comrade who knew the *Fuehrer*'s worth.

As Party poet laureate, Schirach raised flattery to a fine art. He won Hitler's attention by verses on "Germany's greatest son." It was ingenious praise:

> That is the greatest thing about him,
> That he is not only our Leader but a great hero,
> But himself, upright, firm and simple,
> . . . in him rest the roots of our world.
> And his soul touches the stars,
> And yet he remains a man like you or me.

The *Fuehrer* melted under such eulogies. In his estimation the young man had done a remarkable thing—he had rejected his own social caste in favor of National Socialism. He had an admirable sense of what was right. Had he not said that the altar of Christianity was not his church, but rather the steps of the Feldherrn Halle, drenched in Nazi blood during the 1923 Beer-Hall *Putsch*? "This was," the *Fuehrer* said, "a true follower and a dependable lad." He was delighted when Schirach married Henny Hoffmann, daughter of court photographer Heinrich Hoffmann. And his young follower was doing a superb job as head of the Hitler Youth.

Psychologists, psychiatrists, and psychohistorians saw the relationship between Hitler and his youth leader as an excellent example of the power of the ego in human affairs. Hitler was easily one of the greatest egotists of modern times. ("There was a time when there was *only* one Prussian in Europe and he lived in Rome. There was a second Prussian. He lived in Munich and was myself." "When one enters the Reich Chancellery, one should have the feeling that he is visiting the master of the world.")

The wily Schirach knew how to play upon this passionate love of self. There is no doubt whatever that he owed his career in the Third Reich not only to a combination of good fortune and

organizing ability, but even more because of his catering to the
ego of the lord of Berchtesgaden.

Egotist and sycophant. It was a psychic union of bourgeois
master and willing slave.

Baldur von Schirach was born in Berlin on March 9, 1907,
the first of four children of a well-to-do family. He was proud,
at least until 1941, of his three-quarters American origin, and
liked to whistle *Yankee Doodle Dandy* to indicate his American
background. His paternal grandfather had lived for a time in the
United States, fought as a major in the Civil War, and lost a leg
at Bull Run. He married an American girl and returned with her
to Germany. She claimed two signers of the Declaration of Independence among her ancestors.

Baldur's father, Carl Bailey-Norris von Schirach, had been an
officer in the Garde-Kürassier Regiment Wilhelm II from which
he resigned to become a theater director, first in Weimar and
then in Vienna. Young Baldur grew up in a milieu of theater,
music, and literature. In his early years he showed a talent for
writing poetry.

Joining the Young German League at the age of ten, Baldur
took pleasure in its hikes, camp life, and singing sessions. He
turned out to be a romantic and sentimental lad, somewhat plump
in physique and set apart by a kind of banal quality that characterized his verses. As a university student he was forced to
resign from his *Verbindung* (fraternity) under unknown but apparently unpleasant circumstances.

During the revolution that followed World War I, the elder
Schirach lost his job. The once well-to-do family like many others in Germany at the time, was plunged into the bitter status of
the have-nots. Young Schirach became a renegade from Germany's former ruling class, a development that was to be of
some importance in his later career.

Meanwhile, the restless young man, who until then had met
few Jews in his environment, began reading anti-Semitic literature. He was impressed by Houston Stewart Chamberlain's *The
Foundations of the Nineteenth Century*, especially with its fanatical racialism, and Henry Ford's *The International Jew*. Later
at Nuremberg he was to complain that no one told him that Ford
had repudiated his own strictures against Jews, but at the time
Schirach believed the book to be eternal truth. He was even

more convinced by reading the works of Alfred Rosenberg and anti-Semitic articles in the Nazi press.

In 1926 Schirach met Hitler, who had come to Weimar to deliver a speech. He had already read *Mein Kampf*, in which he found added confirmation for views already taking shape in his mind. Hitler, attracted by the handsome young former aristocrat (just the kind of young man he wanted for his Party), advised him to go to Munich, the birthplace of his movement. Schirach agreed and enrolled at the University of Munich.

In Munich the smooth, voluble young man, already a member of the *SA*, the Storm Troopers, became a speaker for the Party. Although lacking the flamboyant oratorical style of Hitler, he was successful enough in drawing fellow students to National Socialism. In 1929 he was made chief of the National Socialist Students' Union, an appointment readily confirmed by Hitler.

By now Schirach was firmly committed to the Nazi Party. In 1931 he was made Reich Youth Leader of the Nazi Party with control over all youth organizations, including the *Hitler Jugend*. Promotion came rapidly for the foppish young aristocrat-turned-Nazi. Like Goebbels, Rosenberg, and other stars in the Nazi firmament, he was shrewd enough to know the proper combination for success in the Nazi world: (1) glorify and extol the *Fuehrer* as a latter-day Siegfried and win the support of the leader morbidly eager for praise; (2) stand forward as a champion of Indo-European, Aryan, Nordic, Germanic racialism; (3) commend the National Socialist Revolution; and (4) denounce and excoriate Jews and Communists. All were of major importance for advancement in the Third Reich, but psychologically the most rewarding procedure consisted of laudation, applause, and panegyric for the *Fuehrer*. Schirach became the master flatterer of the Third Reich.

When Hitler came to political power in early 1933, he promoted Schirach to the position of Youth Leader of the Third Reich. Originally, this post had been under control of the Ministry of the Interior and its leader Wilhelm Frick, but after December 1, 1936, it rated an office in the Reich Cabinet. Now twenty-nine, Schirach had become one of the most important officials in the Third Reich. He had the advantage of reporting directly to Hitler.

Youth Leader Schirach took a series of aggressive steps, which he knew would ingratiate himself even more with the *Fuehrer*.

Using both official pressure and physical violence, he either drove out of existence or took control over all youth groups that might be in competition with his *Hitler Jugend*. As early as February 1933, shortly after Hitler became Chancellor, Schirach led a surprise raid of fifty of his boys on the offices of the National Central Committee *(Reichsausschuss)* of Youth Organizations. He confiscated its records and dismissed General Vogt, its head. At the same time he moved into the central youth hostel office and took over all its functions.

Praise from Hitler for a job well done. But this was not yet enough for the youth leader now fascinated by his success in direct action. There were many boy- and girl-scout associations in Germany at the time, whose political shades varied from middle-of-the-road to nationalist right. Schirach had his eyes especially on the Greater German Youth League, led by Navy Chief of Staff Admiral von Trotha. The admiral, Schirach said, was an admirable man, but he failed to understand the direction of National Socialism. Friction developed when the naval officer refused to allow his organization to join the *Hitler Jugend* as an entity in order to have some independence for his youngsters. Angry reaction from Schirach, who went ahead and dissolved the German Youth League. To appease the admiral, he made the naval officer honorary leader of the Navy Hitler Youth.

In 1934, in conformance with his policy of *Gleichschaltung* (coordination), Hitler issued a decree absorbing the *Stahlhelm* (Steel Helmets), the veteran's organization, into the Nazi war veterans association. At the same time, the deposed head of the *Stahlhelm* was required to place all his youth groups under Schirach. Protestant associations were quickly incorporated, but Catholic youth organizations held out a bit longer. By December 1, 1936, with the Hitler Youth Act, all German youth was organized inside Schirach's *Hitler Jugend*.

Schirach was ecstatic. His beloved *Fuehrer* had called on him "to project National Socialism through German youth into eternity." And now he was in a favored position at the top level of Nazi officialdom to carry out the orders of his demigod in Berlin.

At Reich Party Day in 1936, with Hitler listening intently, Schirach smeared it on thickly: "One thing is stronger than you, my *Fuehrer*. That is the love of young Germans for you. There are so many happy hours in the year of the youth. This, however, in every year is one of our happiest. Because more than any other people, my *Fuehrer*, we feel ourselves to be chained to your person by your name. Your name is the happiness of the youth, your name, my *Fuehrer*, is our immortality.''

Hitler beamed delightedly. This handsome young leader was smart and able. He was the perfect leader for German youth.

There was no limit to Schirach's adulation. Hitler, he intoned at another meeting, was the saviour sent by Almighty God to rescue the German people from the calamities and dangers visited upon them by the most pious parties of the defunct Weimar Republic. In the eyes of the Reich youth leader, Hitler ranked with Wotan and the gods of ancient German mythology.

In speaking to his young charges, Schirach used a tone of classical romanticism, the special quality he saw in his own poetry: ''We interpret the National Socialist Revolution as the rising of German sentiment *[Gemüt]* against the arrogance of the cold intellect. Its victory signifies the triumph of the soul over everything that is only mechanical. Faith has overcome doubt. It rules the lesser forces that dared to defy it. The motto of our lives must be Adolf Hitler's most profound saying: 'Woe to the one who has no faith.' ''

Again the careful catering to his master's beliefs. Like other observant Nazis, Schirach, too, understood that Hitler was always uncomfortable in the presence of professors and scientists, men of cold intellect who were able to recognize the emotional mysticism of the Nazi movement. Schirach, too, expert sycophant, knew how to emphasize the likes and dislikes of the great one.

Schirach controlled the lives of twelve million young people in a population of sixty-six million. For him it was a labor of love to educate them in the principles of National Socialism. Above all, they must be indoctrinated with the *Fuehrerprinzip*, the leadership principle: ''A single will leads the Hitler Youth. The commanding power of every Hitler Youth leader, whether of the smallest or biggest of its units, is absolute—that is he has the unlimited right to issue orders, because he bears unrestricted responsibility. An organization of young people can be successful only if it unreservedly accepts the authority of its leaders. The success of National Socialism is based on discipline.''

With ninety percent of all German youth under his control in 1937, Schirach became a man of substance in the Nazi world. Honors were heaped upon his willing shoulders. He was presented to the German people as a kind of young demigod embodying all that was fine and noble in Teutonic youth. Pictures of him smiling and surrounded by his young charges were displayed throughout the country. In Party newspapers and periodicals he was portrayed as a handsome young Nordic god, who was an inspiration to millions of young Germans. There was no false modesty about him—he accepted all this adulation as proper and merited.

But for Schirach there were some unwholesome flies in the otherwise sweet-smelling ointment. Rivalry among the entourage, common in any gangster environment, was especially strong in Nazi circles. Schirach's success in winning the *Fuehrer*'s trust and admiration by his organization of German youth stimulated jealousy in others who were vying for Hitler's attention. Goering, alienated by Schirach's effeminate manner, was hostile. The envious Dr. Goebbels, Nazidom's most active superstud, hated Schirach not only because of his girlish bedroom but also because he feared that the *Fuehrer* might make Schirach the next Propaganda Minister. An entry in Goebbels's diary for April 4, 1945, shows the extent of Goebbels's contempt for Schirach, then *Gauleiter* in Vienna: "Schirach has long been overdue for dismissal, but the *Fuehrer* has not been able to make up his mind to dispatch him to the wilderness. Now the severest measures must be taken to clean up the situation in Vienna."

Schirach's enemies began a campaign of vilification. He was ridiculed as a transplanted Berliner, who tried to impress Hitler by wearing Bavarian *Lederhosen* (leather breeches). There were crushing attacks on his effeminacy, though he was married and had children. All this he endured and denounced as idiotic envy.

Contemptuous of his critics, Schirach went ahead with his task of winning German youth to Hitler and National Socialism. An able executive, he watched over every detail of his office. He expected each German youth, on March 15 of the year in which he celebrated his tenth birthday, to register with the *Hitler Jugend*. After careful investigation of the boy's family, with special attention to his racial heritage, the lad was admitted to the *Deutsche Jungvolk* (German Young People), including those from ten to thirteen years of age. This honor generally took place on April 20, the *Fuehrer's* birthday.

Then came the *Hitler Jugend* for boys from fourteen to eighteen. At eighteen the young man was graduated and accepted into the National Socialist Party and eventually the *SA*. At nineteen he was called for six months into the State Labor Service, where he was subjected to strict discipline and manual labor. After that came service in the *Wehrmacht*, the armed forces, for two years.

Activities of the *Hitler Jugend* took precedence over any formal education. Its routine filled most hours of the boy's week. Members went on hiking and camping trips, they slept in youth hostels, and always in uniform they attended public demonstrations. Failure of any German boy to join the Hitler Youth was regarded as a serious violation of public responsibility. The uniform, Schirach said, reflected German democracy by doing away with differences between the rich and the poor. "The uniform of the *Hitler Jugend* does not express a war mentality but is the garb of comradeship. It extinguishes class differences. For these young people socialism has been achieved." Here again the Nazi preference for a direct lie. What Hitler wanted from German youth was preparation to right the wrongs of Versailles, achievable only through a war mentality. The dull philistine youth of yesterday, Hitler said, would be succeeded by the lanky, athletic Nordic warrior, "swift as a greyhound, tough as leather, and hard as Krupp steel." Yesterday's degenerate would be eliminated and a new youth created in strict discipline ready to fight for the ideals of National Socialism.

This was the language the Reich youth leader repeated *ad nauseam* in hundreds of speeches. All this was to be achieved by unconditional obedience to the leader. Always the *Fuehrer*. "The young worker," Schirach said, "whose heart beats hotly for the *Fuehrer*, is much more necessary for Germany than the highest German esthete. Much more than the sharpest intellect, we appreciate a true and courageous heart. Those who are cold and intelligent can make mistakes, but the true ones are always right. The intelligentsia want advantages for themselves, the true ones know nothing but their duty."

For the youngest and most impressionable minds, Schirach ordered daily obeisance to the *Fuehrer*. Boys of the *Hitler Jugend* and girls of the *Jungmaedel* were required to repeat a vow of allegiance: "I promise to do my duty in love and loyalty to the *Fuehrer* and our flag." They recited prayers with the evening meal:

Fuehrer, my *Fuehrer*, give me by God
Protect and preserve my life for long.
You saved Germany in time of need,
I thank you for my daily bread.
Be with me for a long time, do not leave me,
Fuehrer, my *Fuehrer*, my faith, my light,
Hail to my *Fuehrer*.

Schirach loved to display his young people in massive pageants, replete with marching bands and ceremonial embellishments. He wrote many of the *Lieder* they sang in unison. In responsive readings the youngsters chanted their faith: "My will is the *Fuehrer's* will!" "The *Fuehrer* of Great Germany is hated, but the forces of evil will not win. We, his true sword-bearers, will protect him."

In the opening months of World War II, Schirach served in the army, starting as a corporal and rising to the rank of lieutenant. After the French had been defeated in Hitler's smashing *Blitzkrieg*, the *Fuehrer* began to look around for someone to serve as *Gauleiter* (district leader) of Vienna. Schirach's record was fine—he was just the man for the job. The young aristocrat-turned-bourgeois had done a remarkable job with young Germans. Besides, he never ceased his campaign of flattery: Hitler was always "Germany's greatest son." And again the laudatory verses about "the genius who has remained a man like you and me."

Hitler asked the question: Would Schirach continue on as Reich leader of youth education, retain all his Party connections, and at the same time serve as *Gauleiter* in Vienna, an important office?

Schirach would.

Accordingly, Schirach, wife Henny, and their four children moved to the governor's palace in the center of Vienna. Their high style of living was what they deemed to be necessary, considering their place in the upper ranks of Nazi officialdom. This was war time and there were strictures but, nevertheless, they hired seventeen servants. Baldur and Henny slept in the bed of the Hapsburgs, took over the gardens of Prince Eugen, and also had a sequestered estate seized from the Rothschild family. Historical justice—and Hitler approved.

The Schirachs appointed themselves arbiters of Nazi taste in the Austrian capital. Just as mouse-general Goebbels saw as his cultural territory all German and Austrian film and radio studios, so did Schirach take as his own province the major opera houses and theaters in Vienna. In 1942, at a time when Jews were being transported from Austria to the gas ovens of Auschwitz, the *Gauleiter* of *Kulturzentrum* Vienna ordered the director of the Burgtheater to put on Shakespeare's *Merchant of Venice*, with special instructions to actors and actresses to emphasize anti-Semitism in their portrayals of the chief character.

For the thirty-five-year-old Schirach it was a head-turning sequence of windfalls. Not only was he *Gauleiter* of Vienna, but at the same time he held national office as a Reich defense commissioner, originally for Military District 17, which included the *Gaue* (provinces) of Vienna, Upper Danube, and Lower Danube. As Reich defense commissioner, the former army lieutenant was to have an important role in planning the war economy. As Reich governor, he headed the municipal administration of the City of Vienna and under supervision of the Minister of the Interior he directed governmental administration in the Austrian capital.

In all these important offices, the young Nazi *Gauleiter* was required to carry out orders from the "Central Ox" in Berlin, even if they involved enslavement and deportation. Under a Fritz Sauckel decree dated April 6, 1942, *Gauleiter* Schirach became the Viennese plenipotentiary for manpower under the policy of forced labor, more accurately the slave-labor program. Workers were to be fed, sheltered, and exploited to the highest degree possible at the lowest expense.

More, Schirach in his new posts was required to implement orders from Berlin on the special matter of Jews. Deportation of Jews from Vienna had already begun when he began his duties there. Some 60,000 of Vienna's original 150,000 Jews were still in the Austrian capital. Schirach got in touch with Hans Frank, Governor General of Occupied Poland, and urged him to take 50,000 Jews from Vienna. To solve his problem, Schirach went straight to the top. Hitler agreed—he issued an order to deport all 60,000 Jews remaining in Vienna to Poland because of the critical housing shortage in Vienna. With word from the great one, Schirach began his deportations in the early fall of 1942.

Though he did not know it, Schirach's speech on September 15, 1942, was to cost him dearly before the International Military

Tribunal at Nuremberg. In that talk he presented in elaborate phraseology his action in driving tens of thousands of Jews into the Ghetto of the East. What he did, he explained, was merely a contribution to European culture.

Meanwhile, the contributor to European culture was receiving reports addressed to him in his official capacity from the office of the chief of the security police describing how the *Einsatzgruppen* (task forces) were exterminating Jews. As late as June 30, 1944, his office was informed that a shipment of 12,000 Jews was on its way to Vienna for essential war work. Those who were incapable of work were to be prepared for "special action," one of the many Nazi euphemisms for extermination. Schirach was well aware of what the term "special action" meant in the Nazi vocabulary.

Schirach was now in dangerous waters over his head—and there was little he could do about it.

On June 14, 1941, came the notorious *Heu Aktion*, or Hay Action, an order from Alfred Rosenberg, then Reich Minister for the Eastern Occupied Territories, for a quota of foreign workers to be sent to Germany. The plan called for apprehension of from 40,000 to 50,000 young workers. Though he had ceased to be active head of the *Hitler Jugend* in 1940, Schirach was accused at Nuremberg of complicity in what amounted to a kidnapping action. The court did not dwell on his responsibility; it merely indicated that he had known about it.

In his cell at Nuremberg the effete narcissist turned into a sullen, fearful introvert interested only in saving his own life in a desperate situation. For a time he pretended allegiance to Hermann Goering, who had appointed himself guardian of the Nazi faith. At the proper time he would astonish his fellow prisoners and the world by a renunciation of his past conduct. He would admit a belated but sincere awakening.

To prison psychologist G. M. Gilbert, Schirach said that in his youth he had moved in an aristocratic milieu and had never come into contact with Jews. But at the same time he noticed a sort of underhanded quiet prejudice against Jews "in the best circles." Then he came under the influence of Julius Streicher, "who had a knack for clothing anti-Semitism in pseudoscientific garb." After Schirach met Hitler he became a confirmed anti-Semite "until the recent bitter tragedy showed me the utter falsity of such a belief." He had changed his mind.

Schirach accused his elders of betraying him. "Why didn't anyone tell us that Henry Ford had repudiated *The International Jew* and that the *Protocols of the Elders of Zion* were a forgery? Why all the historical and scientific lies to brand hatred on impressionable minds? I will not deny my guilt. I made the mistake of approving the Viennese evacuation, and I am prepared to die for it."

The youth leader who had praised Hitler now had a change of heart: "Before 1934 he was *menschlich* [human], from 1934 to 1938 he was *übermenschlich* [superhuman]; from 1938 on he was *unmenschlich* [inhuman] and a tyrant. I believe that power went to his head in 1934 when Hindenburg died and he became *Reichsfuehrer*. About 1942 I began to notice that he was becoming slightly insane. His stare would suddenly go blank in the midst of a conversation and he would wander off."

On the showing of the atrocity film before the Tribunal, Schirach said: "I don't know how Germans could do such things."

Schirach took the stand on May 23, 1946. He began his defense by assuming full responsibility for the education of German youth. Always the esthete, he explained that he was a propagandist not only for National Socialism but also for Goethe and German *Kultur*. The Hitler Youth he headed, he said, was only a kind of Boy Scout organization interested in sports and was not exposed to military training. He had not allowed his boys to participate in the pogrom of 1938, the notorious Night of Broken Glass.

The next day Schirach testified that he and his German youth had expected a peaceful solution to the Jewish problem. He had nothing to do with the Nuremberg Laws, but German youth had been forced to accept them as official policy. He rejected *Der Stürmer* (angry stares from Streicher). He admitted approving transportation of Jews from Vienna to the East while he was *Gauleiter* there. He regretted it now but he had done it out of false loyalty to the *Fuehrer*.

Then Schirach astonished Goering and most of the other defendants by a bitter denunciation of Hitler. The murders at Auschwitz, about which Rudolf Hoess had testified, were not committed by Hoess, who was only the executioner. "The murders were ordered by Adolf Hitler. That can be seen from his Last Testament—that Last Testament is genuine. He and Himmler together committed that crime which for all times is the darkest blot on our history. It is a crime which is shameful to every German.''

Schirach then turned to self-denunciation: "It is my guilt, which I will have to carry before God and the German nation, that I educated the youth of that people; that I raised the youth for a man for whom for many years I considered impeccable as a leader and as head of State; that I organized youth just as I did. It is my guilt that I educated German youth for a man who committed murder millionfold.''

Sensation in the dock. Von Papen and Schacht, both of whom later were found not guilty, agreed that Schirach was absolutely right about Hitler. Goering snorted his defiance. He knew, he said, that "the wimp intended to sell out." Excoriating Schirach, he sought agreement in denouncing this treasonable desertion of the *Fuehrer*.

Schirach was well-satisfied with his performance. It, indeed, saved his life. He felt that his testimony had broken the last moral ties to Hitler. If the Americans were smart, he said, they would capitalize on that to the utmost. "I hope the world will now realize that I only meant well."

The Tribunal found Schirach guilty on Count 4: Crimes Against Humanity. Its judgment:

Von Schirach used the *Hitler Jugend* to educate German youth "in the spirit of National Socialism" and subjected them to an extensive program of Nazi propaganda. . . . The Tribunal finds that von Schirach, while he did not originate the policy of deporting Jews from Vienna, participated in this deportation after he became *Gauleiter* of Vienna. He knew that the best the Jews could hope for was a miserable existence in the Ghetto of the East. Bulletins describing the Jewish extermination were in his office.

Sentence: twenty years' imprisonment.

Schirach's face was tense as he marched to his cell after the verdict. "Twenty," he said to a guard. "Better a quick death than a slow one.''

Glamour boy Schirach, one of the seven Nazis condemned at Nuremberg to prison terms, was sent with them to Spandau, a red-brick, ugly, high-walled prison in a suburb of Berlin. Still arrogant, with an air of aloofness about him, he strode around the compound in crumpled brown corduroy and wearing a dark-colored nylon coat with his monocle dangling from his neck outside it. He was known for the neatness of his cell where his favorite Dunhill pipes were carefully stacked.

His fellow-prisoners were alienated by Schirach's studied air of superiority. He boasted that he had little use for other people: "You see, it is this way. I have never yet seen the man I looked up to, and that includes Hitler or anybody else. I just always feel superior, in my own estimation, to everyone I met." Strange words from the one-time glorifier of Adolf Hitler.

Prisoner Walther Funk, tubby little former president of the *Reichsbank* and a lover of practical jokes, went to some trouble to embarrass Schirach. He arranged with an American warder to place a supply of fresh, smelly horse dung unwrapped between Schirach's bed frame and mattress. When the Russian guard ran his fingers systematically between bed and mattress, there was explosive pandemonium. Schirach was not amused by the case of "the Smuggled Horse Apple."

Schirach served his full term. Released in 1966, he died at Kröv on August 8, 1974.

11

HANGMAN HEYDRICH

Personal power was Heydrich's absolute god.
                                        —Alan Wykes

Many of the rogues who rose to power in Nazi gangsterland were experts in brutality and refugees from decency. Seldom has there been such an assembly of ruffians dedicated to violence in an outlaw regime. In the drive to the top, those who eschewed strong-arm tactics made little headway in Hitler's realm.

Among the most successful who managed to win promotion was Reinhard Heydrich, known as "Hangman Heydrich" and "the Butcher of Prague." This icily cold sadist takes rank with the nastiest criminals of all time. Cynical, suspicious, he trusted no one. He had only contempt for human life—the lives of others—no compassion, no pity.

Tall, slender, and broad-shouldered, Heydrich was presented in Nazi society as the personification of the Teutonic hero, the ideal of Aryan purity. But there was an ironic twist—this representative of Nazi racial superiority was tormented throughout his life by the fear that his body was tainted by Jewish blood and that it was impossible to do anything about it. He was never free from the agony caused by what he saw as biological contamination. It is possible that his savagery in dealing with Jewish victims may have been dictated in part by this stain on his psyche. He was said to be one-quarter Jewish; to him that was a tragic fault in his physical makeup. Others would suffer from the unkind fate that made him a *Mischling*, a German of mixed blood, a mongrel in the eyes of Nazi ideologists.

Reinhard Tristran Eugen Heydrich was born in Halle, Saxony, on March 7, 1904, the son of Bruno Richard Heydrich, a gifted musician and founder of the first Halle Conservatory for Music, Theater, and Teaching. In 1916 Bruno Heydrich was described in Hugo Riemann's *Musiklexikon* as "Heydrich, Bruno, real name Süss." (Süss at that time was a popular Jewish name.) Moreover, according to biographer Charles Wigton, Heydrich had a Jewish grandmother, but was baptized by a Catholic priest and was brought up as a Catholic.

In the Germany of 1904 a Jewish grandmother had no special significance one way or another, especially if the parents or grandchild converted to Christianity. Author Wigton's suggestion of Heydrich's ancestry was based largely on the authority of Dr. Felix Kersten, Himmler's physician. Subsequent efforts to ascertain Heydrich's forebears in the Berlin Documents Center, where the Central Archives of the Nazi Party were kept, were inconclusive, but for Heydrich the charge was critical. For the rest of his life he was engaged in thwarting what was to him an obnoxious accusation. Again and again he brought suit for racial slander against those who spoke of his contaminated blood.

In his early years Heydrich studied music and later showed off his skill at Nazi musical performances. Physically powerful, he was an expert fencer who represented Germany at international fencing contests. He garnered many trophies. He was also an able amateur pilot.

Attracted by a naval career, young Heydrich served under Admiral Wilhelm Canaris in naval intelligence. For two years he studied to become an intelligence officer. He passed from cadet to midshipman in 1924, from midshipman to sub-lieutenant and lieutenant in 1926. Ambitious, the mark of most Nazi rogues, he toadied to anyone in high office who could help him get ahead.

In 1928 naval careerist Heydrich heard Hitler speak at a rally.

He was enraptured. Though not especially politically minded, he had the feeling that this eloquent Austrian could look forward to a great future. He told his sister: "This man alone can save Germany." He had no idea that eventually he was to become one of the *Fuehrer's* chief minions, practitioner of the politics of terror and prime mass murderer of the Third Reich.

By this time Heydrich's character was being molded in a set pattern and a not altogether attractive one. Blond, blue-eyed, with a dolichocephalic skull, he fitted in with Hitler's idea of Aryan racial superiority. He was always neatly dressed and seemingly well-bred. A man of decision once his mind was made up, he went ahead with obstinate purpose. But inside the Aryan superman was a streak of cruelty which later emerged in frightening proportions.

Heydrich's budding career as a naval officer suffered a major reversal in the summer of 1930. Unemployed at the time, he began having problems in his private life. He seduced a girl who became pregnant, but he had no intention of marrying her. At Christmas he became engaged to another girl, Lina von Osten. The situation became uncomfortable when the pregnant girl's father, a shipyard director, threatened Heydrich with a whip and demanded that the naval officer marry the betrayed daughter.

Heydrich refused. It was not compatible, he said, with the honor of a German naval officer that he forsake his betrothed in favor of "a passing fancy." Already there were evidences of Heydrich's special brand of cruelty. At the same time, Lina's parents announced themselves as bitterly opposed to the marriage of their daughter to Heydrich.

The anguished father of the betrayed girl appealed for help to his friend, Vice-Admiral Erich Raeder. The higher officer summoned Heydrich before a naval court. The verdict—marry the pregnant girl or be dismissed from the service. Heydrich sealed his reputation as a consummate cad by choosing dismissal. No one was going to tell him what he must do with his life. Defiantly, he married Lina von Osten.

Unemployed, but still interested in politics, Heydrich was urged by wife Lina, an ardent Nazi, to join the *Schutz Staffel* (*SS*), Hitler's bodyguard. That, she said, would make a great career for him. It happened at the time that Heinrich Himmler, *SS* chieftain, was anxious to draw German aristocrats to his staff.

Meeting the *SS* leader at his poultry farm near Munich, Heydrich accepted the assignment.

That meeting on June 14, 1931, was to change the course of history. Collaboration began between the meek, stuttering Himmler and the tall, blond Aryan Siegfried, a cooperation that was to mean the death of millions of German citizens as well as foreigners. Roots of the tragic Holocaust.

Although he had held rank only as a communications and code officer, Heydrich led Himmler to believe that he had been an important officer in Naval Intelligence. The result was that he was made head of a new *SS* Intelligence unit, whose task it was to spy on members of the Nazi Party, particularly dissidents in the *SA*, the Storm Troopers.

Heydrich started with a small card index of information on Party members. Slowly but carefully he built up a task force of informers and confidential agents. Meanwhile, he kept extensive records for his own use. He compiled a personal treasure of backstairs gossip about governmental officials, army generals, and Party members. He ordered his own army of agents to bring him all the gossip they could find, especially about the sexual life of those eligible for his special brand of blackmail. Soon he had amassed a huge supply of folders concerning the Party's upper echelon.

No one was exempt from Heydrich's secret agents. They brought him photographs, letters, and recordings, to be used one day for the boss's benefit. He had reports on Goering's supposed drug habit and suspected sexual impotence, on Goebbels's hot love affair with "racially impure and sexually perverted film actress Lida Baarova," on Martin Bormann's background. He even accumulated a secret file on his immediate superior *Reichsfuehrer-SS* Himmler, whom he suspected of protecting certain Jewish businessmen. Heydrich gathered evidence to show Himmler's favors for Salon Kitty, a glamorous brothel frequented by high-ranking *SS* officers and foreign diplomats. The house of prostitution was run by Frau Kitty, a butcher's daughter from Munich who managed to win Himmler's support.

There were even closely guarded rumors to the effect that Heydrich kept a file on the *Fuehrer* himself. The folder was said to contain evidence that Hitler's Iron Cross had been awarded retroactively after World War I, as well as medical reports concerning his supposed treatment for syphilis.

This kind of snooping did not prevent Heydrich himself from
attending Salon Kitty as a favored guest. He was seen in the best
nightclubs in Berlin. Though raising a family and fond of his
two sons he sought relaxation in alcohol and sex outside the
Heydrich home. His womanizing was described as straightfor-
ward and violent. Those girls who refused his advances could
expect the attention of the *Gestapo*.

In 1932, just before Hitler became Chancellor, Heydrich was
busy as chief of the *SS* Security Service. As the Nazi movement
of coordination began during the next year, he, as Himmler's
righthand man, incorporated the police departments of the various *Länder* (states) into a national force.

By this time Heydrich had penetrated into the upper ranks of
the Nazi regime. However, there was an annoying blot on the
otherwise happy picture. Rumors began to spread that his grandmother, Sarah Heydrich, was Jewish. Martin Bormann, who had
access to the *Fuehrer*, kept his own set of files which he claimed
proved Heydrich to be Jewish. When Himmler heard about the
critical charge, he went straight to Hitler. The *Fuehrer* ordered
an immediate meeting with Heydrich and Himmler. He told
Himmler privately that Heydrich was a gifted but dangerous man,
"whose gifts should be preserved for the Nazi movement." One
must forget the charge that he had a Jewish grandmother.

Absolution from on high. By the *Fuehrer's* ukase, Heydrich
was purged officially of his tainted blood.

There was more. Hitler told Heydrich that he had all the at-
tributes for a future *Fuehrer* of the Reich. It was a compliment
Heydrich never forgot.

Even this sort of extraordinary appeasement from Hitler himself was insufficient to satisfy the man. Heydrich was driven to
distraction by the persistent rumor. Where once he had been
merely contemptuous of Jews, now he began to hate them with
an intensity that matched Hitler's monomania. He would strike
back at the parasitical people who had ruined his Aryan heritage.
His hatred was lethal. Walter Schellenberg, high *Gestapo* official, described it: "Heydrich's cold eyes glinted with icy pleasure when he gave directions for a Jewish family of shopkeepers,
discovered by the *Gestapo* in a minor infringement of the law,
to be murdered by whipping and strangulation." And further:
"His schizophrenic hatred of his Jewish ancestry led to monstrous actions against Judaism in general."

Admiral Wilhelm Canaris, who had been Heydrich's superior officer in the German Navy and who now was Hitler's chief of military intelligence, described a revealing episode in Heydrich's life. After a hard day's work in Berlin, Heydrich insisted that Canaris accompany him on a drinking spree from bar to bar. "Gradually," Canaris wrote, "he became coldly and calculatingly drunk. He neither stumbled nor slurred his speech but his eyes narrowed until they were almost invisible except as two pinpoints, and his lips twisted as if he were in the grip of an epileptic seizure."

Canaris continued: "When we reached his flat, he persuaded me—'commanded' is a better word—to go in for a final drink. I knew too much about his tainted blood to be fearful of him; but I humored him because I was fascinated by the possible outcome of the evening."

As the two entered the flat and the light was switched on, Heydrich suddenly saw himself reflected in a full-length mirror on the wall opposite the door. "He was swaying a little and I saw rather than heard his mouth twist into the words 'filthy Jew.' Then he snapped the Lüger from its holster and fired three shots at the mirror."

Shattering the mirror and wiping out his reflection could not destroy Heydrich's self-loathing because of his "tainted blood." Psychiatrists would say that his self-hatred could be endured only if he inflicted sadistic torture on others. There were to be many victims of this anguished prisoner of his own body.

Himmler and chief aide Heydrich formed a team of mass murderers, but at the same time there was little sense of friendship between them. Fussy, narrow-minded Himmler, with his rimless glasses and look of discontent, was a colorless philistine. With his peering eyes, weak chin, sloping shoulders, and unprepossessing appearance, Himmler looked contemptuously down on his ambitious subordinate. There was interdependence here, but no respect on either side. Himmler was jealous of his powerful athletic assistant, but found him indispensable. Heydrich adopted a policy of mock obsequiousness and servility. Himmler insisted that he always be addressed as *Herr Reichsfuehrer*: Heydrich often used the form three or four times in one sentence to serve the ego of the man he certainly hoped to replace one day. It was a battle of two sadistic animals for the turf of a rigid territorial imperative.

Like other Nazi rogues, Heydrich was fascinated by the Nietz-schean will to power. He would have others bow to his command. He sought power not only for organizational and political goals, but also for itself. He would allow nothing to stand in the way and he would use any means to his end—blackmail, deceit, even murder. The sense of power he craved might alleviate the curse of his life, his sullied Jewish blood.

In the series of crises which faced Nazism before and after Hitler became Chancellor, Heydrich saw to it that he, himself, was at the center of events. Ambitious for advancement, he took care to avoid the public limelight and, instead, remained in the background. He was careful to learn the moral and political weaknesses of all Nazi leaders. For this purpose he worked like a puppet master to play one against the other.

Roehm and his Storm Troopers were among Heydrich's first victims. By April 1934 Heydrich had become head of the Berlin *Gestapo* under Himmler. His spies alerted him about disaffection among Storm Troopers. At a banquet, *SA* leaders, their tongues loosened by alcohol, uttered wild threats against Hitler because he was opposed to their idea of a Second Revolution. Sensing a personal coup, Heydrich went to Himmler and recommended a preventive strike against the *SA*. He drew up a proposed central death list to destroy treason among Storm Trooper leadership. Typically, he even proposed fake plans for an *SA coup d'état*.

In the Blood Purge of June 30, 1934, Hitler was in Munich and Bad Wiessee conducting the purge of Roehm, Edmund Heines, and other *SA* chieftains. In Berlin, Heydrich was at the side of Goering and Himmler, capturing and executing top *SA* leaders suspected of disloyalty to the *Fuehrer*. Like Goebbels, Heydrich had a talent at being in the right place at the right time.

In 1936 Himmler turned over administration of the *Gestapo* to Heydrich. Now the *SD*, the *Sicherheitsdienst*, Security Service, and the *Gestapo* became one unit. Each worked closely with the other.

Heydrich played a role, if a minor one, in the Blomberg-Fritsch affair, when Hitler in early 1938 dismissed his two senior generals after distasteful personal scandals. Field Marshal Werner von Blomberg, Minister of Defense and Supreme Commander of the *Wehrmacht*, the new armed forces, had married his secretary despite her questionable past. Colonel General Werner von Fritsch, Commander-in-chief of the Army, was accused of disgracing the officer corps by homosexual activities. Hitler decided to sack both top officers and take control himself over the armed forces.

Enter Heydrich. The chief of the Nazi Party Security Service produced a seedy witness named Schmidt, who was prepared to testify that he had observed Fritsch commit a homosexual act with Bavarian Joe, a *Lustknabe* (young boy prostitute), near the Potsdam railroad station in November 1934. Stunned and humiliated, Fritsch hotly denied the charge. Although publicly rehabilitated, his career was at an end. Heydrich had done his work well.

In his memoirs, Field Marshal Wilhelm Keitel wrote about the affair: "As far as Fritsch was concerned, I still believe today that the charge had been trumped up against him in an intrigue designed to make continued tenure of office impossible. I do not know what was behind it, but it was probable either Himmler or Heydrich, his evil genius, for it was well known in the *SS* and in the military, too, that Fritsch was implacably opposed to the military aspirations entertained by the *SS* now that the *Sturmabteiling [SA]* had lost its influence."

Later that year, on November 9, 1938, the hard events of *Kristallnacht*, the notorious Night of Broken Glass. In retaliation for the assassination of the Third Secretary at the German Embassy in Paris by a frustrated young Polish Jew, bands of Nazis on Heydrich's orders systematically destroyed more than a hundred synagogues and smashed and looted thousands of Jewish-owned stores.

As *Gestapo* head, Heydrich wielded the power he deeply craved. He sent his spies to infiltrate the civil service and control it. He needed only a few agents to regulate the entire bureaucracy, which became the quarry of an anonymous terror. He carried on an embittered campaign against the Catholic Church by creating violent incidents involving priests, monks, and nuns. In July 1934, probably on Heydrich's command, Dr. Erich Klausener, head of Catholic Action in Berlin, was murdered in his office. His ashes were sent to his family with the standard Nazi notification that he had committed suicide. Heydrich also issued orders forbidding auricular confession in prisons and camps.

Meanwhile, the once unemployed Heydrich began to build up his personal fortune. In April 1935, along with Himmler, he acquired *Das Schwarze Korps (Black Corps)*, a kind of house organ for revolutionary Nazism. The paper emerged as a competitor for Streicher's *Der Stürmer (The Stormer)* and Goebbels's *Der Angriff (The Attack)*. Like its rivals, it indulged in adulation of Hitler, crude Jew baiting, and directives for "spontaneous violence." Its columns threatened business firms that had not appointed Nazis to their board of directors—a practice close to blackmail. Each issue carried announcements of illegitimate births, obituary notices of *SS* men killed in training, and attacks on Jews, Catholics, and homosexuals. Anyone who refused to contribute to Nazi collection funds was apt to find his name prominently displayed in *Das Schwarze Korps*.

By this time the *Gestapo* chieftain was one of the most feared men in Germany. He was expert in seeking the darkest possible means of achieving his goals. Enjoying his special forms of intimidation, he took pleasure in consigning enemies to *Gestapo* dungeons. Pitiless practitioner of terrorism, he taught his underlings what he called the bylaws of applied terror. He demanded that they learn the proper techniques of deceit. One of his slogans, primitive in its simplicity, was "Pass the buck."

Hans Bernd Gisevius, a diplomat who became an important witness at the Nuremberg Trials, described Heydrich's character; "When Heydrich oppressed, he did so for reasons of discipline. When Heydrich blackmailed, he did so in the name of socialism. When Heydrich tortured, it was to purify the victim. When Heydrich murdered, he acted in the interest of justice. To be German meant to Heydrich, to be a cold-blooded, inexorable terrorist." That was Heydrich's conception of being a "good German."

In typical National Socialist style, Heydrich placed his brutality on the high plane of national necessity. It was important for him to suppress any human instincts. As early as 1935 he said:

> To maintain our nation [*Volk*] we have to be harsh toward our enemy, even at the risk of hurting some enemy . . . If we, as National Socialists, do not fulfill our task in history, because we were too objective and too humane, we shall, nevertheless, not be credited with mitigating circumstances. We will simply be told: You did not fulfill your task in history.

Pleasant, patriotic thought! No humanitarian doubt, no room for pity. Human beings in Heydrich's world were reduced to the category of lower animals—Jews, Communists, and Gypsies—pestilential insects all. Heydrich wanted to eliminate them from the face of the earth for the good of the superior race.

When strategist Hitler needed a *casus belli* for his invasion of Poland in September 1939, Heydrich was there to provide the necessary faked action. In early August 1939 he called in Alfred Helmut Naujocks, described as a typical *Gestapo* product, a sort of intellectual gangster, and outlined to him details of a fictitious Polish attack on a small radio station at Gleiwitz, inside Germany just one mile from the Polish border. The idea was to make it appear that the attacking force consisted of Poles. The scheme was typical of Heydrich's thinking. He had a dozen condemned German criminals dressed in Polish uniforms. Nazi doctors gave them fatal injections, covered them with gunshot wounds, and then placed the bodies in the radio station to make it appear that Polish soldiers had been assaulting German troops.

The next day an excited Hitler informed the German people that they were at war with Poland. Among the reasons, "the attack by regular Polish troops on the Gleiwitz transmitter."

In September 1939, shortly after the war began, state and Party services under Heydrich were merged at his request into a massive administrative unit called the *Reichssicherheitshauptampt* (RSHA), Main Office for the Security of the Reich. Party members were brought together with civil servants in seven bureaus. This vast network meant that the *SS* under Himmler and Heydrich controlled all national administrative agencies. The mighty, many-branched apparatus ultimately became a subsidiary government penetrating into all existing institutions.

Not only was Heydrich active as chief of the most vicious of Hitler's terrorist agencies, but he was also at the beginning of the war the most powerful Nazi in the secret war of espionage. In this sphere he managed to outmaneuver bosses Canaris and Himmler. William Stephenson, famed Allied agent known as "Intrepid," wrote: "The Second World War began with wirelessed intelligence. Heydrich was the evil genius. It as a significant fact that the Nazi *blitz* was launched by coded orders, based on deceit we could not expose, directed by Heydrich. His orders were carried out in the new *Enigmas*. Had we been able to recover these orders, our political leaders might have understood the depth of Nazi wickedness.''

Heydrich, indeed, kept himself busy with matters of espionage. He built hundreds of new portable versions of the *Enigma* cipher machine in a factory near Berlin. He provided the nerve system for the Nazi war effort. Soon, word spread through Nazi officialdom that Heydrich was the man of the hour at the top level, much more powerful than many rivals. Though the Allies built a mock-up of *Enigma* and learned its secrets, they were for a time much troubled by Heydrich's intricate cipher machines.

Like other Nazis, Heydrich did not forget his hatred of Jews. When Hitler, shortly after hostilities began, issued an order for German Jews to be massed in several specified Polish cities having good rail connections for a "final" and secret aim, Heydrich in late September 1939 took pleasure in passing on the word to his SS officers. The man gloried in being in the eye of the hurricane.

In a meeting held at Pretsch in May 1941, Heydrich transmitted orally to his *Einsatztruppen*, task forces of the Security Police, Hitler's order "to carry out the task arising from the conflict of two opposing systems, a process which is to be on the basis of finality." Heydrich then told his 3,000 men to be prepared to liquidate Jews, Asiatic inferiors, Communist functionaries, and Gypsies.

When Hitler in March 1941, even before the invasion of Soviet Russia, issued his famous Kommissar Decree calling for the elimination of Russian commissars, Heydrich was quick to equate Bolsheviks with Jews. He gave orders to his SS officers to the effect that "Western Jewry is the intellectual reservoir of Bolshevism and in the *Fuehrer's* view must be annihilated." No pity for the parasitical enemy.

By mid-1941 Heydrich was on the verge of winning power only subordinate to Hitler. In September 1941 his wife, Lina, and their three children turned Castle Hradcany in Prague into a home when Hitler named Heydrich Reich Protector of Bohemia-Moravia. Hitler wrote to him: "I have accepted your plan to destroy the Czech nation. Basically it will cover three points: the Germanization of as great a proportion of Czechs as possible; the deportation or extermination of those Czechs who cannot be absorbed and of the intelligentsia hostile to the Reich; and the resettlement of the space freed by these measures with good German blood. To that basis I add my decree, that Czechs about whom there exists doubt from the racial standpoint—or who are antagonistic toward the Reich—must be excluded from assimilation. That category must be exterminated.''

The *Fuehrer*'s chief jackal was delighted by the assignment. On October 2, 1941, he delivered a secret speech before Nazi provincial governors, in which he told of Hitler's master plan for dividing Europe into Germans and rejects and of his plans for the Czechs. He would begin a vast screening process to salvage the Sudeten Germans, ''For those of good race and well-intentioned,'' Heydrich said, ''the matter will be very simple— they will be Germanized. For the others, those of inferior origin with hostile intentions, these people I must get rid of.''

Heydrich meant every word of it. He began *Aktion Reinhard*, an eight-months' reign of terror, during which Czech suspects and imprisoned Jews were slaughtered. This became the first of three installments of the Holocaust: *Operation Reinhard*, euthanasia, and the Final Solution. So vicious was Heydrich's behavior in Czechoslovakia that he became known as ''The Butcher.'' Many Czech citizens trembled on hearing his name.

On January 20, 1942, came the infamous Wannsee Conference held at Police Headquarters, Grossen-Wannsee, Berlin, when the Final Solution for the Jewish problem was presented by *SS-Obergruppenfuehrer* (General in the *SS*) Heydrich. The meeting was scheduled originally for December 8, 1941, but it was postponed until late the next month. There were fifteen leading Nazi bureaucrats present under the chairmanship of Heydrich.

Heydrich opened the conference by declaring that he was the plenipotentiary for ''the final solution of the Jewish question.'' He reviewed the emigration problem, especially the earlier plan to deport all Jews to the island of Madagascar, but this scheme had fallen through after invasion of the Soviet Union in June 1941. There was no longer any possibility, he said, of transporting Jews in this fashion. Instead of emigration, the *Fuehrer* had given his sanction (*Genehmigung*) for the evacuation of all Jews to the East as a solution possibility (*Lösungsmöglichkeit*).

Heydrich had it all worked out carefully:

In large labor gangs, with the sexes separated, those Jews who are capable of working will be brought into those areas [the East], employed in road-building, in the course of which a large portion will be eliminated by natural diminution. The ultimate remaining members, being undoubtedly the strongest elements, will have to be treated accordingly [*entsprechend behandelt*], since they represent a natural selection, and would, if released, constitute a germination cell for Jewish reconstruction.

Again the dangerous euphemism: for Heydrich, "treated accordingly" meant simply to be killed. This was the terminology of circumlocution used in official and unofficial papers in the Third Reich to hide the real meaning of genocide.

In Heydrich's protectorate, where he had absolute power as Hitler's deputy, pacification measures were carried out with such brutality that the Czechs reacted with anger. As hostility grew in the conquered country, Czechoslovakian exiles in London decided to strike back by planning to assassinate Hitler's henchman. They would rid their homeland of Heydrich and his terrible reign of terror. Nine Czech agents were selected to undergo hard commando training in England before two volunteers, Jan Kubris and Josef Gabcik, were chosen for the grim task. The two, dropped by parachute near Prague, started on their mission.

On the morning of May 27, 1942, Gabcik carried a Sten gun under a raincoat draped over his arm as he stood waiting at a hairpin bend outside Prague. Kubris had a grenade in the pocket of his jacket. Several hundred yards away two more backup conspirators took their places on opposite sides of the road.

After three days of waiting, the plotters were rewarded. Heydrich had no fear of physical attack. He showed his contempt for Czechs by driving through Prague in the front seat of an open Mercedes convertible. Unlike Hitler, Goering, and Himmler, who traveled everywhere in armored limousines with bulletproof glass, Heydrich preferred to protect himself only with sidearms. He ignored many warnings from his subordinates.

As the Mercedes slowed for the hairpin bend, Gabcik's gun jammed. Kubris immediately hurled his grenade. Heydrich leapt from his car as blood spread over his uniform. No one in the gathering crowd made any move to help.

Eight days later Hitler's viceroy was dead from blood poisoning caused by leather, steel, and horsehair from upholstery forced into his spleen when the grenade exploded.

Consternation in Berlin. Hitler in a rage. Vengeance was grotesque and dreadful. The *Fuehrer* ordered a state of emergency for the protectorate. Six days later, Nazi authorities, alleging that the people of Lidice had helped the assassins, took savage retribution. On the *Fuehrer's* personal order the small village located northeast of Prague was completely destroyed. Every building was razed. All 172 men and boys, the entire male population, were shot. The women were either killed or sent to concentration camps where many of them died. Ninety children were taken off to the camps or in some cases distributed to foster homes. Only a half dozen of these youngsters emerged from concentration camps at the end of the war.

After the systematic destruction of Lidice and its inhabitants, Nazi authorities erased its name from official records. Oblivious to worldwide opinion, they admitted the massacre and called it an act of war.

The two escaping assassins were hidden in a crypt of the Greek Orthodox Church. There they remained for three weeks, with food brought to them by members of the Czech resistance. The *Gestapo*, with its torture instruments ready, soon found the men they wanted. Kubris and Gabcik were executed by the *SS* on June 18, 1942.

Heydrich was given a state funeral the day before the destruction of Lidice. Himmler delivered the funeral oration over the gun carriage. "He was, indeed, a man with an iron heart."

The Nazis were not through. They condemned 860 more Czechs to death at Prague and 395 at Brnö.

12
GORILLA KALTENBRUNNER

Never shall I forget that night, the first night in camp, which had turned my life into one long night, seven times cursed and seven times sealed.

—Elie Wiesel

Throughout history the police force has been the official body in the state dedicated to the task of maintaining order and preventing, detecting, and punishing crime. Hitler's police force took on an added dimension—it became a state within the state. It had a leadership that was itself criminal-minded.

Top Nazi police official Himmler, his *alter egos* Heydrich and Kaltenbrunner, and subordinate Eichmann were mean, depraved human beings who would take prominent places in any encyclopedia of evil. All were obscene bigots. These guardians of the state were responsible for the deaths of millions of their fellow human beings, most of whom were innocent victims of a corrupt political system. They were also accomplished liars who could build stratum after stratum of trickery as a means of avoiding the pain of looking at themselves. Victims of illusions and self-

178

deception, they were also vain peacocks whose ambition it was to get ahead in the Nazi jungle.

Yet, all four regarded themselves as soldiers in a noble cause. They saw the National Socialist attitude to the world as the only one suited to the German nation. Hitler, in their mind, was the most energetic champion of a new society, the only one who could bring the German people back to their proper way of life. They would do his work of biological cleansing even if it meant reducing their victims to the level of lower animals.

In some ways Ernst Kaltenbrunner was the worst of the lot. He was a hulking ox of a man, tall and thin, with a thick neck and a scar running from the left side of his mouth to his nose. His long arms and oversized hands dangling from an elongated body gave him a kind of simian appearance. Even his Nazi colleagues took pleasure in referring to him as "the Gorilla."

But many gorillas have the quality, at least, of being gentle animals. There was nothing soft about this ruthless killer. Kaltenbrunner was the assassin of untold thousands. A common thug, he was an alcoholic who smoked a hundred cigarettes a day to calm his nerves. He regarded himself as an aspiring member of the intelligentsia, but he was actually a shrewd lawyer-on-the-make. Most of his comrades regarded him as stupid. Although he held a higher degree and had some experience as an attorney and judge, many who knew him testified to his lack of intelligence and common sense. Even more, he had no sense of ordinary decency.

Ernst Kaltenbrunner, was born on October 4, 1903, in the village of Ried-am-Innkreis, Austria, near Hitler's birthplace. He attended public school at Raab, then the *Realgymnasium* (semi-classical secondary school) at Linz, an Austrian hotbed of German nationalism. Later, he studied at the *Technische Hochschule* (Technical College) at Graz. He entered the University of Prague (Czechoslovakia) in 1921, and took a law degree in 1926 when he was only twenty-three. Opening a law office in Linz, he served for a time as a junior barrister. He married and sired three children. He then became an assistant judge at Salzburg, another city with pro-German traditions.

It is not known when Kaltenbrunner joined the Nazi Party. His membership No. 300,179 indicates that he was neither a founder nor an early convert to National Socialism. He was attracted especially by its anti-Semitism. Early in life he had developed a virulent hatred of Jews, a sentiment he shared with the leader of the budding National Socialist movement. For him, Hitler's *Mein Kampf*, with its strong denunciation of Jews, was a bible and Hitler a personal hero. There was opportunity here—he could become useful in the Nazi world and rise in the estimation of the leader. For him, Hitler represented ultimate authority. To acquire power on his own became the driving force of his life.

The ambitious young lawyer had little regard for other Nazis at the top echelon. In this soured world he looked upon all Hitler's other henchmen as dangerous rivals. He had only contempt for fat-man Goering with his stale jokes or for thin-man, super-stud Goebbels. At the same time, he envied their lives of luxury. One day, he was sure, he would replace the incompetent Ribbentrop as Foreign Minister. He had only scorn for his sponsor and immediate superior Himmler, but he carefully hid his feelings by an outward show of flattery and patronizing condescension. The Austrian giant was the kind of devious operator who managed to reach the ear of Hitler—the formula for success in the Nazi milieu. This critical achievement enabled him to circumvent boss Himmler whenever he thought it necessary. He was expert in getting exactly what he wanted. In a gangster environment he knew how to improve his own status.

The "Gorilla's" rise to fame and fortune was rapid. By 1933 he was already a "district stumper," legal adviser of the 8th Division of the *SS*, and leader of *Standarte 37*, a unit of twelve hundred men. Later he was promoted to command of the 8th Division, the Austrian Legion of Storm Troopers.

Nazi activities in Austria were illegal, but they were promoted even after Hitler had agreed by treaty to disclaim the activities of Austrian National Socialists. Kaltenbrunner emerged as one of the most zealous Austrian champions of *Anschluss*, the proposed union of Germany and Austria. On July 25, 1934, Austrian Nazis, dressed in the country's army uniform, invaded the Federal Chancellery in Vienna and assassinated Chancellor Engelbert Dollfuss. Although Dollfuss was bleeding from a wound in the throat, his killers refused to allow any medical assistance. The diminutive Austrian Chancellor bled to death on a sofa. Kaltenbrunner was among those arrested by the Viennese police immediately after the assassination.

Austria became a hotbed of Nazism. The illegal party was led by an executive committee of which Kaltenbrunner was an important member. In early 1937 its headquarters, which housed a secret printing press, were raided by the police. Meanwhile, Kaltenbrunner was secretly reorganizing Austrian Storm Troopers. All the while Hitler continued to deny any interest in Austrian affairs.

Viennese police raided Kaltenbrunner's office and discovered details for a proposed Nazi *Putsch* in the capital city. Arrested on a charge of high treason, he was sent to prison, where he remained for a year. When word of his plight reached Berlin, Hitler decided to reward his fellow Austrian for his loyalty to National Socialism.

His prison experience was not enough to make Kaltenbrunner change his mind. He resumed Nazi activities immediately upon his release. On the night of March 11, 1938, with orders from Berlin to take over the Austrian government, five hundred Austrian *SS* troops under Kaltenbrunner's command surrounded the Federal Chancellery. The next day Hitler entered Austria. In a speech before a huge crowd at Linz he proclaimed the union of his homeland with Germany. On March 13, Austria was formally incorporated into the Third Reich. Hitler had finally achieved his much-desired *Anschluss* (Union)

Great day for Ernst Kaltenbrunner. He sent word to Hitler that his Austrian Storm Trooper units were awaiting orders from Berlin. Hitler was mightily pleased by the offer—this was the kind of language he wanted to hear. He saw to it that Kaltenbrunner was included in Arur Seyss-Inquart's new cabinet as State Secretary of Security for Austria. In that office Kaltenbrunner was responsible for implementing Austria's *Gleichschaltung*, the policy of political and cultural coordination. When his post was abolished in 1941, he was appointed Police Leader. Meanwhile, he was being promoted rapidly on Hitler's *SS* (Elite Guard) staff. By the spring of 1942 he was second officer in Himmler's organization, in rank just below Reinhard Heydrich.

Promotion and power! The Gorilla was on his way.

Though the country was at war, Kaltenbrunner had no intention of changing his lifestyle. He worked hard on his many duties, but simultaneously added to his reputation as a Nazi playboy. He enjoyed an expensive apartment, rounds of night clubs, and excessive drinking. When funds ran low, he could always go to Himmler for financial help.

Kaltenbrunner was still unknown to the general public, but what was more important was the fact that he had access not only to boss Himmler but also to the sacred presence of the *Fuehrer*. To satisfy both, he adopted the familiar pattern of expressing increasing hatred for Jews. He knew instinctively, as did other Nazi chieftains, that this was a sure way to Hitler's heart.

Kaltenbrunner was determined to push his way ahead among Nazi leaders and he was successful. When Reinhard Heydrich, chief of the *Reichssischerheitsamt* (RSHA), the Reich Security Office, was assassinated by Czech patriots in May 1942, Hitler needed a replacement, a man without sentiment and a brutal killer who could take orders. Himmler proposed the name of Kaltenbrunner.

January 30, 1943—a brown-letter day in the life of the Austrian Gorilla. Hitler approved Himmler's recommendation for the successor to Heydrich's key post. Again, great news for Kaltenbrunner: he had been dissatisfied with his role as an underling. His scar-faced eminence now held a dizzying variety of offices. He had the rank of *SS-Obergruppenfuehrer* (OGRUF), general of the *SS*. He was master of the Secret Police of the Reich with responsibility for all concentration and extermination camps. He was head of the *Gestapo*, the secret State Police. He controlled the *SIPO* (Security Police), *KRIPO* (Criminal Police), and the *SS* Security Service. He was still subordinate to *Reichsfuehrer-SS* Heinrich Himmler, but he felt he knew how to handle that. Below him in rank was Adolf Eichmann, chief of Amt IV-B-4 of the RSHA, who would later make waves of his own.

There was more. In addition to these powerful offices, Kaltenbrunner controlled the dreaded *Einsatzgruppen*, special mobile units and task forces used for extermination in the East. These troops were responsible for ''special handling'' of Jews, Poles, Gypsies, and such undesirables as Soviet prisoners of war. Orders went out from Kaltenbrunner's office under his signature for protective custody or release from the camps.

In his high police offices Kaltenbrunner literally had the power of life and death over millions of unfortunate victims. Witnesses later testified that he visited Mauthausen concentration camp to observe how prisoners were killed in various ways—hanging, shooting in the back, and gassing. He put on a show of indifference while the executions were going on.

At his Nuremberg trial Kaltenbrunner denied any participation in the program of extermination. He insisted that he was concerned only with matters involving foreign intelligence. Nevertheless, he was accused of being tireless in hunting victims for the gas chambers. One specific charge was that he had 5,000 Jews transferred from the relatively safe concentration camp at Theresienstadt to Auschwitz with its gas ovens working around the clock. His reason—all Jews over sixty, he said, were disease carriers and had to be eliminated.

Kaltenbrunner continued his denials despite accusations that he had played a major role in the "Final Solution of the Jewish problem." Evidence was presented showing that his special missions scoured the occupied territories and Axis satellite countries arranging for deportation of Jews to death camps. On June 30, 1944, he wrote a letter describing the shipment of some 12,000 Jews to Vienna, and ordering that all who could not work be held in readiness for "special action," his code word for extermination. Kaltenbrunner denied his signature on the letter. He did the same thing for a large number of orders on which his name was stamped or typed and, in some instances, written. He declared emphatically that he scarcely knew Adolf Eichmann. Besides, he insisted, Himmler had told him that he would not be burdened by anything concerned with concentration camps. Not only that, he claimed that the criminal program of extermination had started long before he took high office. Why blame him for the excesses of the dead Himmler?

It was a lame defense. Kaltenbrunner was head of the *RSHA* and controlled its activities. Unless he was a complete idiot he was certainly aware of what it was doing. The claim of innocence was preposterous. When Kaltenbrunner was asked by *Gestapo* chieftain Heinrich Mueller what to do with twenty-five French prostitutes who were infected with syphilis, he replied, "Shoot them!" When in early 1945 he was approached by *Gestapo* officials at headquarters in Berlin and asked whether prisoners they held should be transported or shot, Kaltenbrunner decided for execution. Innocent bystander?

There was much more incrimination. An *RSHA* order issued during Kaltenbrunner's regime set up the so-called Bullet Decree, by which escaped prisoners of war who were recaptured were taken to Mauthausen and shot. This order resulted in the summary execution of Allied commando troops, including parachutists. Kaltenbrunner signed an edict instructing his subordinates not to interfere with attacks on Allied flyers who had bailed out of their planes. He recommended that the death of such troops be explained as "prisoners shot while attempting to escape." One charge held that Kaltenbrunner had personally participated in the murder of a French general held as a prisoner of war. The evidence was damning.

The master killer of Nazidom denied all accusations. He pleaded innocence as "a victim of war hysteria." His reaction to the indictment became the theme of his defense: "I do not feel guilty of any war crimes. I have only done my duty as an intelligence organ, and I refuse to serve as an *Ersatz* [substitute] for Himmler."

On the day the Nuremberg proceedings began, Kaltenbrunner had a slight cerebral hemorrhage, but he recovered and was able to attend most of the sessions. When he returned to the dock he expected to get a hearty welcome from his fellow prisoners. Instead—silence and eyes staring straight ahead. He was amazed and dismayed by his reception. He tried to start a conversation with those near him, but they pretended not to hear.

Psychologist G. M. Gilbert, who tested the prisoners, rated Kaltenbrunner's IQ at 113, the lowest of the twenty-one defendants except for Julius Streicher (IQ-106) in mechanical efficiency of the mind. That agreed well with the estimate of his comrades who often spoke of his stupidity.

In his cell Kaltenbrunner told Gilbert that he knew nothing about the killings at Auschwitz. "The people," he said, "who did are all dead—Hitler, Himmler, Bormann, Heydrich, Eichmann. I had nothing to do with it. Concentration camps were not my responsibility. I never found out anything about any of this."

Strange talk from the chief of the RSHA. Rudolf Hoess, Kaltenbrunner's agent, testified in a previous trial that *under Kaltenbrunner's orders* he had gassed two and a half million human beings at Auschwitz extermination camp.

Kaltenbrunner took the stand on April 11, 1946. His defense counsel, Dr. Kauffmann, introduced as evidence affidavits from several *Gestapo* officials testifying that Kaltenbrunner was a nice man and that he was not Himmler's right hand man but merely a weak underling. The contention was that Himmler wanted no rival to his own power, such as Heydrich, and selected Kaltenbrunner as Heydrich's successor because he (Kaltenbrunner) was weak and indecisive.

Kaltenbrunner then took the stand and began his defense. He was only an Austrian motivated by purely nationalistic concerns. He was a moral man who meant the best for mankind. He was loyal and obedient to his superiors. Admittedly, he was Himmler's second-in-command as formal head of the *RSHA*, but he knew absolutely nothing about the concentration camps. His duties were limited to the intelligence service, and therefore he could not possibly know anything about mass killings. As far as he understood it, recalcitrant workers were sent only to "labor education camps."

Astonishment in the court. There had been clear-cut testimony that, in fact, Kaltenbrunner had been responsible for transmitting orders for extermination. And here he was shifting the blame to his superior, predecessor, and subordinates.

Even the prisoners in the dock reacted with ridicule. "Just listen to that!" exploded Goering. Doenitz: "He ought to be ashamed of himself." Schacht: "Was he the superior officer or was he not?" Fritsche: "He is lying." Sauckel: "*Ach*, you devil—you swine!" Speer: "He is not suffering from some prison psychosis—he is just lying."

Kaltenbrunner again denied his own signature on documents introduced as evidence. It was possible, he said, that he may have signed them, but he did not recognize the signature and he had signed so many things. Under cross-examination he was presented with documents, inconsistent statements, and direct accusations, to which he reacted with flat denials. Even as chief of the Intelligence Service under Himmler, he said, he knew nothing about atrocities committed by his own organization.

It was a miserable performance, a perjured defense which could have only one outcome. Here is a condensed version of the Nuremberg judgment:

When he became Chief of the Security Police and *SD* and head of the *RSHA* on January 30, 1943, Kaltenbrunner took charge of an organization which included the main offices of the *Gestapo*, the *SD*, and the Criminal Police. During the period in which he was head of the *RSHA*, it was en-

gaged in a widespread program of War Crimes and Crimes
Against Humanity. These crimes, including the mistreatment and murder of prisoners of war, Jews, commissars,
and others who were thought to be ideologically hostile to
the Nazi regime, were reported to the *RSHA*, which had
them transferred to a concentration camp and murdered.

The order for the execution of commando troops was
extended by the *Gestapo* to include parachutists while Kaltenbrunner was Chief of the *RSHA*. An order signed by
Kaltenbrunner instructed the police not to interfere with
attacks on bailed-out Allied fliers.

The *RHSA* played a leading part in the "final solution" of
the Jewish question by the extermination of Jews. A special
section under the AMT [Office] IV of the *RSHA* was established to supervise the program. Under its direction ap-
proximately 6 million Jews were murdered, of which 2
million were killed by the *Einsatzgruppen* and other units
of the Security Police. Kaltenbrunner was informed of the
activities of these *Einsatzgruppen*. The murder of 4 million
Jews was under the supervision of the *RSHA* when Kaltenbrunner was head of that organization.

Verdict: guilty on Count 3: War Crimes, and Count 4: Crimes
Against Humanity.
Sentence: death by hanging.
As the sentence was pronounced, Kaltenbrunner whispered:
"Death." He could say no more.
At 1:30 A.M. on the morning of October 16, 1946, Kaltenbrunner entered the execution chamber at Nuremberg. He wore
a sweater beneath his double-breasted coat. He glanced nervously around the room before mounting the gallows. Turning
around on the platform, he faced an American army chaplain
clad in a Franciscan habit.
Asked if he wished to say anything, he replied: "I would like
to say a word. I have loved my German people with a warm
heart. I have done my duty by the laws of my people and I am
sorry my people were led this time by men who were not soldiers and that crimes were committed of which I have no knowledge."

As the black hood was about to be placed on his head, Kaltenbrunner, speaking in a low, calm voice, said: "Germany, good luck."

The trap was sprung at 1:39 A.M.

The case of Ernst Kaltenbrunner falls within a similar pattern of other leading henchmen of Hitler who took part in the scramble for power and in the excesses of the Nazi regime. These were morally and politically corrupt men, dangerously cynical and indifferent to any sense of humanity. All were afflicted with a deadened conscience and they were driven by opportunism. At Nuremberg, Kaltenbrunner presented the familiar plea that he had no blood on his hands—it was all the fault of his superiors. The poor innocent soul was only contributing his mite to European culture.

13

KILLER ADOLF EICHMANN

I will leap laughing to my grave, because the feeling that I have five million people on my conscience is for me a source of extraordinary satisfaction.

—Adolf Eichmann

Boss Himmler. Subordinates Heydrich and Kaltenbrunner. Underling Eichmann. Few human beings have inspired more revulsion and contempt. All are raw material for experts in behavioral pathology.

There were some common characteristics among these insensitive clods with their ultimate capacity for evil. All were otherwise unremarkable men who became major war criminals. All emerged from respectable middle-class surroundings. Each had a fairly good education. In their early years they were moral in personal life, law-abiding, and devoted to their families.

All four were infected with the obedience syndrome, a severe failing in German society. Americans with their traditional freedoms tend to underestimate the power of the submissive commitment; they must turn to psychiatrists for explanations of such behavior. In the grotesque environment of Naziland these once-normal citizens turned into inhuman brutes because of blind obedience to higher authority. They felt no sense of responsibility for their own conduct. They saw themselves as good soldiers carrying out orders from above. How could one object to a trooper of high or low rank who was only doing his duty?

True, they were executioners, but "someone had to do the necessary work." One could slaughter subhumans and still represent what was good and decent in national life. The SS officer, after a day spent working at the gas ovens, could go home to family and wife for a good dinner, romp with the children, and play the violin for relaxation. Or he might make the rounds of night clubs and drink himself into a stupor.

These mass killers were confused by numbers. They might take pause at the murder of a single individual, but the guilt of suffocating thousands eluded their conscience. It was all in a day's work, no more exciting or immoral than placing flypaper in the kitchen or rat traps in the cellar. Had not the noble *Fuehrer* condemned their victims as worthless, pernicious animals?

Once exposed to Hitler's mind, these once normal citizens embraced his simplistic pan-German ideology, his fixation on racial theory. They became hardened against humanitarian sentiment or pity for inferior "races" that had damaged Germany's bloodstream. Led on by their leader's frenzied words, these average Germans became soldiers in a new world of racial values. They saw Jews not merely as social parasites, but as detested rats, roaches, and insects to be exterminated for the good of society.

Karl Adolf Eichmann, obedient tool at the lower level of the SS officialdom, was born at Solingen in the Rhineland on March 19, 1906. After his mother died when he was four, the family moved to Linz, Austria, in the area where Hitler had spent his youth. Father Eichmann was then director of the streetcar and power company in Linz.

As a youngster Adolf went to four classes of secondary school (*Realshule*). Although obedient to authority, the boy was a muddled disaster, shy, clumsy, and colorless. He was a loner, a melancholy lad who seldom played with other students. Because of his dark complexion, he was called *"der kleine Jude"* ("the little Jew") by his comrades. On one occasion he reacted violently by leading a gang of boys to attack a Jewish classmate.

Eichmann spent two years at the Linz Higher Institute for

Electro-Technical Studies, but had to leave either because he was a poor student or as a result of the postwar Depression. From 1925 to 1927 he was a salesman for the Upper Austrian Electrical Construction Company. He then took a job as salesman for the Vacuum Oil Company. In this capacity the once colorless young man came out of his shell and emerged as a loud-talking, hard-drinking extrovert who loved to ride his red motorcycle from Linz to Vienna.

In his work Eichmann came into contact with Jews, but at the time had no unpleasant experiences with them. There were comparatively few Jews in Upper Austria. At first Eichmann had little interest in them. But hearing lurid tales in the cafes of Vienna about Jews, he changed his attitude and had a sense of growing antipathy. "After hearing Hitler speak," he said later, "I began to hate myself for mixing with those Jews who were the enemies of the German people and who defiled our blood. I began to feel that these foreign-looking people were, indeed, the enemies of us all. They all seemed to be traders and financiers, people willing to take little part in the real work of the community."

Joining the Austrian National Socialist Party in early April 1932, Eichmann was sworn in as member of the SS. To avoid attention by the Austrian police, he made his way to the border and thence to Berlin. Here he was attached to the SD, *Sicherheitsdienst*, the Security Service of the SS under Reinhard Heydrich dedicated to intelligence work.

In his SD post, Eichmann was assigned the task of collecting material on "the global conspiracy of Freemasons." It was a dull job as a filing clerk ordered to type data on suspects under Nazi surveillance. Eichmann began to read all the material he could find on the Freemasons. Soon he began to regard himself as an expert on their "conspiracy." This work further stimulated his interest in what he called Jewish problems. He was convinced that Freemasons worked with Jews to dominate the world.

The serious filing clerk was complimented by his superiors for his good work. When Heinrich Himmler created his Scientific Museum for Jewish Affairs as an agency of the SD, he appointed Eichmann to head the project.

Delighted and fired with enthusiasm, Eichmann extended his research on Jews and Judaism. His associates began to speak favorably of his encyclopedic knowledge of Jewish history.

Whenever he could, he attended Jewish meetings and visited the Jewish quarters of many towns and cities. He made copious notes and set up systematic files. By now he had won a reputation in Nazi circles as the Party's leading expert on Jewish affairs. He thoroughly enjoyed the work. He even learned to speak some Hebrew, although haltingly. His immediate goal was to combine his work as an intelligence agent with his growing knowledge as an expert on Jews. He regarded it as a special achievement when he discovered in a report filed as "Top Secret" that the *Fuehrer's* diet cook was 1/32 Jewish.

At this time in the mid-1930s Hitler's solution for his Jewish problem had not yet been formulated. In Nazi circles it was felt that the best way to defeat Jews in what was called the Semitic drive for world power was to know more about them. It was necessary to challenge them and destroy their power. To learn even more about "the internal enemy," Eichmann in 1937, using a falsified press card indentifying him as a staff member of the *Berliner Tageblatt*, went to Palestine. He spent just two days there, during which he visited the German Templars' Colony near Tel Aviv and also a Jewish settlement. Then he went to Cairo to meet Amin el Husseini, the Mufti of Jerusalem, known as Jew-hater and admirer of Nazism. When the Palestine Mandate authorities refused to allow Eichmann to return to Jerusalem, he went back to Berlin, angry and disgusted with what he believed to be an unsuccessful mission.

It was important for Eichmann to impress his colleagues as well as the Jewish community in Berlin with his status as expert on all Jewish matters. He began to spread word that he was from Palestine himself and knew all about Jews and Judaism. He had been there for only forty-eight hours, but more and more Nazis began to believe in his Palestinian origin. So pervasive was the myth that some of his Nazi comrades suspected him of being a Jewish spy. The legend persisted. Later, even some Jews in Budapest asserted that Eichmann had been a student of rabbinical literature in Jerusalem.

Originally a typical underling, pedantic and punctilious in his card-filing work, Eichmann began to take on the attitude of an important bureaucrat. He was coming up in the world and it was necessary to push his way in a highly competitive milieu. By now he was a shrewd manipulator, who knew instinctively those superiors who were to be flattered and those who could be safely ignored. He looked forward to promotion. At the same time, he was certain that he had the Jewish community and the Zionists under his control.

Eichmann was in Vienna on November 7, 1938, when Legation Third Secretary Erwin vom Rath, a diplomat at the German Embassy in Paris, was assassinated by a young Polish Jew. A nationwide pogrom called *Kristallnacht* (Night of Broken Glass), took place on November 9–10, 1938. Some 20,000 Jews were arrested and at least 36 killed. In the process, 119 synagogues were burned down, more than 900 shops owned by Jews destroyed during the rampage, 7,500 stores looted, and 171 dwellings set aflame. Reinhard Heydrich ordered Eichmann to lead the raids in Vienna. Eyewitnesses reported that Eichmann was seen moving from one synagogue to another to supervise the destruction. He was described as exhilarated by the assignment.

Within a few days after *Kristallnacht*, Eichmann sent his first shipment of Jews to a concentration camp. From then until the beginning of the war he controlled emigration from Austria as supervisor of the departure of some 100,000 Jews. Superior officer Heydrich, highly satisfied with Eichmann's work, began to urge his promotion.

The transformation in personality was now complete. The once shy clerical filer of reports appeared on the Nazi scene as a coarse and brutal despot. Success in his chosen work went to his head. He never forgot the taunts of his classmates—*"der kleine Jude."* Now "the little Jew" had control over the life and death of hundreds of thousands of Jews. He was somebody. Curses on those subordinates who did not respond quickly to his orders. "Sacks of dung," he called them.

Eichmann had performed important service for his Nazi masters. His assignment to Vienna came at a time when the Nazi campaign against Jews was being changed into a more dangerous form. He stimulated the mass emigration from Europe of much of its Jewish population. Jews by the thousands, in deadly fear of Eichmann, began to leave their homeland. By 1939 only 100,000 were left in Austria, most of them in Vienna.

Both Hitler and Himmler were impressed by Eichmann's processing system in Vienna. The man was energetic and showed satisfactory initiative. Most of all, he could be counted on to follow orders implicitly. Here was a model technician who could ease the way to a biological cleansing of the Third Reich.

In early 1939 Hitler established a new Reich Central Office for Jewish Emigration modeled on Eichmann's office in Vienna, with sub-offices in Prague. He appointed Reinhard Heydrich as a nominal head of the new unit. But he also brought Eichmann from Vienna as captain in charge of the entire operation with control over local *Gestapo* chieftains.

In the opening months of 1940, with World War II under way, Eichmann went to work to expel as many Jews as possible from Germany. On the night of February 13, 1940, he forced a thousand Jews in Stettin from their homes after requiring them to waive their property rights. Several hundred died in a brutal march in subzero temperature. Both Hitler and Heydrich were pleased by reports of Eichmann's efficiency in the emigration process.

There was more important work for the energetic little man from Linz. In June 1940, after the fall of France, Hitler was told of a plan by which France would cede Madagascar to Germany "for the purpose of solving the Jewish problem." Frenchmen on the island, more than 25,000 of them, would be required to leave so that German Jews brought in would have no contact with white Europeans. Responsibility for implementation of the scheme was given to Eichmann, who for the next year was busy in this task. This was important planning at the highest level and he, Eichmann, was in a position of authority to carry it to fruition. He would organize a special fleet of German ships to transport four million Jews to Madagascar after paying their own way. The *Fuehrer* would surely reward him for his magnificent work.

Nothing came of the proposed Madagascar Plan despite Eichmann's efforts. For a time Hitler continued to play with the idea, but it was eventually rejected. There would be another solution.

On July 31, 1941, nearly six weeks after invasion of the Soviet Union, Hermann Goering called in Reinhard Heydrich and informed him that the earlier policy of emigration of Jews was finished. There would be a new approach for the "complete solution of the Jewish problem" in the German sphere of influence in Europe. "I request that you send me an overall plan for implementation of the desired final solution of the Jewish question."

"Final Solution." The words were clear-cut, meaningful, and deadly.

Heydrich summoned Eichmann to his Berlin office. By this

time Eichmann, reputed to be the leading Nazi expert on Jewish affairs, had been promoted to Chief of Subsection IV-B-4 of the *Reichssicherheitshauptamt* (*RSHA*), the Reich Central Security Office. That subsection was to become the most notorious agency of the Nazi killing apparatus. Heydrich opened the interview with the remark that emigration of Jews from Europe was no longer possible because of the war with the Soviet Union. The *Fuehrer* had ordered the physical extermination of Jews and his word was law. Heydrich was pleased to inform Eichmann that he was chosen for the task of destroying the remnants of European Jewry. The days of deportation were finished.

It did not occur to Eichmann to challenge the order. This was a command from the All-Highest and one had to obey. "I was free of all guilt," he said later at his trial. "Who was I to judge? Who was I to have my own thoughts in the matter?" The obedience syndrome was at work in full force.

With the thoroughness of the born bureaucrat, Eichmann prepared himself for his assignment. He watched his first executions at Minsk. "Although I was wearing a leather coat which reached almost to my ankles, it was very cold. I watched the last group of Jews undress down to their shirts. They walked the last 100 to 200 yards—they were not driven—then they jumped into the pit. It was impressive to see them all jumping into the pit without offering any resistance whatsoever. Then the men of the squad banged away into the pit with their rifles and machine pistols."

There was more preparation. At Lodz, Eichmann watched as Jews were gassed and their bodies thrown into a trench about two meters deep. "Some Poles threw the corpses into the pit. Another Pole with a pair of pliers in his hands jumped into the pit. He went through the corpses opening their mouths. Whenever he saw a gold tooth he pulled it out and dumped it into a small bag he was carrying." Eichmann's recital was dry and indifferent.

That same winter Eichmann went to Auschwitz to confer with commandant Rudolf Hoess on necessary details for constructing the largest and most important death camp in Poland. The expert on Jewish affairs became the responsible officer for the new program of genocide. The one-time card-filer was now somebody.

The procedure was frozen at the Wannsee Conference held on January 20, 1942, when Heydrich convened a meeting of top-ranking Nazi bureaucrats to hear his plan for final solution. There would be, he said, deportation to the East, forced labor, and mass executions. Eichmann was among the lower-ranking Nazis present. The task for implementation would be delegated to him.

Eichmann was elated by the news. Never before had he been present with such a distinguished gathering of "big personages." He was flattered. "After the conference your humble servant sat with them cozily around a fireplace, not just talking shop but giving ourselves a rest after the taxing hours." The men were tired after the hours of discussion about extermination.

The happy bureaucrat went to work at once. He was gratified to see the end of forced emigration. That was too good for the despicable Jews—why give them their lives? He would do his job and he would do it well. In his new post of authority, he set up a network of stations all over Europe. He issued orders to round up Jews, deliver them to transports, and then dispatch them to the East. There they would be worked to death and the survivors executed. "The people who were loaded on those trains," he said later, "meant nothing to me. It was really none of my business." His business was to set up the timetables of death.

The little man of Linz held the power of life or death over literally millions of human beings. He urged his subordinate: "Don't be sentimental—this is a *Fuehrer* order." Spoken in awe—godlike Siegfried in Berchtesgaden had willed it.

Eichmann introduced a note of speed in his work. A few hours after the disposal of a transport, a special message would arrive from *RSHA* in Berlin signed by Eichmann. The teletype might say that the foreign press had learned that a transport was on its way from Paris to Auschwitz. Eichmann appended a list of those who were Aryans and who should on no account be executed. Another list for the transport officer included the names of those who were to receive "special treatment."

By this time Eichmann was even more impressed with his own importance. In the summer of 1942 he became impatient with the Foreign Office in Berlin. The authorities, he said, had the wrong attitude toward Jews in such countries as Italy, Switzerland, Spain, Portugal, Sweden, Finland, Hungary, and Turkey. He lectured the bureaucrats of the Foreign Office: "We ask that you put aside any possible scruples of the interest of finally solving the Jewish problem, because in this matter the Reich has met the governments in the most generous matter." It was necessary, he said, that all Jews living in European countries outside of Germany be given special treatment. The man was talking big: quotas had to be met.

Eichmann felt strong enough to make major decisions. In May 1944 he became involved in a proposed blood-for-goods deal with Joel Brand, leader of a Hungarian Jewish relief committee. Brand was the negotiator in an attempt to exchange Jews for trucks. After escaping from Germany, he went to Budapest, where he became active in a semiclandestine organization for helping German Jews escape through secret contacts with Nazi agents in Hungary.

Brand was called in for an interview with Eichmann, now in a position of awesome power. Eichmann spoke bluntly: "I suppose you know who I am. I am prepared to sell you one million Jews. Not the whole lot—you would not be able to raise enough money for that. But you can manage a million. Goods for blood; blood for goods. Whom do you want to save? Sit down and talk."

Brand would go to Istanbul to meet Jewish leaders who had contact with the Allies. Eichmann warned him that his mother, wife, and children would be held in custody until his return. He later handed the astonished Brand $120,000 in cash "to help Jewish children." In return he wanted ten thousand trucks, complete with spare parts and equipped for winter conditions. "If you return from Istanbul and tell me the offer has been accepted, I will close Auschwitz and bring ten percent of the promised million to the frontier. You can take one hundred thousand Jews away, and afterward bring me one thousand trucks. We'll go on like that. A thousand trucks for every hundred thousand Jews."

The deal for trucks, desperately needed in Germany, fell through. Brand was arrested by the British, who suspected him of being a Nazi agent. He was released the following October.

Eichmann went back to his death factories. In the summer of 1944 Himmler ordered him to report on the total number of Jews who had died or had been given "special treatment" in extermination camps. Eichmann was vague: he set an approximate figure of six million, four million of whom had died from natural causes and the rest shot by mobile units. Himmler was dissatisfied with the report and informed Eichmann that he would send a statistical expert to work out the exact figures.

Eichmann was satisfied with his own work. He had no sense of contrition. On one occasion, talking with a subordinate, he uttered words that accurately described his own character: "I'll die happily with the certainty of having killed almost six million Jews." At heart he preferred dead Jews to live ones.

Eichmann's luck ran out temporarily with the fall of the Third Reich. He was arrested at the end of the war, but managed to escape unrecognized from an internment camp in the American Zone of Occupation. Then he disappeared for fourteen years.

The search for Eichmann and the final disposition of his case rate a footnote in the history of the twentieth century. The story brings to mind a fictional counterpart—the implacable police-man Javert and his prey Jean Valjean in Victor Hugo's *Les Misérables*. There was, however, an important variation from this tale. The Eichmann hunter (*der Eichmann Jäger*) was not a trained gumshoe detective wise in the thousand ways a criminal could avoid capture, but a gifted amateur. Simon Wiesenthal, born in Polish Galicia, was of Jewish background and well-versed in the nature of the Nazi regime—he had spent four years in a series of concentration camps. After the war he decided to devote his life to the task of retribution. He would search out the many Nazi criminals who had been successful in avoiding Allied attention and bring them to justice.

In 1947 Wiesenthal, acting with some modest volunteer help, set up a small documentation center in Linz, Austria, to assist fellow Jews trace missing relatives. After this early start he planned to track down the thousands of Nazi killers he knew were still at large. The name of Adolf Eichmann appeared again and again in the testimony of those who had suffered under the Nazi lash, Wiesenthal learned that eighty-nine of his own relatives had been killed under orders by the chief of Subsection IV-B-4. The Nazi hunter set out to find him.

It was a long and laborious task filled with dramatic moments. In the Spring of 1948 Wiesenthal knew enough to reconstruct Eichmann's wanderings since the end of the war. The man had arrived at Theresienstadt concentration camp on April 20, 1945, and had remained there for a week. Then Prague—Budweis—the Ebensee camp near Bad Ischl—Altausee. Afterward he managed to hide in American internment camps until the end of June, when he escaped from the compound at Cham. Wiesenthal followed the trail with the perspicacity of a bloodhound. He would not allow his quarry to escape him and avoid ultimate retribution.

The amateur detective then turned his attention to Eichmann's wife, father, and family. He learned through his connections that Eichmann intended to spend New Year's Eve with his family at Altausee. With the assistance of the local police he managed to come within several hundred yards of his prey only to lose him among the holiday celebrants.

Once again the trail ran cold. Wiesenthal could barely look at the large file he kept on his desk. He was convinced that Eichmann was no longer in Europe and that he had escaped with the help of ODESSA, the secret organization that found sanctuary for former *SS* officers in South America or elsewhere. Possibly, Eichmann was hiding in the Near East, where he had friends in the Arab world.

One by one Wiesenthal's colleagues left him to start a new life. Even those he counted as his friends indicated that he might well be suffering from a persecution complex. But the Nazi hunter refused to give up his search for his phantom prey. In January 1951 he learned from a former *Abwehr* officer, wise in counterintelligence and with contacts among ODESSA agents, that Eichmann had been seen in Rome. It was possible, Wiesenthal learned, that Eichmann had moved there along a well-known monastery route. In Rome, Eichmann obtained a Vatican identity card necessary for a visa to a South American country. He probably sailed on a transport with other *SS* men for Brazil or Argentina.

Unfortunately for his goal, Wiesenthal did not have resources enough to follow Eichmann to Brazil or Argentina. The search would have been a difficult one anyhow. The only photograph of Eichmann available was one taken fourteen years before and proper identification was becoming more and more difficult.

Wiesenthal persisted. His remaining hope was Eichmann's family. Sooner or later the man would get in touch with his family. In the Spring of 1952 he learned that Frau Eichmann and her three sons has disappeared from Altausee. That was news of enormous importance. There were rumors that the Eichmanns had gone to Brazil to meet husband and father. But the lead soon flickered out. Again deep disappointment.

Late in 1953 Wiesenthal received a tip from an old Austrian baron, a monarchist and devout Catholic who lived in the Tyrol, that "this awful swine Eichmann who commanded the Jews" *(diese elende Schwein Eichmann, der die Juden kommandierte)* was living in Argentina near Buenos Aires and was working for the water company.

The Nazi hunter was in a dilemma. What could he, a private citizen, do under the circumstances? German immigrants had become a powerful political force in Argentina. After the war many Nazis, fearing retribution for their misdeeds, had moved to Argentina and set themselves up in business there. It was said that wealthy Nazis had presented $100 million to dictator Juan Domingo Perón, who was inclined to overlook their records during the war years. Buenos Aires had become the terminal point for ODESSA, the Nazi travel organization. Escaped Nazis took over hotels and boarding houses and provided new *SS* comrades with identity papers, Perón's army was being trained by former German officers. Argentine industries were run by Germans. To find Eichmann in this pro-Nazi milieu seemed to be an impossible task.

At this point, Wiesenthal realized that his work as a private investigator had come to an end. Others with more clout and money would have to take over. He prepared two reports on every aspect of the Eichmann case as he knew it; he turned one over to the Jewish World Congress in New York and the other to Israeli authorities.

For some time Wiesenthal heard nothing from Israel. He was beginning to feel that no one really cared about Eichmann any longer. He was mistaken. The Israelis had not forgotten. They had too many reports in their files of what this man had done in the Holocaust. They wanted Eichmann alive to face the consequences for his treatment of Jews.

What the Israelis wanted most of all was a current photograph of Eichmann as he looked now. The solution was a brilliant piece of detective work accomplished by Wiesenthal as his final effort in the case. He sent expert photographers in disguise to a funeral, where they took pictures of Adolf's four brothers, including Otto, whose resemblance to Adolf was striking. Wiesenthal arranged a composite photograph and sent it to Israeli's investigators.

An Israeli team of secret service men went off to Buenos Aires. In a dramatic confrontation they captured Eichmann, who was using the name "Ricardo Klement," and smuggled him back to

Israel. On May 23, 1960, Prime Minister David Ben Gurion informed the Israeli *Knesset* (Parliament) that Eichmann had been caught and was now in an Israeli prison.

Global sensation. Israeli agents had pulled off an astonishing coup, praised by some as a magnificent feat and denounced by Argentinians as a violation of their sovereignty.

The trial took place from April 11 to August 14, 1961. Eichmann was charged with crimes against the Jewish people, crimes against humanity, and war crimes. The spectacle of the little man sitting in a glass cage for his own protection aroused worldwide attention. This was something unique in the history of jurisprudence.

The once confident bureaucrat was reduced to a sullen, angry hulk, staring at the many witnesses who appeared for the prosecution. A half dozen psychiatrists certified him as normal. "After having examined him," one of them testified, "I find him more normal than I am." Another stated that "his whole psychological outlook, his attitude toward his wife and child, mother and father, was not only normal but most desirable." Psychiatrists said that Eichmann suffered no conflict of conscience because, on the level of the laws of nature, he was doing what his conscience, the conscience of any National Socialist, prescribed.

In his defense Eichmann recapitulated the pleas of most of those who were accused of mass murder in the Third Reich:

1. He admitted his role in what had taken place in concentration and extermination camps.

2. He had never acted from base motives.

3. He had never had an inclination to kill anybody; he had never hated Jews.

4. Still, he could not have acted otherwise and he did not feel a sense of guilt.

5. His role in the Final Solution was an accident and almost anybody could have taken his place so that potentially all Germans were equally guilty.

6. He had only done his duty. He had obeyed the laws of the land based on the *Fuehrer*'s orders.

7. He had no pricks of conscience about his work. "I am free of all guilt."

The Israeli court was not convinced. It found the prisoner guilty. "Suffering on so gigantic a scale is beyond human understanding." And further:

The fact remains that you have carried out, and therefore actively supported, a policy of mass murder. For politics is not like the nursery; in politics obedience and support are the same. And just as you supported and carried out a policy of not wanting to share the earth with the Jewish people and the people of a number of other nations—as though you and your superior had any right to determine who should and who should not inhabit the world—we can find no one, that is, no member of the human race, can be expected to want to share the earth with you.

That is the reason, and the only reason, you must hang.

Shortly after midnight on May 31, 1962, Adolf Eichmann mounted the gallows at Ramle. After asking for a bottle of red wine and drinking half of it, he walked to the ceremony with dignity. He refused any religious consolation. When the guards tied his ankles and knees, he asked that they loosen the bonds so that he could stand up straight. When the black hood was offered him, he rejected it: "I don't need that."

He began his last words with the statement that he was a *Gottgläubiger*, expressing the common Nazi fashion that he believed in God but was no Christian and had no belief in life after death. He then went on: "Gentlemen, after a short while, we shall meet again. Such is the fate of all men. Long live Germany, long live Argentina, long live Austria! I shall not forget them."

Hannah Arendt commented: "It was as though in those last minutes he was summing up the lessons that this long course in human wickedness had taught us—the lesson of the fearsome word-and-thought-defying *banality of evil*."

Eichmann's body was cremated. The ashes were scattered in the Mediterranean—outside Israeli waters.

14

EXTERMINATOR RUDOLF HOESS

Auschwitz: That was far away. Somewhere in Poland.
                                                    —Rudolf Hoess

The man worshipped his family. "To them I was securely anchored. My thoughts were always with their future, and our farm was to become their permanent home. In our children both my wife and I saw our aim in life. To bring them up so that they could play their part in the world, and to give them all a stable home, was our one task in life."

Rudolf Franz Hoess, commandant of the extermination camp at Auschwitz, did not have the same regard for other families. Under the regime of this monstrous aberration of a human being, many thousands of victims went to the gas ovens in what he, himself, described as "the greatest institution for human annihilation of all time." He never quite understood the horror of his crimes. His was a curious double standard. He saw himself as a "normal," pedestrian bourgeois: "Even while I was doing this extermination work, I led a normal family life." He admitted his role as a professional killer, but, at the same time, spoke of his love for children and animals.

Hoess claimed that he was trained to obey orders without even thinking. "The thought of disobeying an order simply never occurred to anybody." Besides it was all the fault of Heinrich Himmler. No real expression of remorse, sorrow, or regret. Only schizoid apathy, unbelievable insensitivity, and lack of ordinary decency.

The exterminator was aware of the fact that he was not an idol of his people: "Let the public continue to regard me exactly as a bloodthirsty beast, the cruel sadist, the mass murderer. They could not understand that he, too, had a heart and that he was not evil." He pointed to the commendation in his personal file in 1944: "Hoess is not only a good commandant but a true pioneer in the field because of his new ideas and methods of education [*Erziehungsmethode*]."

Rudolf Franz Hoess was born in Baden-Baden on November 23, 1900, the son of shopkeeper Franz Xaver Hoess. The father, pious Catholic, hoped that his son would become a priest. Mass murderer Hoess later complained that he grew up in the shadow of his parent's extreme piety.

In his Nuremberg cell Hoess told psychologist G. M. Gilbert that he was brought up in a rigorous Catholic tradition:

> My father was really a bigot. He was very strict and fanatical. I learned that my father took a religious oath at the time of the birth of my younger sister, dedicating me to God and the priesthood, and after that leading a Joseph married life [*celibacy*]. He directed my entire youthful education toward the goal of making me a priest. I had to pray and go to church endlessly, do penance over the slightest misdeed—praying as punishment for any little unkindness to my sister, or something like that.

When asked if his father ever beat him, Hoess replied that he was only punished by prayer. "The thing that made me so stubborn and probably made me later on cut off from people was his way of making me feel that I had wronged him personally, and that, since I was spiritually a minor, he was responsible to God for my sins. My father was a kind of higher being that I could never approach, and so I crawled back into myself—and I could not express myself to others."

Young Hoess was trained in total obedience, a trait that eventually led him to the gallows. He had to renounce his own mind in favor of complete subservience to authority. He told about it in his autobiography:

I had been brought up by my parents to be respectful and obedient toward all grown-up people, and especially the elderly, regardless of their social status. I was taught that my highest duty was to help those in need. It was constantly impressed upon me in forceful terms that I must obey promptly the wishes and commands of my parents, teachers, priests, etc., and indeed of all grown-up people, including servants, and that nothing must distract me from this duty. Whatever they said was always right.

These basic principles on which I was brought up became part of my flesh and blood. I can still clearly remember how my father, who on account of his fervent Catholicism was a determined opponent of the Reich government and its policy, never ceased to remind his friends that, however strong one's opposition might be, the laws and decrees of the State had to be obeyed unconditionally.

From my earliest youth I was brought up with a strong awareness of duty. In my parents' house it was insisted that every task be exactly and conscientiously carried out. Each member of the family had his own special duties to perform.

Hoess had a modest education, including six *Gymnasium* (grammar school) classes. When World War I began he was not yet fourteen, but after a year he managed to hide his age and join the army. He fought with the Turkish Sixth Army at Baghdad, Kutal-Amara, and in Palestine. Wounded three times and a victim of malaria, he was awarded the Iron Cross Second Class and the Iron Crescent.

After the war, like so many other discontented veterans, Hoess joined the *Freikorps*, paramilitary freebooter units devoted to nationalism and the search for "traitors" to the Fatherland. From

1919 to 1921 he fought for the Rossbach group of the *Freikorps* in the Baltic area, Silesia, and the Ruhr.

In 1923 while in the Ruhr, Hoess got himself into serious trouble. Albert Leo Schlageter, a young *Freikorps* officer in the Ruhr region during the French occupation, was arrested by the criminal police, tried for espionage and sabotage, and executed on May 26, 1923, near Düsseldorf. Nazi leader Adolf Hitler was infuriated: "The German people don't deserve this sacrifice."

Hoess and his *Freikorps* comrades were equally angered. He and Schlageter had been friends active in illicit gunrunning. The *Freikorps* units decided that Walter Kadow, a former teacher in elementary school, was really a Communist spy who had infiltrated its ranks and had betrayed Schlageter to the French. They demanded vengeance.

Accordingly, Hoess and others (Martin Bormann, later to become Hitler's most trusted assistant, was indirectly implicated) spent the night of May 31–June 1, 1922, drinking. They then abducted Kadow into the woods, where he was beaten with clubs and his throat was cut. He was finally finished off with two revolver bullets. It was an especially brutal murder. There is not the slightest scrap of evidence to prove that Kadow was in any way connected with the denunciation of Schlageter. It may well have been a case of mistaken identity.

Within a month Hoess was arrested and sentenced to ten years' imprisonment. He served five years.

"I was certainly there myself," Hoess admitted later, "but I was neither the ringleader nor the person chiefly concerned. When I saw, during interrogation, that the comrade who actually did the deed could only be incriminated by my testimony, I took the blame on myself, and he was released while the investigation was still going on. I need not emphasize that I was in complete agreement with the sentence of death being carried out on the traitor." Hoess saw himself as merely a good, upstanding citizen carrying out a necessary execution.

In captivity Hoess regarded himself as a political prisoner found guilty of a "crime of conviction." I had been taught since childhood to be absolutely obedient and meticulously tidy and clean; so in these matters I did not find it difficult to conform to the strict discipline of prison. I conscientiously carried out my well-defined duties. My cell was a model of neatness and cleanliness." He remained in touch with Bormann, who as collaborator in the crime was serving one year in a Leipzig prison. The contact was to serve him well later on.

In his cell Hoess read voraciously on all manner of topics. What interested him most of all were books on ethnology, racial research, and heredity. What he learned became important for his later career when he was Himmler's man designated for the task of "cleansing the Aryan race."

Released in 1928 under a general amnesty, Hoess became a farmworker. He had joined the NSDAP in November 1922 as Party Member No. 3240, but had not been especially active in its affairs. By now he was more and more impressed by Hitler's doctrines. For years he had read Goebbels's editorials in *Das Reich*, as well as his books and speeches. He was also influenced by Alfred Rosenberg's *Myth of the Twentieth Century* and by Hitler's *Mein Kampf*. This reading gave him, he said, "food for thought."

"I took it all as fact," Hoess said, "just as a Catholic believes in his church dogma. It was the truth without question. I had no doubt about it." Sooner or later, he was sure, there would be a conflict between National Socialism and World Jewry. Other peoples, too, he believed, would be convinced of the Jewish danger and would likewise take a stand against it. The Jews were a pestilential enemy. "Everybody was convinced of this."

Hitler's charge that World Jewry had started a showdown with National Socialism made sense to Hoess. If the *Fuehrer* in his wisdom wanted the Jews eliminated, that was proper guidance for the impressionable family man. In Hoess's mind this was enough to justify his own implication in mass murder.

On September 20, 1933, Hoess joined the SS as candidate (*Anwärter*). On April 1, 1934, he was accepted as an *SS-Mann* and promoted three weeks later to *SS-Sturmmann* (private first class). As a former cavalryman he was asked to form a troop of Mounted-*SS*. While reviewing the *SS* unit in Stettin, Himmler urged Hoess to join the concentration camp administration. Great idea! Hoess came to Dachau in November 1934.

By this time Hoess was a member of an *SS* Death's Head unit. Under the strict discipline of Theodore Eicke, he was taught that every *SS* man must be able to destroy even the members of his own family if they transgressed against Hitler's beliefs. The promoted *SS-Unterscharfsfuehrer* (corporal) was happy in his work. "Once more I was a recruit, with all the joys and sorrows that

that entails, and soon I was myself training other recruits. The soldier's life held me in thrall.'' He became a block leader in the ''protective custody camp.''

The once pious Catholic, even as Goebbels and Himmler, deserted his early belief for the religion of Nazism. As a National Socialist of long standing he was convinced of the need for concentration camps. It was necessary, he said, to lock up opponents of the State to safeguard the rest of the people from their evil deeds.

In 1936 the efficient Hoess was promoted to *Untersturm-fuehrer-SS* (2nd lieutenant). He was also named an Old Fighter of the Nationalist Socialist Party. On August 1, 1938, he was given the post of adjutant at Sachsenhausen concentration camp.

In the summer of 1941 Hoess was suddenly summoned to *Reichsfuehrer-SS* Himmler for personal orders. Evidently, Hoess was rising in the Nazi world. He was delighted. He was told by Himmler in effect: ''The *Fuehrer* has ordered that the Jewish question be solved once and for all and that we, the *SS*, are to implement that order. The existing extermination centers in the East are not in a position to carry out the large actions which are anticipated. I have therefore marked Auschwitz for this purpose, both because of its good position as regards communications and because the area can easily be isolated and camouflaged *['weil es Bahntechnisch und Günstigsten liegt']*. I have decided to entrust this task to you. You will treat this order as absolutely secret, even from your superiors.''

Himmler went on to denounce the Jews as sworn enemies of the German people and said that they must be eradicated. ''Every Jew we can lay our hands on is to be destroyed now during the war, without exception. If we cannot now obliterate the biological basis of Jewry, the Jews will one day destroy the German people.''

Immediate acquiescence by the obedient robot. He would oblige. This was an order and his role was not to reason why.

Hoess discussed the necessary details with Adolf Eichmann, protegé of Ernst Kaltenbrunner, chief of the *SD*, the Security Service. They talked of ways and means of effecting the extermination. This could be done only by gassing, because it would have been impossible, they agreed, to dispose of the large number of people by shooting. That would place too heavy a burden on the *SS* men "because of women and children among the victims." The two inspected the area of Auschwitz that offered space of "measured isolation." Surrounding the complex was a large and dense wood which discouraged escape. They chose a likely spot—a peasant farmstead at nearby Birkenau, isolated and screened by woods and hedges and not far from the railroad.

Promoted to the rank of *Obersturmfuehrer-SS* (1st lieutenant), Hoess ordered all camp personnel to maintain complete secrecy. He, himself, never spoke of his task. Only once did he break his word. In late 1942 his wife, whose curiosity had been aroused about Auschwitz, asked him if rumors she heard about his activities were true. He admitted that they were.

The camp commandant declared one large area to be a special sphere of influence (*Interessengebiete*), from which everyone was evicted so that they would not be in the way of "necessary political tasks." That meant annihilation of selected enemies of the National Socialist state. The camp complex was enlarged to 19.9 square miles and declared to be Reich (*SS*) property.

Hoess went ahead with the construction of extermination installations at Birkenau. For compactness he built combination units, each containing an anteroom, a gas chamber, and an oven for body disposal. The first chambers of death were two remodeled old peasant houses, whose windows were filled in, the interior walls removed, and special airtight doors built. Nearby, a barracks served as a dressing room for the victims. These provisional gas chambers were later replaced by specially built cremation furnaces manufactured by Topf and Sons, Erfurt. After gassing, bodies were hauled up to the furnaces by elevators.

Proud of his sparkling neatness, the commandant ordered a green belt of trees planted around two of the crematories. At the front gate of his domain he placed large letters over the entrance: ARBEIT MACHT FREI (WORK LIBERATES). Hoess was expressing his humanitarian motives: he was pleased to let his victims, as well as all the world, know that his camp was devoted to beneficial labor. "Work," he said, "is not only an effective disciplinary method, but it is educational as well, for those who go through the blessed effectiveness of work can still be rescued from criminality." It never occurred to him that what he was doing at Auschwitz might come under the category of criminal behavior.

The new commandant was most anxious to impress his superiors by improving the extermination process. On a visit to the camp at Treblinka, he noted that carbon monoxide was being used as the death gas because presumably it could overwhelm its victims and cause them no pain. He expressed doubt about this procedure. His attitude brought him into conflict with Christian Wirth, chief of the Criminal Police Section (*Kriminalkommissariat*) at Stuttgart. Wirth was an important official, designated by Hitler to prepare technical means for euthanasia, or gas killings, at Belzec, Sobibor, and Treblinka. Wirth constructed carbon monoxide gas chambers. He was satisfied with the results.

Hoess, however, made it plain that he did not favor the use of carbon monoxide. Instead, he chose Zyklon B, hydrogen cyanide (prussic acid), which he believed to be more quick-working. This was a direct challenge to Wirth and an immediate threat to his authority. Wirth replied by ordering all Zyklon B in his possession to be burned on the pretext that it had been spoiled. He demanded that all his subordinates never propose to Berlin the use of any other gas than carbon monoxide.

From that moment on, Hoess and Wirth were bitter enemies. Where Hoess spoke of his "improvements," Wirth denounced him as a neophyte newcomer and "an untalented pupil." No matter. Hoess turned out to be the victor in this fierce rivalry among the two architects of mass killing. His Zyklon B became the approved method of extermination at the death plants.

Hoess's work at Auschwitz was so appreciated in Berlin that eventually he was promoted to *Obersturmbannfuehrer-SS* (lieutenant-colonel). Some 2,000 *SS* men were posted there during the war. From 20,000 to 25,000 prisoners were confined at the base camp, while Birkenau housed 30,000 female and 50,000 to 60,000 male prisoners.

It was truly an incredible camp of death with an indescribable stench. Around the prisoner compound was a long concrete wall, with guard towers and searchlights placed at intervals. There were twenty-eight blocks to house the prisoners, used variously as offices, storerooms, and hospitals. The entire compound was surrounded by two high, electrified barbed-wire fences, brightly lit at night. Along the inner fence ran a ten-foot wide gravel strip, called the neutral zone. Any prisoner found there was promptly shot.

At nearby Birkenau, three and a half miles away, was the

adjunct camp. Here, prisoners were housed in windowless stables and stone buildings. There were three units—a women's compound; an area for sick prisoners, for quarantine, and Gypsies; and barracks for those who worked in textile mills.

The first shipment of Polish prisoners arrived at Auschwitz on June 14, 1940. After adoption of the Final Solution at the Wannsee Conference in January 1942, endless hordes of prisoners, mostly Jews, flowed into the camp. The mass killing was under way.

Under Hoess's administration, inmates were beaten and tortured, given injections of poison, or made guinea pigs in medical experimentations. Many died under the primitive sanitary conditions. Witnesses at postwar trials testified to the horrible conditions at Hoess's ''model'' camp. With every step one took in the compound, prisoners would sink more deeply into the viscous mud. They had little water for washing. They slept on three tiers of wooden slabs, six to each tier, and for the most part without any straw pallets. There were roll calls twice a day, which meant that unfortunates had to stand for hours in the wet, cold mud. When it rained, they had to lie on their wooden bunks in their wet garments.

Hundreds died daily. The prisoners saw posters decorated with skulls and warning: AUSCHWITZ CONCENTRATION CAMP AREA—DO NOT CROSS THIS LINE—FIRE WILL BE OPENED WITHOUT WARNING. Outside work details were accompanied by as many guards as prisoners. Trained dogs trailed those who missed roll call. When anyone escaped, all others were kept standing in the open all night.

Life expectancy was calculated at several weeks. Because of the unsanitary conditions and inadequate diet, combined with hard labor and torture, many prisoners died within a few weeks or months after arrival. Women dressed in rags had to carry rocks and dig trenches. Only those who became trusties could stay alive for longer periods. Weak inmates tried to commit suicide after only a few days by ''going into the wires.'' An electric charge and a burst of machine-gun fire saved them future torture.

Everyone at Auschwitz knew the meaning of Hoess's Block 11. From the outside it looked much like any other block, but inside the windows were sealed off and only a narrow slit permitted a little light to filter in. The basement windows were heavily barred. This was the scene of executions. Against one of the stone walls in the yard was the Black Wall—for thousands the last sight on their road through life. Prison guards used small caliber rifles. In the background were the frightened stretcher-bearers waiting for their cargoes. The executioners showed no pity—instead, abysmal contempt and sadistic fury.

One eyewitness described the fate of Russians brought to Auschwitz in 1941–42:

> The misery there was indescribable. People went out of their minds with hunger. They fell on every scrap of food, every piece of beet root, like vultures. The dead were taken off to the crematory by the cartful every evening. The dying, who could no longer take the indescribable suffering, crawled on the carts voluntarily and were then slaughtered like animals.

Literally hundreds of witnesses testified about the horrendous conditions at Auschwitz under Hoess. In his posthumous autobiography, *Commandant at Auschwitz* (London: Weidenfeld & Nicolson, 1959), Hoess substantiated much of the testimony by horrified eyewitnesses:

> From time to time women would suddenly give the most terrible shrieks while undressing, or tear their hair, or scream like maniacs. They were immediately led away behind the building and shot in the back of the neck with a small-caliber weapon. . . .

> I had to see everything. I had to watch hour after hour, by day and by night, the removal and burning of the bodies, the extraction of the teeth, the cutting of the hair, the whole grisly, interminable business. I had to stand for hours on end in the ghastly stench, while the mass graves were being opened and the bodies dragged in and burned.

> I had to look through the peepholes of the gas chambers and watch the process of death itself, because the doctors wanted me to see it.

> I had to do all this because I was the one to whom everyone looked, because I had to show them that I did not merely

issue the orders and make the regulations but was also prepared myself to be present at whatever task I had assigned
to my subordinates.

Call for sympathy. Hoess wanted the world to know that he
had an iron determination to carry out Hitler's orders, which
could be implemented only "by stifling all human emotions."
In late 1943, at the urging of Martin Bormann, Hoess was
named Deputy Chief Inspector of Concentration Camps. The
pioneer of Auschwitz was rewarded for his great contributions
at that death complex. His new job was to assist the comman-
dants of all concentration camps. He was also responsible for
necessary changes in personnel. He reported Bergen-Belsen, under the regime of Josef Kramer, as a picture of wretchedness.
"The barracks and the storerooms and even the guard's quarters
are completely neglected. Sanitary conditions are far worse than
at Auschwitz."
On April 23, 1945, at a time when Russian troops were moving on East Berlin, Hoess tried to establish contact with the
International Red Cross. At the same time he ordered that killings cease. Invited to Ravensbrück to discuss details, he was
injured in an automobile accident and disappeared.
Like Boss Himmler, Hoess attempted to sink into anonymity.
It was not until March 11, 1946, that he was found dressed in
the clothes of an agricultural worker and using the name of Franz
Lange. Captured by the British, he considered himself fortunate
not to fall into the hands of the Russians. Still, he complained
of beatings at the hands of his British captors.
After three weeks Hoess was taken by truck to Nuremberg,
where he was called upon to act as a witness for the International
Military Tribunal. From his cell he gave depositions about his
work of extermination. He was anxious to confess all—as if that
would find favor in the eyes of the British. He readily confirmed
that some two-and-a-half million Jews had been executed under
his direction. When asked how it was possible to kill that many
people, he replied that it was not at all difficult: "It would not
have been hard to exterminate even greater numbers." It was
possible, he said, to gas up to 10,000 in one 24-hour period in
the larger extermination chambers. "The killing was easy. You
didn't even need guards to drive them into the chambers. The
whole thing went very quickly."

Boss Himmler told him, Hoess said, that the Final Solution must be accomplished, otherwise Jews would later destroy the German people. When asked if he showed any reluctance, he replied: "I had nothing to say. I could only say *'Jawohl!'* ['Yes, indeed!']. We could only execute orders without any further consideration. That is the way it was. [Himmler] often demanded impossible things, which could not be done under normal circumstances, but once given the order, one set about doing it with his entire energy, and often did things that seemed impossible."

When asked if he could refuse to obey orders, Hoess replied: "No, the thought of refusing an order just did not enter one's head. I guess you cannot understand our world—I naturally had to obey orders and I must now stand to take the consequences."

Hoess took the stand on the morning of April 15, 1946. He told how he had acted on direct orders of Himmler, who had passed on a *Fuehrerbefehl* (leader's command) for a final solution of the Jewish problem. He spoke in a calm, matter-of-fact tone, as if he were describing a military campaign. He told how he was ordered in June 1941 to establish extermination facilities at Auschwitz. He visited Treblinka to study its methods of extermination, mostly liquidation of Jews of the Warsaw Ghetto. Unimpressed by the use of carbon monoxide gas, he recommended Zyklon B, crystallized prussic acid, to be dropped into the death chamber from a small opening.

Another improvement Hoess made over Treblinka was to build his gas chambers at Auschwitz to accommodate 2,000 people at one time, whereas at Treblinka the chambers could only hold 200 prisoners each. "Still another improvement we made over Treblinka was that at Treblinka the victims almost always knew that they were to be exterminated, while at Auschwitz we endeavored to fool the victims into thinking that they were going through a delousing process. Of course, frequently they realized our true intentions, and we sometimes had riots and difficulties. We were required to carry out these exterminations in secrecy, but of course, the foul and nauseating stench from the continuous burning of bodies permeated the entire area and all of the people living in the surrounding communities knew that exterminations were going on at Auschwitz."

Dead silence in the prisoners' dock. Then outburst from the defendants. Hans Frank: "Two-and-a-half million people in cold

blood! That is something people will talk about for a thousand
years." Alfred Rosenberg: "A dirty trick to put Hoess on the
stand just before me. That places me in a difficult position to
defend my philosophy." Others among the accused denied that
Hoess could have been a Prussian, for "a Prussian could never
do things like that." He must have been a southern German.

In his cell the next night Hoess tried again to justify his conduct: "For me as a fanatical National Socialist, I took it all as
a fact—just as a Catholic believes in his church dogma. It was
plain truth without question. I had no doubt about that. I was
absolutely convinced that the Jews were the opposite pole from
the German people, and that sooner or later there would have to
be a showdown between National Socialism and World Jewry.
After getting the clear and direct order for the extermination of
Jewry, there was nothing left to do but to carry it out."

In his autobiography, Hoess presented an apologia for his career. He had adhered to National Socialism for nigh on twenty-
five years, had grown up with it, was bound to it completely,
and could not throw it aside simply because its leaders had used
their powers wrongly, and even criminally. "I can see that the
leaders of the Third Reich, because of their policy of force, were
guilty of causing this vast war and all its consequences. I see
that these leaders, by means of exceptionally effective propaganda and of limitless terrorism were able to make the whole
German people so docile and submissive that they were ready,
with very few exceptions, to go wherever they were led, without
voicing a word of criticism."

Besides, Hoess continued, it was all the fault of Heinrich
Himmler. "Himmler was the crudest representative of the leadership principle. Every German had to subordinate himself unquestionably and uncritically to the leaders of the State, who
alone were in a position to understand the real needs of the
people and to direct them along the right path."

Hoess described himself as guided by two lights—his Fatherland and his family. His unalterable love for his country brought
him into the Nazi Party and the SS. He spoke of his intense love
for his family and his thoughts for its future. Both he and his
wife were interested in only giving their children a stable home
life.

The good family man was calling for understanding. "Un-
knowingly I was a cog in the wheel of the great extermination

machine created by the Third Reich.'' Here he was, an innocent underling only doing his duty, and he was being condemned as an animal and brutal sadist—even as a mass murderer. It was all most unfair. How could a man be condemned merely, as a good citizen, for following orders?''

Nor did the court at Poland, before which he was tried, understand the man. On March 29, 1947, he was condemned to death. Several days later he was brought to the Old Crematory at Auschwitz. Nearby, on the ruins of the Political Section of the death camp, was constructed a gallows, as specified by the Polish court. Here, in surroundings he knew well, Hoess paid with his life for his pioneer work at Auschwitz.

This was the self-described innocent who could operate without second thoughts amidst the stench of burning bodies and even wax poetical in the process: ''In the spring of 1942 the people walked under the blossoming trees of the farmstead, and most of them went with no premonition of their death.'' Historian Ernst Nolte described Hoess as ''on the whole less of a criminal in the conventional sense than a sentimentalist.''

Hoess, indeed, saw himself as a sensitive human being, who was forced to hide this ''defect'' under an icy exterior. He had a difficult job to perform and he would do it without sympathy or pity. ''When Hitler called me to him. I just took it as a realization of something I had already accepted, not only I, but everybody. Even though it did frighten me momentarily, it fit in with all that had been preached to me for years. The problem itself—the extermination of Jewry,—was not new but that it was *I* to be the one to carry it out, that frightened me at first. But after first getting the direct order and even an explanation with it—there was nothing to do but carry it out.''

That his behavior might be judged as criminal never occurred to the poor, frightened man. He must overcome any notions of pity for Jewish children and their mothers, because ''such ideas came close to being treason to the *Fuehrer*.'' And over and over again *Reichsfuehrer-SS* Himmler had explained that the task was precisely the same as exterminating vermin. Hoess repeated the dictum of Himmler: ''Anti-Semitism is exactly the same as delousing. Getting rid of lice is not a question of ideology. In just the same way anti-Semitism for us has not been a question of ideology but a question of cleanliness.''

Hoess's telescoped thoughts while on the gallows at Auschwitz

might well have included some perplexed questions. Why the
outcry against a simple soldier doing his duty? If one refused to
follow orders, was he not committing treason? Was not his beloved country at war with Jewry? Was not all permissible in the
crucible of war? What about the barbaric Allied bombing of
Hamburg and Dresden and those firestorms that took the lives
of German men, women, and children? Why execute a good
family man?

One may well wonder if the hangman at Auschwitz, who presided over the execution, might have been able to answer Hoess's
agonized questions.

15

JOSEF KRAMER: THE BEAST OF BELSEN

I had no feelings in carrying out those things because I had received an order.

—Josef Kramer

Great novelist Thomas Mann, representative of that other Germany, was appalled by, thoroughly ashamed of, and disgusted with the Nazi regime. In his diary he denounced "the primitiveness, the disappearance of a culture, the increase in stupidity, and the reduction to a petit bourgeois mentality." And again: "Cryptic sciences, pseudosciences and frauds, formation of sects and quackery were the vogue and had a mass appeal. Intellectuals did not consider this a low, modern fad or as a cultural degradation. Instead, they welcomed it as the rebirth of mystic powers of life and of the soul of the people. The soil was ready for the most absurd and lowest political mass superstition. That was the faith in Adolf Hitler."

What Thomas Mann was worried about was that National Socialism would educate the German people in a moral sansculott-ism and in an apathy to all cruelty. That is what happened to

217

the assorted thugs and ruffians described in these capsule biographies. In addition to the incorruptible citizens who followed the Nazi line in the belief that they were patriots, others of questionable background were attracted to the Nazi movement by the possibility of improving their status in a wildly changing society. There was a place for those of stunted intelligence and morals who, without questioning, would carry out orders for mayhem and murder. For them the prospect was inviting—legalized murder, not punishment, but promotion, glory, and money.

Josef Kramer was one of them.

Little is known about his early life. Born in 1907, his first vocation was that of bookkeeper. Of stocky build, with staring eyes and thin lips, he was a misfit in German society, but he was always on the lookout for any kind of deal that might enhance his material well-being.

In 1932, a year before Hitler's accession to power, Kramer volunteered for membership in the *SS*, the Nazi Elite Guard. He learned quickly that if he kept his mouth shut and followed orders, he could advance rapidly in his unit. His first assignment was to guard concentration camp inmates. In the months preceding the outbreak of World War II he served at various camps, including Sachsenhausen, Dachau, and Mauthausen. In each camp, the energetic lieutenant gained a reputation as a strict disciplinarian.

In the Spring of 1940 Kramer was assigned to the new camp at Auschwitz. Together with Rudolf Hoess he was ordered to inspect Auschwitz as a possible site for a new synthetic coal-oil installation and a rubber plant. But Boss Heinrich Himmler had something else in mind. He needed a special camp to be used for physical elimination of Jews, Gypsies, Communists, and other enemies of the state—an idea then rapidly gaining favor in Hitler's mind. Those who did not meet the *Fuehrer*'s specifications for the proper blood type were to be given special treatment. Presumably, the report by Hoess and Kramer was favorable—Auschwitz was later selected as a special center for extermination.

In Berlin *Reichsfuehrer-SS* Heinrich Himmler was much impressed by reports of Kramer's toughness and his insistence on discipline and obedience. At the time, Himmler was sponsoring typhus experiments on human beings. In August 1943 he ordered Kramer, then serving at Natzweiler concentration camp in Alsace, to receive some eighty inmates from Auschwitz. In a letter accompanying the assignment he was requested to communicate at once with Professor August Hirt, anatomist of the Strassburg Medical Faculty, who was conducting typhus experiments. Kramer's job was to provide prisoners for typhus immunization to test a new serum. The human material had to be healthy, in a normal state of nourishment, and in bodily vigor corresponding to the physical condition of soldiers. The prisoners were limited to ages between twenty and forty.

Kramer went to Strassburg, where he was greeted by Professor Hirt. The anatomist told him that a prisoner convoy was en route from Auschwitz to Natzweiler. These people were to be killed by poison and their bodies sent to the Anatomical Institute for experimentation.

At the end of the conversation the professor gave Kramer a bottle containing about half a pint of salts. This was Zyklon B, crystals of hydrogen cyanide, or prussic acid. Kramer was already familiar with its use, he said, for Hoess had brought it to Auschwitz. The professor then recommended an appropriate dosage to be used on the prisoners arriving from Auschwitz.

The victims were brought to Natzweiler in the dead of night. Kramer selected fifteen women, informed them that they were to be disinfected, and sent them to the gas chambers. Assisted by several *SS* guards, he, himself, stripped the women and then shoved them into the death rooms.

Kramer was indifferent to the cruelty. Later, during his court examination, he described what had happened:

> When the door was closed they began to scream. After the door had been closed, I introduced a certain amount of salt installed to the upper right of the peephole. I then closed the opening of the tube with a cork attached to the end of the tube. This cork had a metal pipe. This metal pipe projected the salt and water toward the opening in the chamber of which I have spoken.

> I illuminated the inside of the room by means of a switch installed near the tube and observed through the peephole what had happened inside the room.

I saw that these women breathed for about half a minute before they fell to the ground.

After I had turned on the ventilation inside the flue, I opened the doors. I found the women lying lifeless on the floor and they were covered all over with excrement.

The next morning I told the *SS* orderlies to place the bodies in a small car—it was about 5:30 o'clock—so that they would be taken to the Anatomical Institute, as requested of me by Professor Hirt.

No compassion, no regret, no mercy. Good soldier Kramer, in approved Nazi fashion, was only doing his duty.

Several days later Kramer took more women to the gas chambers. He repeated the process until fifty were killed. Questioned about his reaction, Kramer replied that he was not concerned about what Professor Hirt meant to do with the bodies. "On the basis of what Professor Hirt said, I did not think it was any of my business to ask him." Replying to another question, he remarked that he paid no attention to the nationality of the inmates. "I believe they came from southern Europe, but I cannot tell you the country."

Shown an album of photographs of a gas chamber, Kramer admitted that he recognized a Struthof unit in the pictures which, he said, was built in the middle of 1943 for gassing inmates intended for Dr. Hirt. When asked whether he would have used bullets if some victims survived the gas, Kramer said: "I would have tried once again to suffocate them with gas by throwing another dose into the chamber. I had no feeling in carrying out those things because I had received an order to kill the eighty inmates in the way I already told you. That, by the way, was the way I was trained."

Classic response of the icily cold robot. No remorse. No sense of shame. Kramer's attitude was querulous: how in the world could anyone accuse him of murder when he was only being obedient to proper, legal authority? This was a war situation— he had to do what he was told or he would forfeit his own life. It was stupid to charge him with making decisions on life or death! It was utterly unfair to accuse him, a simple soldier, merely for carrying out his orders.

Kramer's pattern of behavior brought him exactly what he wanted—promotion. In November 1943, while serving as adjutant to Hoess at Auschwitz, he was placed in charge of gas chambers at Birkenau (Auschwitz II). In late 1944 came the assignment he wanted—commandant of the concentration camp at Belsen. Originally a small, privileged camp, Belsen was located near the village of Bergen on the road from Celle to Hamburg. It had been enlarged to serve as a convalescent depot for sick inmates as well as displaced persons from the whole of northwestern Europe transferred from other concentration camps, factories, and farms.

There were no gas chambers at Belsen. But prisoners brought there had to face the wrath of the new commandant. Arrogant in his new post of authority, Kramer turned out to be a bestial sadist. He detested the prisoners assigned to his care as "scum and parasites," and handled them accordingly. He introduced the Auschwitz routines he had learned from Hoess, including lengthy roll calls, during which weakened prisoners had to stand for hours after answering to their names. It was torture for those who had been subjected to back-breaking work and who had insufficient food. The adamant camp director would accept no excuses.

Conditions at Belsen deteriorated drastically within a few months after Kramer arrived. As administrator he was clumsy, narrow-minded, and coarse. He expected all inmates and guards to comply instantly with his orders. He would run the kind of camp that would bring him praise from Berlin. A cruel taskmaster, he had only contempt for his prisoners. He had obstreperous inmates hung from large hooks, suspended by their arms, for hours at a time. Many of his charges died after pitiless beatings. Others, in deadly fear of his violent nature, took care to avoid him in the compound.

Belsen was overcrowded with prisoners brought in from both East and West. Some arrived in the camp after a five-day train journey without food or water. Many had marched on the roads for days. The supply of food in the camp was limited mostly to raw, uncooked roots, for which the inmates fought bitterly. The water was inadequate for the thousands of prisoners.

Following approved concentration-camp procedure, Kramer divided his charges into three categories: the healthy, who managed despite harsh conditions to keep themselves in fairly good condition; the sick, who had to be cared for by their fellow-prisoners; and the vast majority, who lived in squalor and without any sense of normal behavior, crawled around the camp in helpless rage. It was a miserable existence. The camp commandant did nothing to better conditions.

Kramer showed considerably more interest in the work of his doctors, who were studying the effects of mustard gas and other agents on inmates. On one occasion a physician assigned to the camp tried to avoid working on the experiments by pleading a stomach disorder. He expressed his objection to Kramer, when he saw his name on a list of doctors assigned to test a large number of prisoners transported from Hungary. The camp commandant reacted angrily: "I know you are being investigated for favoring inmates. I am now ordering you to go to the ramp and if you fail to obey the order, I shall have you arrested on the spot."

Again the obedience syndrome, most sacred of all Nazi obligations. Kramer expected his own subordinates to obey him without question just as he respected any order from Boss Himmler.

Despite his efforts, Kramer was faced with one critical emergency after another. When a typhus epidemic broke out in the compound, he was at a loss on how to handle it. He would have to execute the entire to camp to control spread of the disease. He became more and more perplexed as one inmate after another died. The most important service the former bookkeeper could perform was to keep careful records. He devoted much of his attention to the task of noting the number of prisoners under his jurisdiction, how many attended roll calls, and how many died each day. In one report dated March 1, 1945, he entered a total of 45,000 prisoners and 250 to 300 dead of typhus.

By this time Kramer had lost control of his camp. He found it impossible to keep up with the overwhelming flow of prisoners. By March 15, 1945, the number rose to 60,000. During the week of April 13 more than 20,000 additional prisoners were brought to the camp. It was just too much for the commandant. He ordered roll calls stopped and left the prisoners to their own devices. Corpses rotted in the barracks. Bodies were piled on the floor of the children's hut and the guards had no time or inclination to move them. Reduced to filth and squalor, Belsen became a veritable hell on earth.

Only Dante's *Inferno* could match the gruesome scene. Moaning skeletons shuffled around the grounds. Many prisoners went mad. There were dead bodies everywhere—it was impossible to dispose of so many of them. Some were disfigured by terrible sores and bullet marks. Typhus and dysentery took a fearful toll of life. Throughout the compound there was the smell of death.

By mid-April 1945 Kramer had given up in disgust. He was frustrated and angered not so much by the condition of his charges but by the annoying fact that he had not won promotion beyond the office of *Hauptsturmfuehrer-SS* (captain). He had held that rank since May 1944, but had not been promoted since then despite what he deemed to be his superior work at Belsen. Moreover, he had to face the scorn of his wife, who was upset because other *SS* officers had advanced in rank over her husband.

The terrible conditions at Belsen under Kramer's administration came to light in mid-April 1945 when troops of the British Oxfordshire Yeomanry moved into the compound. The liberators could scarcely believe what they saw. Oxford historian Patrick Gordon-Walker, BBC commentator and chief editor of Radio Luxembourg, described the scene in Kramer's Belsen. Here is a condensed version of his report:

I went to Belsen. It was a vast area surrounded by barbed wire. The whole thing was being guarded by Hungarian guards. They had been in the German Army and now immediately and without hesitation were serving us.

Outside the camp, which is amidst bushes, pines, and heather, all fairly recently planted, were great notices in red letters: DANGER: TYPHUS.

The first night of liberty, many hundreds of people died of joy.

Next day some men of the Yeomanry arrived. The people crowded around them, kissing their hands and feet and dying from weakness. Corpses in every state of decay were lying around, piled up on top of each other in heaps. There were corpses in the compound in flocks. People were falling dead all around, people who were walking skeletons.

One woman came up to a soldier who was guarding the milk store and doling the milk out to children, and begged for milk for her baby, black in the face and shriveled up. The woman went on begging for milk. So he poured some on the dead lips. The mother then started to croon with joy and carried the baby off in triumph. She stumbled and fell dead in a few yards.

Dead bodies, black and blue and bloated, and skeletons had been used as pillows by sick people.

An enormous buried dump of personal jewelry and belongings was discovered in suitcases. When I went to the camp five days after its liberation, there were still bodies all around. I saw about a thousand.

In one place hundreds had been shoveled into a mass grave by bulldozers; in another, Hungarian soldiers were putting corpses into a grave that was sixty feet by sixty feet and thirty feet deep. It was almost half full.

Other and similar pits were being dug. Five thousand had died since we got into the camp. People died before my eyes, scarcely human, moaning skeletons, many of them gone mad. Bodies were just piled up.

In one compound I went, I saw women standing up quite naked, washing among themselves. Nearby were piles of corpses. Other women were defecating in the open and then staggering back, half dead, to their blocks. Some were lying groaning on the ground. One had reverted to the absolute primitive.

I went into the typhus ward, packed thick with people lying in dirty rags of blankets on the floor, groaning and moaning. An amazing thing is the number who managed to keep themselves clean and neat. All of them said that in a day or two more they would have gone under from hunger and weakness.

Other prisoners were dying like flies. They can hardly walk on their legs. Thousands still of these cannot be saved, and if they were, they would be in lunatic asylums for the short remainder of their pitiful lives.

The next morning I left this hellhole, this camp. As I left, I had myself deloused and my recording truck as well.

To you at home this is one camp. There are many more. This is what you are fighting.

None of this is propaganda. This is the plain and simple truth.

Such was the result of a pernicious combination—Hitler's will, Himmler's orders, and Kramer's administration. It was a literal hell on earth, where the moral universe had collapsed, a Nazi black hole, concentrated pressure of the worst evil in this world.

Ashamed German officials proposed to the victorious Allies that the camp at Belsen be by-passed. The suggestion was refused. British troops disarmed the *SS* guards, many of whom naïvely believed that they would go on with their duties elsewhere and then be set free.

Commandant Kramer thought so, too. He believed that his captors would respect his office. He took them on a tour of the compound, but made no effort to explain the scene of degradation. They, of course, as military men, would know that it was impossible for him to control a camp infected with typhus. Surely they would understand and give him sympathetic approval.

The unimpressed British arrested Kramer and all his *SS* guards. The commandant was astonished and chagrined when he was placed in an icebox with some stinking fish. He was told that he would be kept there until he was sent back to the rear.

Kramer's *SS* guards also received special attention from the British. At first, male and female guards were held in confinement to protect them from attacks by outraged prisoners. Then they were put to work shoveling corpses into lorries. There were some 35,000 bodies to be buried. *SS* men were forced to ride on top of the loaded corpses and then hurl them into huge open graves. Exhausted, surrounded by jeering inmates, some of them fell among the dead. Two committed suicide in their cells. There was instant retaliation for others. Several who jumped from lor-

ries and tried to run away and get lost in the crowd were shot
down. One who threw himself into a concrete pool was riddled
with bullets.

Kramer's tough *SS* women guards were forced to carry heavy
loads and cook meals for the prisoners. Angry inmates reported
to their liberators that female guards, all in their twenties, were
even more brutal than the men. One *SS* woman, who tried to
escape disguised as a prisoner, was denounced and arrested.
Another tried to take her own life.

Kramer was brought before a court at Lüneburg. The British
handled such trials with dispatch. Their military tribunals, unlike their American counterparts, were staffed exclusively by officers. The accused were given competent counsel, who did their
best to save the lives of the defendants.

Kramer was brought to trial before one of these British military courts. The evidence against him was so overwhelming that
little could be said in his defense. He presented the usual Nazi
case—this was war; he was an officer; he had taken an oath of
loyalty; he had merely carried out his orders from above; he was
an innocent arm of the laws of his country. The only alternative
was his own death. No effect on the British. Verdict—guilty.
Sentence—death.

Kramer was hanged on November 27, 1945. He went to the
gallows together with eleven *SS* guards and Dr. Bruno Tesch,
supplier of Zyklon B.

Josef Kramer, like his Nazi comrades, knew nothing of human
kindness or commiseration. His character shortcomings were
typical of a system that defied morality of any kind. An eyewitness who observed him in his days of glory testified: "Captain
Kramer never missed an execution. He generally stood by beaming, slapping his thighs with glee when the scene grew especially
exciting."

16

ILSE KOCH: THE BITCH
OF BUCHENWALD

*This bestial woman's guilt in specific murders is irrefutably
established.*
—*U.S. Senate Committee, Dec. 27, 1947*

In his summation on July 20, 1946, at the Nuremberg Trials,
U.S. prosecutor Robert H. Jackson spoke of the difficulty in
outlining the details of the defendants' mad and melancholy records. He denounced the intellectual and moral bankruptcy of
the Nazi regime which attempted to goose-step the supposed
Herrenvolk (master "race") across international frontiers. He
described the philosophy of National Socialism, which for years
had deceived the world, masking falsehoods with plausibilities.
The men in the dock, he charged, were guilty of planning, executing, and conspiring to commit a long list of crimes and
wrongs.

Jackson continued: "They stand before the record of this trial
as blood-stained Gloucester stood by the body of the slain king.
He begged of the widow, as they beg of you: 'Say I slew them

not.' And the Queen replied: 'Then say they were not slain. But dead they are.' ''

The prosecutor presented the widow in traditional terms—as outside the periphery of aggressive behavior. There were no women in the dock at the Nuremberg Trials. But later at subsequent proceedings, there would surface a number of females who more than matched their male counterparts in cruel and aberrant behavior. Thus far our collection of Nazi rogues includes only males. To find a female of this species may be shocking to those who customarily tend to place women on a pedestal. Women are credited with creating, not destroying, life. They bear the pains of childbirth and give life instead of snuffing it out. Ordinarily, they do not take part, as do their male consorts, in the barbaric sequences of war. They are rated the gentler sex.

As always there are exceptions to the norm. On occasion, women do resort to the extremity of murder, but the number of cases is minuscule when compared with the masculine melancholy record of mayhem, killing, slaughter, and massacre.

The case of Ilse Koch represents a new low for womankind. While her commandant husband went about the business of gassing thousands of fellow human beings, this woman, called ''The Bitch of Buchenwald,'' swaggered through the camp compound with whip in hand to beat any unfortunate who stood in the way. According to witnesses, Ilse Koch in her spare moments nurtured her collection of lamp shades made from the skin of executed prisoners.

It is an ugly story—the lifestyle of this lady of the lamp shades.

Ilse Koch was born in Saxony in 1906, the daughter of a laborer. Her earliest known occupation gave no indication of what was to happen to her later. For a time she engaged in the placid work of librarian, checking out books, keeping records and, with prim modesty, meeting the public.

Then in 1936 at the age of thirty, Ilse fell in love with and married a tough character. Karl Koch, at the time a *Standartenfuehrer-SS* (colonel), was assigned as senior officer at Sachsenhausen concentration camp. Little is known of his early life. As commandant of what was then called a correction camp, he turned out to be a vicious sadist with a reputation for coarse and brutal conduct. Much of his boorish quality influenced his spouse.

Karl Koch's conduct may be judged by a typical case. Peter Schneider, a confessional minister considered to be an enemy of the state, was sent to Sachsenhausen in September 1937. At the time, Commandant Koch decreed a daily flag-raising ceremony. When Schneider refused to take off his cap in honor of the Nazi emblem, he was sentenced by Koch to receive twenty-five lashes. He was thrown by guards into a bunker, where he lay for months suffering agonizing torment. His cell was kept dark day and night. The floor was covered with two inches of water. During this entire time he was not allowed to bathe. His clothes were infested with lice, his body was covered with sores. Eventually he was killed.

When the pastor's wife begged permission to have her children view their father's body, she received Koch's permission. The camp commandant regarded his own acquiescence as a useful propaganda gesture. The corpse was brought to an *SS* barber, who applied makeup to the face and covered the head with a wig to conceal mutilations. Koch then told the grieving family: "Your husband was my best prisoner. I was about to inform you of his discharge when he died of heart failure." Warm words from the considerate custodian.

In 1939 Koch was transferred to a new and more important post. The camp at Buchenwald was located on a wooded hill four miles from Weimar, shrine of German culture associated with the names of Goethe, Schiller, and Wieland. This was one of the three camps set up by Hitler (Sachsenhausen in the north, where Koch had already served; Dachau near Munich in the south; and Buchenwald in central Germany). They formed the nucleus of the *Fuehrer*'s system of concentration camps. At first, these were to be convenient detention centers to re-educate enemies of the state. Later, they would be used for a more deadly purpose.

As World War II staggered on, Buchenwald was changed from a correction camp to an all-out extermination factory. The new goal was genocide, the annihilation of European Jewry, Gypsies, and assorted dissidents. Under orders from *Reichsfuehrer-SS* Heinrich Himmler, Karl Koch presided over beatings, torture, and starvation of prisoners. He required them to work in an adjacent factory producing machine guns, small arms, ammunition, and other war matériel for the German armed forces. His prisoners worked around the clock in twelve-hour shifts.

Both the commandant and his wife had only contempt for prisoners entrusted to their care. They worked the inmates to death and then saw that the bodies were buried. They consigned inmates too weak to work, straight to the gas ovens. No pity for women or children. The major concern of the Koch team was to win the approbation of superior SS officers in Berlin up to and including Himmler.

In 1941 the Nazi euthanasia program for extermination of feeble-minded and crippled Germans was put into effect. Behind it was Hitler's plan to ''cleanse the Aryan race.'' In Germany at the time there were about a million feeble-minded people, a quarter of a million hereditary mental defectives, ninety thousand epileptics, and many thousands of cripples. For Hitler these people were dangerous for the country's health and had to be eliminated.

Orders were forwarded to Koch at Buchenwald. Calling all his SS officers together, he informed them that he had received secret instructions from Himmler to eliminate debilitated and crippled prisoners. Because at the time Buchenwald did not have gas ovens, Koch, in compliance with the order, had more than three hundred prisoners of various nationalities (but all certified as Jews) shipped to the euthanasia station at Bernburg for extermination.

Like military installations throughout the world, there was in Buchenwald a special hierarchy of social status among the wives of senior officers. For them the promotion of their husbands was a matter of major importance. There was bitter rivalry among women for whom advancement was too slow. Commandant Hoess's wife at Auschwitz complained angrily that her spouse was not given the high status he deserved.

Ilse Koch, too, was infected with the promotion bug. She enjoyed the importance of her husband's exalted post at Buchenwald, but she wanted even more. She expected other wives to cater to her rank and status. Whatever Karl Koch did in his masculine way, she felt free to imitate in her favored position as the commandant's consort.

Ilse became the camp's character. With her power of life or death over prisoners, she went far beyond the boundaries of what is regarded as normal feminine conduct. The strapping red-haired woman of ample proportions rode horseback through the compound, whip in hand, lashing out at anyone who as much as glanced in her direction. She saw herself as mistress of this dark world, and heaven help any prisoner who did not defer to her wishes.

Witnesses later charged that Frau Koch participated in the killings that took place at Buchenwald. In 1947 a United States Senate Committee investigating her case reported that she had helped beat and kill hundreds of prisoners. The committee made no use of the term "probably"; its members on the basis of evidence presented to it judged her guilt as established beyond a shadow of a doubt.

Even more shocking was the accusation that Ilse Koch kept herself busy at Buchenwald indulging in her special hobby of collecting lamp shades, book covers, and gloves made from the skin of dead prisoners. This was said to be her most satisfying pleasure in private life. Witnesses testified that when newly arrived prisoners were hustled from trains moving into the compound, they were met by Ilse's agents, who were assigned to make lists of those with "interesting tattoos." The commandant's wife, it was said, was enormously attracted by tattooed skins.

A German prisoner who had been liberated from Buchenwald testified before the International Military Tribunal at Nuremberg that all those who had tattoos were required to report to the dispensary. "After the prisoners had been examined, the ones with the best and most artistic specimens were killed by injection. The corpses were then turned over to the pathology department, where the tattoos were removed from the bodies. The finished products were turned over to Ilse Koch, who had them made into lamp shades or other ornamental objects."

Ilse Koch apparently started a trend in Naziland. Another witness stated that when word got to other concentration and extermination camps about the tattoo rage at Buchenwald, demand for skins began to outrun the supply.

No one in the Buchenwald camp dared openly to criticize the commandant's lady. Those who were shocked by her conduct only whisper in bewilderment: "*Hexe*!" ("witch" or "sorceress"). She was the chief's wife, *nichtwahr*?

How can one explain this morbid behavior? Again, one can only turn for enlightenment to the behavioral scientists and their analysis of mental disease. Here was a classic case of an overpowering fetish, the tendency in human nature to aggrandize the virtue of one thing above all others. Those addicted to the worship begin to collect odd objects—old garters, toothbrushes, corsets, gloves, any one of a thousand things. It is conduct one expects in a theater of the absurd, not in normal human relations. There is apparently no end to eccentricities of the human mind. Slaughtering of prisoners for the sake of collecting their tattooed skins represents sadism carried well into the realm of insanity. Such aberrations would seem to have no place in civilized society.

Conditions at Buchenwald under the regime of Karl and Ilse Koch eventually became so bad that higher German officials began to become alarmed. Rumors about Buchenwald were spreading rapidly—and they were not at all favorable to National Socialist prestige. In 1941, top SS officers and authorities at Police Court XXII in Kassel decided to investigate the Koch administration at Buchenwald. Something had to be done to counter the increasing tales of corruption, brutality, and worse at the camp. It was a sensitive matter. Himmler, in his perverse way, regarded his SS as an honorable institution of moral rectitude dedicated to the safety of the German nation. He was concerned especially about rumors of bribes and financial irregularities at Buchenwald.

The investigation got nowhere. The commandant was even congratulated for his "fine work." The report stated that no unemployed lawyer would be allowed "to stretch the hangman's hands to grasp the white body of Koch." The man was a good National Socialist and he was doing an excellent job for his country. So much for the objective inquest.

There was just one concession to guilt. For a time the Kochs were transferred to another killing center. But they were soon back at Buchenwald to continue their interrupted tasks.

Again charges and recriminations. Commandant Koch was brought before an SS tribunal and accused of racketeering, insubordination, and murder, including the killing of an SS man. It was one thing to execute "Jews and other parasites," but it was too much when the victim wore the SS uniform. There were some suspicious developments in this case. A material witness scheduled to testify against Koch about conditions at Buchenwald was found murdered in his cell. Samples of chemicals found in the deceased man's body were fed forcibly to Soviet prisoners of war, all of whom died quickly.

This time Koch was unable to escape. Tried for brutal behavior in his post as commandant, he was found guilty, sentenced to death, and executed in early 1945. The verdict provided that he was to be given the choice of serving on the Eastern front, but Prince Waldeck, *SS* leader in the district, insisted on the death penalty.

Accomplice Ilse was arrested and tried along with her husband. She was acquitted on the charge of receiving stolen goods.

The damage at Buchenwald had already been done. When troops of the U.S. Eightieth Division entered the camp on April 10, 1945, they found it difficult to believe what they saw. Murder had been conducted on a mass production scale. Liberating troops saw weak, staggering, almost dead prisoners moving forward slowly to greet them. Some inmates, the excitement too much for their frail bodies, died on the spot. Carloads of unburied corpses lay throughout the compound. It was a nightmarish scene. CBS correspondent Edward R. Murrow described the liberation of Karl and Ilse Koch's Buchenwald:

We drove on, reached the main gate. The prisoners crowded up behind the wire. We entered.

And now let me tell you this in the first person, for I was the least important person there, as you can hear. There surged around me an evil-smelling crowd; men and boys reached out to touch me. They were in rags and the remnants of uniforms. Death had already marked many of them, but they were smiling under their eyes. I looked over that mass of men to the green hills, where well-fed Germans were ploughing.

As I walked down to the end of the barracks, there was applause from the men too weak to get out of bed. It sounded like the hand clapping of babies.

As I walked into the courtyard, a man fell dead. Two others, they must have been over sixty, were crawling towards the latrine. I saw it but will not describe it.

The children clung to my arms and stared. We crossed to the courtyard. Men kept coming up to speak to me . . .

professors from Poland, doctors from Vienna, men from all of Europe.

Most of the patients in the hospital could not move.

I asked the cause of death. A doctor shrugged and said: "Tuberculosis, starvation, fatigue, and there are those who have no desire to live."

I pray you to believe what I have said about Buchenwald. I reported what I saw and heard, but only part of it. For most of it I have no words.

Other reporters told similar stories about Buchenwald's gallows, torture chamber, dissection units, and laboratories where experiments were made on live prisoners. They described the area of the camp where inmates were allowed to starve to death. This was the domain of Karl and Ilse Koch, male and female angels of death. Both insisted in their courtroom appearances that they were merely soldiers doing their duty. Like other Nazis participating in mass executions, they saw themselves as loyal citizens implementing the laws of a sovereign state.

After the war Ilse Koch at first sank into obscurity. For two years she enjoyed freedom in the Federal Republic of West Germany. But there was retribution in the air of the new Germany. Sensitive to world public opinion, authorities of the Bonn Republic were dismayed by the record of the "Lady of Buchenwald." They arrested her and brought her to trial for crimes against German nationals. Ilse Koch was being tried by her own peers.

The trial of Ilse Koch attracted global attention. There was no way she could escape this time. She presented a spirited defense, but the evidence of her brutal conduct at Buchenwald was so damning that her guilt was established to the full satisfaction of the German court. Psychiatrists called to examine her described her before the court as "a perverted nymphomaniacal, hysterical, power-mad demon." The facts were overwhelming. On January 15, 1947, she was found guilty and sentenced to life imprisonment.

The condemned woman never ceased to protest her innocence. She appealed to the International Human Rights Commission and asked for protection of her rights. Ironic request from the lady who had showed little concern for the prerogatives of prisoners in the hell hole of Buchenwald.

Then came an extraordinary break for Ilse Koch. General Lucius D. Clay, military governor of the U.S. Zone during the occupation of Germany, reduced her sentence to four years. The decision aroused international controversy. Critics denounced the general's "lack of severity" in a case where guilt had been proved before a German court.

In prison Ilse finally gave up all hope. On September 1, 1967, at the age of sixty-one, she latched a bed sheet to the door of her cell in the Bavarian prison at Aichach and hanged herself.

In her last note to her son Uwe, born in prison in 1947, she wrote: "I cannot do otherwise. Death is the only deliverance."

17

AUSCHWITZ DOCTOR
JOSEF MENGELE

The Jews go through this door and out the chimney.
— *Josef Mengele*

The Hippocratic oath, ethical code or ideal, although in no sense a law, guided the practice of medicine for more than two thousand years. The legacy of an ancient Greek physician, it was a charter of medical conduct adopted as a pattern by doctors everywhere for many centuries:

> The regimen I shall adopt shall be for the benefit of my patients according to my ability and judgment, and not for their hurt or for any wrong. I shall give no deadly drug to any, though it be asked of me, nor will I counsel such. . . . Whatsoever house I enter, there I will go for the benefit of the sick, refraining from all wrongdoing or corruption.

But not in the land of the crooked cross.

The Hitler regime was notorious for its own kind of special medical science. Nazi doctors who practiced their profession in concentration and extermination camps, were not adjusted to the practice of healing as advised by the good Hippocrates. Without a thought on the well-being of their patients, they sent those inmates unable to work directly to gas ovens. They ordered elimination of anyone showing symptoms of typhus or other contagious diseases, and showed the same attitude toward those who had any contact with the terminally ill. Auschwitz physicians did not hesitate to inject poison or air into the veins of inmates. Like the camp commandant, those practitioners of Nazi medicine were themselves infected with germs of the obedience-syndrome.

Camp doctors were expected to carry out a special major task. It was their responsibility to meet incoming transport trains and examine the new prisoners. Their work was perfunctory and their decisions speedy. They sent prisoners able to work to one side and consigned the weaker ones to gas ovens. In addition, these doctors were expected to work in laboratories supplied with human beings instead of animals for experimentation. The callous sons of Hippocrates pursued such tests as heating and freezing of inmates, practices they regarded as contributions to scientific research.

Among Hitler's medicine men was Dr. Josef Mengele, head physician at Auschwitz, whose specialty was what he called the science of twins. The doctor's goal was the artificial creation of Aryan children distinguished by blond hair and fair features— the type favored by the *Fuehrer*. Mengele was known among camp inmates as "the collector of blue eyes."

Josef Mengele was born on March 16, 1911, in Günzburg, a quaint medieval town of some twelve thousand inhabitants on the banks of the Danube in Bavaria. His father founded the farm-machinery factory of Karl Mengele and Sons, an enterprise employing many townspeople. The family was noted both for its wealth and its public spirit. Soon after World War I the Mengele business acquired an interest in an assembly plant in Buenos Aires, Argentina. That move was to be of critical importance later for Dr. Mengele when he fled from prosecution after World War II.

Young Josef was regarded with pride by the Mengele clan. He showed promise as a student and much was expected of him. In the mid-1920s he went to Munich to study philosophy. There he was attracted by the racial ideology of Alfred Rosenberg, up-and-coming philosopher of the Nazi movement. He also met budding politician Hitler. He soon became a fanatical follower of the Nazi chieftain.

The young man was bothered by one annoying problem. Though he praised the Aryan "race," he, himself, was short, swarthy, and dark complexioned, just the opposite of the tall, blond Nordic superman he worshipped. Because he was often mistaken for a Gypsy, he developed a lifelong bitter hatred for the wandering, dark-skinned people. He was trapped by his physical appearance—and there was no way he could change it.

Mengele moved from Munich to Frankfurt-am-Main, where he attended the university and took a degree in medicine. He had a vague idea of combining interests in both philosophy and medicine. In common with Alfred Rosenberg's idea of racial superiority, he developed a theory that human beings, like dogs, had distinct pedigrees. This became the basis for his later experimentation designed to breed a race of Nordic-Aryan giants.

In the early months of World War II Mengele enlisted in the armed forces, for which he served in the *Waffen-SS* as an *Untersturmfuehrer* (2nd lieutenant). He was initially assigned to France as a medical officer and later to the Russian front. In 1943 he received an important promotion when Heinrich Himmler appointed him chief physician at extermination camp Auschwitz.

The deterioration of Auschwitz had already begun when Mengele was sent there to supervise its medical facilities. Situated on a marshy tract between the Vistula and tributary Sola, the camp was surrounded by stagnant and smelly ponds. Originally housing a military barracks, it was later the site of a tobacco factory. Under Commandant Rudolf Hoess, hundreds of thousands of prisoners were executed in this hell hole. Many others were allowed to starve to death.

Conditions in Auschwitz were chaotic. Inmates died of malnutrition and illnesses, including typhus, diarrhea, typhoid fever, and tuberculosis. It was a nightmare for any normal physician. There were sickening scenes in the compound. Prisoners, reacting like dogs, lapped up what little food they could find. Their only source of water was next to the latrines. They fought for a taste of water while their fellow sufferers sat in the latrines next to them. Hardened guards, including females, lashed out with clubs on the inmates. *SS* officers looked on with cold indifference.

Hannah Arendt denounced the grotesque behavior of *SS* guards at Auschwitz. These were no desk murderers, she wrote. Nor, with some exceptions, were they regime criminals who carried out orders. Rather, Arendt wrote, they were parasites and profiteers of a criminal system that made mass murder, the extermination of millions, a legal duty.

There were some chilling reports about conditions at Auschwitz:

—There was the case of the boy who knew that he would die. The lad wrote with his blood on the barracks wall: "Andreas Rappaport—lived sixteen years."

—There was the nine-year-old boy who felt that he knew a lot but "won't learn any more."

—There was Dr. Friedrich Boger, Mengele's colleague. A witness later testified that when he found a child eating an apple, Boger grabbed him by the leg, smashed the child's head against the wall, and calmly picked up the apple to eat it himself an hour later.

This was the atmosphere into which the good Dr. Mengele settled to do his stint for the glory of the Third Reich. Long forgotten was the normal physician's concern for people in trouble. He was now chief of a medical staff of ten men and they had a job to do.

Ten men. Ten doctors. Few were convinced Nazis or fanatical anti-Semites—except Mengele. Most had little taste for the work they were required to do. But they deemed it to their own best interest to obey. The authorities *(die Obrigkeit)* had issued orders, and it was their duty to do what they were told to do. Most of the ten, upset by their assignment, remained continually drunk.

But not Dr. Mengele. Eyewitnesses reported that he was always sober—even under the most horrifying conditions. He took delight in ending the lives of those he believed unfit to live under National Socialism. It was a pleasure to get rid of biologically impure Jews and Gypsies. Especially Gypsies. Why had an unkind fate given him a physical appearance so close to that of a people he scorned?

The man later described as a medical murderer was a stickler for neatness and cleanliness. He strode around the compound in immaculate uniform, carefully pressed, with shiny boots and white gloves. He had a habit of keeping his thumb in his pistol belt. His private office was impeccably clean. He could smile at an innocent while giving a lethal injection with a carefully disinfected syringe. He admired subordinate Dr. Vetter, who was known for his exquisite manner of handling patients before they were executed.

Spotless Mengele and his nine assistants were responsible for the selective process which meant the difference between life and death for prisoners. First came the Canada Detail,* composed of inmates trained to handle incoming prisoners. Meeting arriving transports, they searched the victims for booty. They also cleaned the filthy railroad wagons and then loaded them with anything of value taken from the prisoners. One report told how in February 1943 exactly 781 wagonloads filled with booty left Auschwitz for Germany; 245 were filled with clothing, others with human hair and gold fillings extracted from the mouths of executed prisoners.

After the work of the Canada Detail came the selective medical process. Dr. Mengele, anxious not to miss any important assignment, was always there day and night. He and assistants Drs. König, Thile, and Klein, among others, took part in this elaborate charade. Their main task was to select prisoners for the industrial machine. Those fit to work ("positive selection") were separated from those too weak or ill for manual labor. The scene was one of grotesque and ultimate cruelty. Victims were paraded before the doctors for instant decisions. In the spot selection "Right" meant work in the factories—and life itself. "Left" was the word of doom—removal to subcamp Birkenau and its gas ovens.

The prisoners chosen to go left were immediately deprived of their luggage. Then came separation of men and women. The unfortunates were led to an area where they could see great flames belching from chimneys and could smell the odor of what was called the "bakery." Some believed the large sign: "WASH AND DISINFECTING ROOMS." Guards who collected clothing and valuables always gave careful receipts. Women had their

---

*"Canada Detail" was the term used by guards to describe those inmates assigned to manage incoming prisoners. The detail confiscated all booty and took it to a building called "Canada." From there it was sent back to Germany.

hair cut off. The irregular lines were then led to the "disinfecting rooms."

Inmates throughout the camp were terrified of Dr. Mengele and his small band of killer-physicians. An eyewitness later recalled that in October 1944 Mengele, leading the selective process with other officers, came to Barracks 11, where presumably healthy Jewish children between the ages of sixteen and eighteen were housed. "They probably sensed what they were in for and dispersed. Thereupon the camp leader rounded them up like dogs. That happened on a Jewish holiday. After two days vans came, and the boys were put in the vans and taken to the gas chambers. This was done amidst laughter. They were probably amazed because these children cried out for their mothers."

Other witnesses gave additional details about Mengele's behavior at Auschwitz. Hermann Langbehn, a Viennese, later general secretary of the International Auschwitz Committee, worked there as a clerk. He told how Mengele and other camp officials kept precise records: day and night, in shifts at seven typewriters, clerks filled out forms with notations of day and hour of death on file cards. Records were considered to be far more important than lives.

Nazi hunter Simon Wiesenthal interviewed Langbehn about Mengele's work at Auschwitz: "Langbehn told me that once Mengele came into the children's block at Auschwitz to measure the boys' height. He became very angry when he found many of them too small for their age. He made the boys stand against a doorpost marked with nails for each group. If the boy's head did not reach the proper nail, Mengele gave a sign with his riding crop. The child was taken away to the gas chambers. More than a thousand children were murdered at that time."

The very sight of Gypsies aroused Mengele to fury. He decided eventually to liquidate the entire Gypsy compound. What happened was described by seventy-one-year-old Maximilian Sternol, who testified at a postwar trial: "On the night of July 31, 1944, there were terrible scenes at the Gypsy compound. Women and children were on their knees before Mengele and Boger, crying 'Take pity on us, take pity on us!' Nothing helped. They were beaten down, brutally trampled upon, and pushed into the trucks. It was a terrible, gruesome sight."

Mengele had his own special solutions for camp problems. When he came to Auschwitz, he found six hundred sick women

in 180 beds in the hospital barracks. Most were plagued with
lice, carriers of typhus. Mengele did not hesitate. He met the
problem by gassing the entire block. He then disinfected the
area, put in a bathtub, and allowed inmates of an adjoining block
to bathe there.

Some charges against Mengele seem incredible. One witness
informed Wiesenthal that he had seen the doctor throw a baby
alive into a fire. Another swore that Mengele killed a fourteen-
year-old girl with a bayonet.

Mengele kept himself busy at Auschwitz with his own race
purification program. He would win the *Fuehrer*'s eternal gratitude by his work in promoting a race of biologically superior
Nordic men and women. Collecting corpses of what he called
subhumans, he sent them to the Institute for Racial Biology in
Berlin for further examination. Most important for him was his
specialty of medical experimentation on twins to find a means
of multiplying the population of the German nation. He was
accused of supervising an operation by which two Gypsy children were sewn together to create Siamese twins. The purpose
of the procedure was not entirely clear. Its only result was said
to be that the hands of the children became badly infected where
their veins had been resected.

With these and other reports it is easy to see why Mengele
became one of the most wanted Nazis in the postwar period.
For Nazi-hunter Simon Wiesenthal, capturing the Auschwitz
doctor became a matter of major importance. In his memoirs,
The Murderers Among Us (New York: McGraw-Hill, 1967),
Wiesenthal described his unsuccessful search for Mengele. The
amateur detective, motivated by those four years he had spent in
Hitler's concentration camps, was angered by the evidence he
had accumulated about Mengele's conduct at Auschwitz. He began a search to bring the doctor to justice.

Using skills he had learned in tracking other Nazis, Wiesenthal found that at the end of the war Mengele had gone home to
Günzburg. Here, Mengele's relatives and friends, unaware of his
ghastly work at Auschwitz, greeted him as a returned war hero.
The doctor had done his duty for his country. Although Günzburg was in the U.S. Zone of Occupation, American authorities
apparently knew nothing about Mengele's record.

For five years Mengele remained in the old Bavarian town. He
made occasional visits to nearby Munich. Then his name began

to emerge again and again during trials of Nazis for war crimes. Testimony taken at these trials revealed much about his activities at Auschwitz.

By this time Mengele thought it expedient to disappear. Like other wanted Nazis, he turned to ODESSA, the secret escape organization of the *SS* underground, a clandestine travel bureau set up to enable former *SS* officers to avoid arrest by the Allies. The most favored terminal point was Buenos Aires in Argentina. The usual escape route was Italy-Spain-South America.

In 1952 Mengele, fortified with a set of false identity papers, arrived in Buenos Aires. Posing as Dr. Friedrich Edler von Breitenbach, he set up a practice as a physician-without-license. He was not especially worried because he was on good terms with dictator Perón's police. Later, he assumed a large number of pseudonyms, including Helmut Gregor-Gregori, Fausto Rindon, José Aspiazi, Sebastian Alvez, Walter Hŭsek, Heinz Stobert, Fritz Fischer, and Lars Balistroem. He was advised by ODESSA officials to change his identity as often as possible. He hoped to sink into anonymity and escape the vengeance of those who had not forgotten what he had done at Auschwitz.

There was danger in the air for Mengele. When Perón was overthrown and went into exile in September 1955, Mengele and many of his Nazi comrades began to fear for their own safety. The once easily-bribed Argentine authorities were now gone; there were problems about remaining in the country. Most Nazis residing in Buenos Aires began moving to Paraguay, especially to capital city Asunción. Mengele was among them. Finding it dangerous to practice medicine illegally, he, instead, took over management of his family's local business office.

Meanwhile, Mengele's work at Auschwitz was being fully documented in German courts. Authorities of the Federal Republic, sensitive to its reputation, offered a reward of 60,000 marks (at that time worth about $16,000) for his capture. Nazi-hunter Wiesenthal, never forgetting the search for Mengele, urged Bonn authorities to demand extradition. The German officials were willing to bring him back for trial. Early in January 1960 an urgent request was sent from Bonn to Argentina for Mengele's extradition.

The German Embassy in Buenos Aires was told to pursue the matter. It soon ran into a stone wall. The Argentine *Procurador de la Nación* informed embassy officials that Mengele's offenses were political rather than criminal. Admittedly, he said, the evidence against the doctor was impressive, but it was not his place to overcome the psychological attitude throughout South America, which made extradition virtually impossible. Mengele, after all, was a "guest," and even though he had a dark past it was not in the interest of Argentina to grant the request. Faced with this tortuous reasoning, the German officials gave up in disgust.

Meanwhile, Mengele returned to Paraguay where, aided by influential friends, he managed to obtain Paraguayan citizenship. He disappeared in Bariloche, a resort in the lake district of the Andes, where many wealthy Nazis had settled on large estates. The area, close to the borders of Chile, provided means for a further escape in case of necessity.

Authorities in Argentina belatedly took additional interest in Mengele. In June 1960 they issued a warrant for his arrest. It was too late. The doctor-on-the-run moved into Brazil. Once again he disappeared.

From Brazil, Mengele fled to Cairo and then to a Greek island. Again he returned to the safe haven in Paraguay, whose authorities notified Bonn that he was a citizen "with no criminal record." All efforts to obtain his extradition to Germany were unsuccessful. Paraguay's President, General Alfredo Stroessner, threatened to break off diplomatic relations with the Federal Republic of West Germany if it persisted in its efforts for Mengele's extradition.

There was a complicating factor for the Paraguayan government. It was interested in obtaining a three-million dollar development loan from Bonn. Hence, it decided to delay a decision on Mengele. He was isolated in a heavily guarded area of eastern Paraguay, where no foreigners were permitted. Interpol, the international police agency, indicated that it would like to get its hands on Mengele, but Paraguay was not a member of that organization.

The wanted doctor had escaped retribution from both the Bonn Republic and Israel, but he was not altogether a free man. Wiesenthal described Mengele's life in Paraguay in recent years:

Mengele now lives as a virtual prisoner in the restricted military zone between Puerto San Vincente on the Asunció-Sao Paolo highway and the border fortress of Carlos Antonio López on the Paraná River. Here he occupies a small white shed in a jungle area cleared by German settlers. Only two roads lead to the secluded house. Both are patrolled by Portuguese soldiers and police, who have strict orders to stop all cars and shoot all trespassers. And just in case the police should slip up, there are four heavily armed private bodyguards with radios and walkie-talkies. Mengele pays for them himself.

Despite Wiesenthal's report, Paraguayan authorities continued to deny that they knew of Mengele's whereabouts. The Minister of the Interior and the head of the Supreme Court asserted that he could not be found. In late February 1984 a criminal judge in Asunción, Anselmo Aveiro, reissued a 22-year-old order for the arrest of the Nazi fugitive.

Another Nazi pursuer joined the hunt. *The New York Times* reported on February 23, 1984, about the efforts of a West German woman to find Mengele:

Beate Klarsfeld, a pursuer of Nazis, who recently went to South America to campaign against sanctuary for war criminals, said yesterday in New York that Paraguayan officials had assured her they would arrest and deport Josef Mengele, the former Austrian doctor, if they could find him. . . .

Mrs. Klarsfeld said that it was the first such assurance from the Paraguayan government, which she said had protected the Nazi fugitive since his arrival from Argentina in 1960. Survivors say Dr. Mengele conducted medical experiments at Auschwitz and selected new arrivals to be put to death in the gas chambers.

In a letter to *The New York Times* dated February 24, 1984, Nazi-hunter Wiesenthal told of his frustration in the task of finding his elusive quarry:

With reference to the matter of Dr. Josef Mengele, I might add that in 1979 I managed, with the help of then U.N. Secretary General Kurt Waldheim as well as a number of U.S. senators, to persuade the Paraguayan Government to revoke Dr. Mengele's citizenship and to issue an arrest order.

On Jan. 5, 1983, people working with me in South America found out that Mengele was in Philadelphia, Paraguay, a Mennonite village. I immediately asked my colleagues to contact the Paraguayan police to check whether Mengele was really on their wanted list.

A police agent did indeed accompany my colleagues in Philadelphia, prepared to arrest Mengele, but unfortunately they arrived five days too late—Mengele had left on Dec. 31, 1982.

The search for Mengele was yielding no results. In 1979, under pressure from abroad, the Paraguyan Supreme Court had stripped him of his citizenship. That year one report had it that he had flown from Asunción to Miami. From 1981 to 1985 checks on his whereabouts were made in Miami, West Germany, as well as in Paraguay, Chile, Brazil, Ecuador, Bolivia, Uruguay, Australia, and other countries. No success.

Late Bulletins, 1985

London (United Press International, Feb. 11, 1985.) Nazi death camp doctor Josef Mengele lives "fairly openly" in Paraguay, where he is guarded by the military and divides his time between a jungle hotel and a log cabin, it was reported yesterday.

The Sunday Times said its information came from Domingo Laino, a leading Paraguayan political exile living in Argentina, and from a senior diplomat at the Israeli Embassy in Buenos Aires.

Meanwhile, an Israeli Nazi hunter was quoted on Israel radio as saying he had received information that Mengele was serving as Paraguayan president Alfredo Stroessner's personal physician.

Hamburg (Deutsche Allgemeines Sonntagsblatt, March 3, 1985). Since the beginning of last month the Hesse Land government has offered DM 1,000,000 for information leading to Mengele's arrest. In the United States a million dollar reward also is on his head.

New York (The New York Times, May 8, 1985). Tel Aviv, May 7. Israel offered a $1 million reward for the capture of Josef Mengele, the notorious concentration camp doctor.

The offer brings to $3.4 million the total reward money put up for seizure of the longtime fugitive.

Washington (Special to The New York Times, May 27, 1985). United States marshals [*who*] routinely track fugitives wanted by the Justice Department, have been assigned a fugitive case that possesses unusual problems. The target, Josef Mengele, the infamous Nazi death-camp doctor, has been hunted for more than four decades, and it is not even clear that he is still living.

Embu, Brazil (The New York Post Wire Services, June 7, 1985). Gravediggers yesterday smashed open a coffin that investigators believe may contain the body of the Nazi ''Angel of Death'' Dr. Josef Mengele, the world's most wanted fugitive.

Sao Paulo, Brazil (Associated Press, June 8, 1985). Coroners yesterday began cleaning the bones unearthed in a nearby town to determine whether they belong to Josef Mengele, the infamous Angel of Death in the Nazi concentration camp at Auschwitz.

Time, July 1, 1985. The 16 forensic experts (six of them American) who have been examining the skeletal remains announced their unanimous conclusion: ''The skeleton is that of Josef Mengele ''within a reasonable scientific certainty.'' Later, the Americans reported that they had ''absolutely no doubt'' of their findings.

The extraordinary search for Josef Mengele was supposed to have ended in this way. But serious doubts still existed as to whether the bones and teeth really were the remains of the notorious camp doctor. Some observers believe that it was useless to keep hunting for the old man who once ran Hitler's murder machine. The evil empire lay buried and its former servants now posed no further threat. Even if the barbarous Angel of Death were still alive, they say, it is as a reclusive fugitive.

Others disagree. It does matter, they insist, that the escaped murderer be traced down. To shrug him off as a harmless old man would be to condone his crimes and to evade the world's debt to his victims. The man was an example of the indifferent boorishness that was the public face of Nazism. This point of view remains—the butchers must be hunted to the end of their days.

18

QUACK DOCTOR
THEODOR MORELL

If Hitler had to deliver a speech on a cold or rainy day, he would have [Morell's] injections tho day before, the day of the speech, and the day after. The normal resistance of the body was thus gradually replaced by an artificial medium.
                                                    —Dr. Karl Brandt

In addition to Auschwitz Doctor Josef Mengele there were other rotten apples in the barrel of Nazi medicine. Hitler's favorite physician, Dr. Theodor Morell, was one of them. Fat and gross, cringing in manner, inarticulate in speech, he managed to include among his patients the top and lesser gods of Nazidom. Not all of them were impressed with "Dr. Feel Good." Hermann Goering, No. 2 Nazi, who knew something of drugs himself, sarcastically called him "Herr Reich Injection Master."

For years the corpulent court physician fed Hitler drug after drug which served to impair an already damaged mind and body. Among the thirty or more drugs he administered to his patient were these dozen:

1. *Orchikrin*: extract of the seminal testicles and prostrates of young bulls, reinforced male hormone, to promote potency and combat exhaustion.

2. *Brom-Nervacit*: potassium bromide, sodium barbitone, aminopyrinen, as tranquilizer and hypnotic.

3. *Chamomile*: for enemas.

4. *Mutaflor*: for symptoms connected with abnormal intestinal flora.

5. *Sympatol* (p-hydroxyphenyl methylamino ethanol tartrate), to promote cardiac activity.

6. *Eupaverin*: for spasms and colic.

7. *Glyconorm*: metabolic enzymes, to ease digestion of vegetable foods and reduce flatulence.

8. *Septoid*: for respiratory infections and slowdown of arteriosclerosis.

9. *Luizym*: enzyme preparation, to combat digestive weakness.

10. *Omnadin*: combination of proteins, lipoids from the bile, and animal fat, to ward off colds.

11. *Intelan*: vitamins, to stimulate appetite.

12. *Eukadol*: chlorohydrate of dyhydroxycodeine, narcotic and anti-spasmodic.

For the hypochondriacal *Fuehrer*, Morell was a medical magician. "Go see him," he urged Eva Braun, his mistress and future bride-for-a-day. Always the obedient *Mädchen*, she consulted the doctor who had won the confidence of her lord and master. Morell tried in vain to diagnose Eva's complaint. In reality, she was in good health and did not even suffer from headaches during her monthly period. But her adored one had spoken and his word was law.

Eva found the doctor disgustingly dirty. "His office was like a pig sty," she complained. She would never let him treat her again.

But not Hitler. For him the doctor-with-the-dirty-fingernails represented the staff of life. All day long he swallowed or sucked on brightly colored pills supplied him by his faithful physician. He felt that he could not live without Morell's injections. The doctor, he told those in his intimate circle, was simply a genius, a superman, who unlike other members of the medical profession, knew exactly what ailed his patients and how to treat them.

Hitler's obedient yes-men, always anxious to remain on his good side, went to Dr. Morell because of the *Fuehrer's* glowing recommendation. They submitted themselves willingly to his regimen of drugs and vitamins. They made it a point to report back to Hitler about his marvelous doctor—just the right words the *Fuehrer* wanted to hear. Calls to Dr. Morell became fashionable for leading Nazis and their wives. After all, the demigod of Berchtesgaden made no mistakes.

Little is known about Morell's early life. After obtaining a medical degree, he began to take long voyages as a ship's doctor. He made it plain to all who would listen that he had studied under the great Russian bacteriologist Ilya Mechnikov, professor at the Pasteur Institute and Nobel Prize winner. From Mechnikov, Morell said, he had learned the secrets of combatting bacterial infection. It was effective publicity.

Meanwhile, Morell dedicated himself to the art of making money. After practicing medicine in Munich for a time, he came to Berlin and opened an office on the Kurfürstendamm, the smart, centrally located street located near the Gedächtniskirche. A sign at the entrance to his office read: DR. THEODOR MORELL, SKIN AND VENEREAL DISEASES. On the walls of his waiting room were displayed inscribed photographs of famous film stars, actors, and actresses he had treated. He quickly built up a lucrative practice in his Berlin office. Characteristically, he was partial to the treatment of wealthy and important patients, including the former German Crown Prince. Many came to him for nervous complaints—he knew how to handle these fidgety patients. Word got around among the Nazi brass that here was a great doctor, one who had Hitler's confidence and who miraculously could cure their illnesses.

The money-conscious doctor found other profitable sources of income. He discovered a powder that could be used to rid German soldiers of fleas and other troublesome vermin. Later, with Hitler's approbation, "Dr. Morell's Flea Powder" would be used extensively in the armed forces. One word from on high and the way to wealth was open.

Morell was fortunate in the way he came to Hitler's attention. In 1935 Heinrich Hoffmann, the *Fuehrer's* favorite court photographer, became seriously ill. He came to Morell, who used sulfonamides to cure him. Among Hoffmann's assistants was a young girl named Eva Braun (who privately called her boss "the mad drunkard"). Hoffmann told Eva about what the wonderful Dr. Morell had done for him. Eva's mother, too, was Morell's patient. Through mother and daughter the doctor managed to get an invitation to Berchtesgaden. Eva would later change her mind about Morell.

That was all the ambitious medic needed. Thus began a relationship between patient and doctor that was to last until Hitler's final days in the Berlin bunker.

Status of the *Fuehrer's* health? Experts do not agree. Some conclusions have merit, others are shrouded in mystery.

According to psychohistorian Rudolph Binion, Hitler was a self-punitive hypochondriac throughout his life. From his early days as an unfulfilled artist to the dark nights when he was a louse-ridden tramp in Vienna to the final days below the Berlin Chancellery, Hitler suffered from severe stomach pains. He was said to believe that his lifelong case of excess stomach gas was due to cancer and that he would die of that disease.

Other historians, including biographer Alan Bullock, mention reports that Hitler had contracted syphilis while a young man in Vienna. This rumor was passed on by Ernst Hanfstängl, Hitler's court jester in the early days of the Nazi movement. Bullock admits that this may well have been malicious gossip, but also points out that medical specialists believe Hitler's later symptoms, psychological as well as physical, may well have been those of a man suffering from the tertiary stage of syphilis. In his autobiography, *Mein Kampf,* Hitler wrote emotionally about "the scourge of syphilis." This is not evidence, of course, that he, himself, was a victim of the disease. The issue remains unresolved.

Hitler's health suffered a severe setback in World War I. On October 13, 1918, while serving as a lance corporal, he was caught in a heavy British gas attack during the Battle of Ypres. "I stumbled back with burning eyes, taking with me my last report of the war. A few hours later, my eyes had turned to glowing coals; it had grown dark around me." He was cured after hospitalization. From then on he often expressed annoyance about his watery eyes.

There was an outburst of Hitler's psychogenic behavior during the unsuccessful Beer-Hall *Putsch* at Munich on November 8–9, 1923. When he saw the police fire on his followers, his left arm began to tremble and the movement of his forearm began to become constricted. Perhaps the sudden death of sixteen of his comrades on that fateful march may have contributed in part to his psychological reaction.

During his string of victories in the early stages of World War II, Hitler remained in comparatively good health. But there were repercussions—the strain of conducting campaigns, as well as the later defeats, took a toll on his health. He complained of bouts of giddiness. "I noted," wrote Dr. Goebbels in his *Diaries*, "that he was already becoming quite gray and that merely talking about the cares of winter makes him seem to have aged very much."

As news from the war fronts grew ever worse, Hitler began to give way to outbursts of hysteria, invariably accompanied by trembling of hands and feet. General Heinz Guderian described what seemed to be bouts of animal rage:

> His fist raised, his cheeks flushed with rage, his whole body trembling, the man stood there in front of me, beside himself with fury and having lost all control. After each outburst Hitler would stride up and down the carpet edge, then suddenly stop immediately before me and hurl his next accusation in my face. He was almost screaming, his eyes seemed to pop out of his head and the veins stood out in his temple.

By the time he had retired to his Berlin bunker, Hitler was a physical wreck. His health deteriorated rapidly in the cramped quarters as he faced his *Götterdämmerung*. His head wobbled, his left arm hung slackly by his side, his face gave the impression of total exhaustion. Apparently, the effects of the bomb blast on the July 20, 1944, attempt on his life were much more serious than he had thought. There were also evidences of increasing senility.

Was the man insane? Experts in the behavioral sciences differ in responses to this key question. Some are convinced that he suffered from several kinds of insanity. Most believe that he was highly neurotic but not actually insane. They see his character and personality as molded in his early years by an accumulation of frustrations, hostility, and hatreds, all of which contributed to growing neuroses. But they are not convinced that he had moved over the line between neurosis and insanity.

British historian Hugh R. Trevor-Roper caught the quality of

Hitler's mind in a classic one-sentence analysis: "A terrible phenomenon, imposing indeed in its granite harshness and yet infinitely squalid in its miscellaneous cumber—like some huge barbarian monolith, the expression of giant strength and savage genius, surrounded by a festering heap of refuse—old tins and dead vermin, ashes and eggshells and ordure—the intellectual detritus of centuries."

This was the man to whom the Germans entrusted their destiny as a nation. It was also the hypochondriacal patient who came to Dr. Theodor Morell, "Specialist in Skin and Venereal Diseases," for help in conquering his many complaints.

At the time when Eva Braun recommended Dr. Morell, Hitler was having his usual intestinal trouble as well as an annoying foot rash. The physician gave his patient a thorough examination. Diagnosis—the *Fuehrer* was suffering from complete exhaustion of intestinal flora. That, Morell informed his patient, was at the root of his trouble. Replace the lost bacteria and all symptoms would fade away.

This gave the doctor an opportunity to inject his own product called "Multiflor," composed of intestinal bacteria derived from the best stock of animals owned by Bulgarian peasants. This was followed by a restorative process consisting of varied pills and injections of hormones, vitamins, phosphorus, dextrose, and many other drugs.

Eureka! Within a few days Hitler's foot rash vanished. In a matter of weeks the crippling stomach pains disappeared.

Hitler was ecstatic. He had found a true medical genius. "Nobody has ever told me before, so clearly and precisely, exactly what was wrong with me. His method of cure is so logical that I have the greatest confidence in him. I shall follow his prescriptions to the letter."

And follow the doctor he did. From then on, Morell was Hitler's revered medicine man. Now at long last the *Fuehrer* could eat the heavy Viennese chocolate cakes he craved and not be subject to those damnable gastritis attacks. "How lucky," he said, "I was to meet Morell. He has saved my life. Just great the way he has treated me."

The doctor, too, was delighted. At last he had found the open sesame to riches. To be in the *Fuehrer's* good graces was money in the bank for any doctor. Now Morell could have his pick of patients of substance among top Nazi officials. When word got around that Morell enjoyed the complete confidence of the *Fuehrer*, leading Nazis vied with one another for the doctor's attention. The matter was simple—when in Berlin do as Hitler does. Hence, the parade to the Kurfürstendamm office of the successful doctor.

Hitler praised Morell to all who listened. He refused to allow any criticism of the doctor. No matter how slight the ailment of a colleague or one of his secretaries, he or she was urged to seek an appointment with the great physician.

Even Albert Speer, Hitler's architect, although he had some reservations, decided to see Morell at the urging of the *Fuehrer*. Like others in the charmed circle, Speer was careful not to offend the master. He told about it in his memoirs:

> In 1936, when my circulation and stomach rebelled against an irrational working rhythm and adjustment to Hitler's abnormal habits, I called at Morell's private office. . . . After a superficial examination, Morell prescribed for me his intestinal bacteria, dextrose, vitamins, and hormone tablets.
>
> For safety's sake I afterward had a thorough examination by Professor von Bergmann, the specialist in internal medicine at Berlin University. I was not suffering from any organic trouble, he concluded, but only from nervous symptoms caused by overwork.
>
> I slowed down my pace as best I could and the symptoms abated. To avoid offending Hitler I pretended that I was carefully following Morell's instructions, and since my health improved, I became for a time Morell's showpiece.

Others in Nazi officialdom were not quite as considerate of the *Fuehrer's* feelings. Goering joked in public about the Third Reich's injection specialist. His sarcastic remarks goaded Morell to outbursts of anger. Others ridiculed the doctor's use of bulls' testicles as well as his official flea powder. But the criticism was limited to areas away from Hitler's ears. There could be trouble for those who spoke against the master's medical specialist.

Other doctors, including those who also served Hitler, were

appalled by Morell's methods of treatment. Judging his unusual ministration to be risky, they warned about the dangers of addiction. They were right—Morell's injections for the *Fuehrer* had to be given more and more frequently. There was little indication that the treatment was working. Morell's rivals were skeptical of his chemicals and plants, which, they said, were tainting Hitler's bloodstream. But those doctors who dared hint about their reservations to Hitler were summarily dismissed. When an ear specialist tested the pills Morell was giving Hitler, he confirmed that the patient was being poisoned. He and two colleagues were straightway denied access to the *Fuehrer*'s presence. Hitler was adamant: "You can say what you will about Morell. He is and remains my only personal physician, and I have full confidence in him."

Meanwhile, Hitler's symptoms were becoming even more alarming. His skin was more and more discolored. Unconcerned, Morell continued his regime of drugs and more drugs. Let his jealous colleagues rant and rave and criticize. He, not they, had the patient's confidence.

Despite the many drugs he forced upon Hitler, Morell was never quite convinced that his patient was seriously ill. "In reality," he told another doctor, "Hitler has never been ill." The trouble, he said, was psychogenic. This was a case of hypochondria, he asserted, which he was forced to treat with drugs because Hitler wanted them.

The doctor did not always satisfy his unruly patient. There was the case of the unused mushrooms. At Berchtesgaden, Hitler's aides constructed a large greenhouse specifically for the purpose of raising mushrooms. The project was costly. The reason: Dr. Morell had suggested that a mushroom diet might be a good thing for his patient. But the *Fuehrer*, fearing that he might be poisoned, refused to touch mushrooms. Scrapped—one expensive unused greenhouse.

Morell was much concerned about his rivalry with Dr. Karl Brandt, who at one time had been Hitler's personal physician and who was retained along with other doctors. In August 1933, Brandt, then aged twenty-nine, had been summoned to Upper Silesia to treat Hitler's niece and his adjutant, Wilhelm Bruckner, both of whom had been injured in an automobile accident. The young doctor made so favorable an impression that he was invited to join the *Fuehrer's* personal staff. By the next year he

was a permanent member of Hitler's Obersalzberg circle. Eventually, he was given the rank of major-general in the *Waffen-SS*,
and despite his limited experience he was appointed Reich Commissioner for Health and Sanitation.

Brandt and Morell were soon locked in competition for
Hitler's favor. Though both remained with him until the final
days in the Berlin bunker, they were always at odds on the
matter of medical treatment. There were mutual recriminations: Morell criticized Brandt's ability and Brandt responded with angry denunciations of his rival's drugs and
vitamins. There was real danger, Brandt warned, that Morell
was systematically poisoning his patient. Hitler rejected
Brandt's advice. As always, the *Fuehrer* used his special
brand of divide-and-rule in dealing with competitive subordinates. The battle between the two doctors would later come
to a head in the Berlin bunker.

Morell was at Hitler's side on important occasions. One of
them took place in March 1939 when the independent state of
Czechoslovakia was proclaimed under German protection. Faced
with the disintegration of his country, President Emil Hácha
made the fatal mistake of asking for a personal meeting with
Hitler. Summoned to Berlin, the old man was brought into the
Fuehrer's presence. Hitler went into a hysterical rage. The
Czechs must surrender immediately, he shouted. His patience
was at an end. Hácha must sign the surrender document or the
German army would march.

Stunned, Hácha sat as if turned to stone. He protested weakly
against the outrage. Talked down by Goering and Ribbentrop,
he fainted.

Morell was in the wings for just such an emergency. Goering
called him in and ordered him to give Hácha an injection. Ironic
twist—Goering had only contempt for the doctor. It was a grisly
scene as Morell fussed over the old man. The injection may well
have paralyzed Hácha, who had just enough strength to sign the
fatal document. He had been browbeaten into turning his country into a German protectorate. A triumphant Hitler proclaimed
himself Protector of Bohemia and Moravia. He also "accepted"
the new status for Slovakia. Simultaneously, the German army
entered Prague. Czechoslovakia ceased to exist as an independent state.

Morell was also on stand-by service at critical moments in

Hitler's personal life. One had to do with an embarrassing sequence of events concerning a blond, blue-eyed English girl, the very model of Hitler's craze for Nordics. Unity Valkyrie Mitford, one of the aristocratic Redesdale girls, all of whom led a turbulent life, fell hopelessly in love with Hitler. The *Fuehrer* was flattered by the attentions of the English *Mädchen*. For reasons of state he at first encouraged her or at least gave that impression.

Then tragedy. On September 3, 1939, Unity Mitford was found slumped over as if asleep on a bench in the *Englischer Garten* in the middle of Munich. She had fired several bullets into herself, and one of them still in her skull had paralyzed her whole nervous system. She was in desperate condition.

Shocked and concerned, Hitler ordered that the English girl be attended by the best doctors, among whom he included Dr. Morell. She was given a luxurious room in a clinic at government expense. For months she lay in a coma, without speaking or recognizing anyone. Hitler ordered Eva Braun to send her flowers, a request that must have aroused considerable resentment in his young mistress. He also charged Morell with taking part in all consultations on the condition of the English girl.

Then Hitler decided to send the critically ill Unity back to her parents in England. The bullet was still lodged in her head when she was taken to Switzerland on April 16, 1940. Morell was there to make all medical arrangements for the trip. Unity survived, unmarried, until May 28, 1948. On her grave was placed a stone reading: "Unity Valkyrie Mitford. Say not the struggle nought availeth."

Throughout World War II Morell continued his service for Hitler and his circle. There was much psychic illness among leading Nazis as it became increasingly clear that the war was not going to be won. The doctor was so busy that he even made diagnoses by telephone. Albert Speer told how in early 1944 he became desperately ill of what his own physicians described as muscular rheumatism. Dissatisfied with the treatment by Dr. Karl Gebhart and suspecting a pulmonary embolism, he decided to consult Dr. Friedrich Koch, a well-known internist at Berlin University.

Once again Speer accidentally became involved with Morell, for whom he had little regard. Dr. Gebhart, annoyed by Speer's action in turning to another doctor, tried to force Dr. Koch out of the case by contacting Dr. Morell. He invited Morell to a consultation. Morell replied that he was too busy and could not be spared from other duties, but he asked to have the case described by telephone. "Sight unseen," Speer wrote, "Morell prescribed vitamin K injections to stop me from spitting blood. Dr. Koch rejected this suggestion and a few weeks later he described Morell as a total incompetent."

Speer recovered without the use of Morell's telephoned prescription.

In the Berlin bunker all was chaos and Morell contributed to it. The burly doctor hustled busily in and out of cramped quarters administering his pills and injections to increasingly hysterical patients. The atmosphere was psychologically oppressive. Incessant air raids, added to deadly fear of the Russians, led to nervous exhaustion and despair among the trapped Nazis. More work for Morell.

The *Fuehrer*, himself, was in a badly weakened condition. He was hit hard by one military shock after another as the situation deteriorated—defeats in Africa and the Mediterranean, retreat in Russia, failure to halt the Normandy invasion, resistance movements, the stalled Ardennes offensive. These setbacks, plus the attempt on his life on July 20, 1944, left scars on Hitler. His health was undermined by Morell's flow of drugs. His face became pallid, his hands shook, his eyes were clouded and lifeless. An overstrained life and Morell's nostrums were taking a heavy toll.

A bitter medical battle continued in this dank atmosphere. Morell and Brandt confronted one another in mutual recriminations in a struggle for Hitler's confidence even at this late date. On April 16, 1945, Hitler was told that Brandt had left his wife and child in Thuringia in an area where they could give themselves up to the advancing Americans. Enraged by the news, Hitler called for a summary court-martial to try Brandt on a charge of treason. Brandt, he said, instead of sending his wife to Berchtesgaden as ordered, had tried to use her as a courier for secret documents intended for the Americans.

The court-martial condemned Brandt to death. He was brought to a villa in West Berlin, but his life was saved by Heinrich Himmler, who stalled the execution by calling for new evidence.

Morell was clearly the victor in the battle of doctors in the Berlin bunker. Brandt did not escape Allied vigilance. One of the main defendants in the trial of twenty-three *SS* physicians and scientists in Nuremberg after the war in what was called the Doctors' Trial, he was sentenced to death and hanged on June 2, 1948. His last words before the black hood was placed over his head: "It is no shame to stand upon this scaffold. I have served my Fatherland as others before me."

Meanwhile, triumphant Morell was again No. 1 doctor in the bunker. He treated Goebbels, now pale and sunken, his temples graying, living almost exclusively on brandy and cigarettes. He could do little for the Propaganda Minister. But the caring doctor gave Frau Magda Goebbels a quick-acting poison for herself and her children.

Eva Braun remained antagonistic. Following Hitler around the gloomy rooms, she was worried because he seemed to be transformed into a living ghost. "Morell is poisoning you," she warned. "Don't take any more of his medicines." The *Fuehrer*, frustrated and resigned, paid no attention.

On April 20, with the Russians surging into Berlin, there was a general exodus from the bunker. Among those who fled were Ribbentrop, Hitler's adjutants, his two stenographers, two of his four secretaries, and Morell. "I don't need drugs to see me through"—those were Hitler's last words to his doctor.

After the war, Morell was arrested and placed in an American internment camp. The medic who with supreme confidence had pressed his assortment of nostrums upon his patients could not help himself. His health deteriorated rapidly. Liberated but paralyzed, he died miserably at Tagernsee in May 1948.

Morell becomes eligible for this collection of Nazi rascals primarily because of the way he practiced medicine and because of his acceptance into Hitler's inner circle. Unlike Dr. Josef Mengele, Auschwitz's "angel of extermination," Morell was not guilty of performing outrageous medical experiments on helpless prisoners. Nor was he guilty, as were other criminal doctors, of complicity in the joint murder of thousands of concentration camp inmates. But in his medical practice he showed himself to be an inadequate, careless scamp, a doctor motivated by the greed of a slick confidence man. He was more quack doctor than professional physician. At one point in his career he claimed to be the true discoverer of penicillin. He complained that his secret had been stolen from him by the British Secret Service.

19

OTTO SKORZENY: SOLDIER OF FORTUNE

*I knew my friend Adolf Hitler would not leave me in the
lurch.*

—Benito Mussolini

He was a giant of a man, all of six-feet-four inches tall. His
comrades knew him as "Scarface." The most publicized adventurer in the Third Reich, he managed to win national fame in
the Third Reich as well as global attention because of his exploits. Delighted Germans saw him as a Teutonic swashbuckler
capable of the most outrageous conduct. For his countrymen he
was a swaggering, blustering, fighting man but a genuine patriot; for his enemies he was a dangerous terrorist without conscience.

Otto Skorzeny was a very special *SS* man in the gang that
surrounded Adolf Hitler. He had no ideology. A soldier-of-
fortune with a devil-may-care attitude, he was interested primarily in money, risk, and glory—in that order. Let naïve Nazis
prate about politics, Jews, and Communists. Skorzeny was con-

siderably more interested in material advantages and the pleasures of sabotage.

Scarface Skorzeny won fame for four operations with the Nazi Special Forces, of which three were commando-type affairs. In two of them he acted against Italians and Hungarians. But in all four he showed a toughness, resourcefulness, and resiliency that won him even the grudging admiration of his foes.

He had his own share of good luck. He was a native Austrian, which in itself made him a special favorite of the *Fuehrer*. But along with good fortune he had intelligence and determination, both of which made him a successful commando leader in a new kind of warfare.

Otto Skorzeny was born in Vienna on June 12, 1908, the son of an engineer of Slavic background. The family suffered during the miserable post-World War I years, at a time when defeated Austrians had to face hard years of currency inflation and unemployment. The Skorzeny family managed to survive mainly through assistance from the International Red Cross.

The teenager tasted butter for the first time when he was fifteen. Meanwhile, he was growing into a giant. At eighteen, aiming to follow in his father's footsteps, he applied for an engineering course at the University of Vienna.

At the university the strapping young Skorzeny was attracted by the student dueling fraternities, which had become popular among Austrians as well as Germans. For a century and a half the *Mensur*, or student duel, had been a traditional pursuit at both German and Austrian universities. This kind of fighting was forbidden in the Weimar Republic and postwar Austria, but the authorities generally turned their eyes away if such duels were held outside university towns. Students regarded them merely as sporting events.

Duels were fought with a *Schläger*, a sword blunt at the end but sharp-edged with a basket hilt. Vital organs of the duelist were protected by a suit of stuffed leather—only his face and breast were exposed. No feinting, no side-stepping: the student had to hold his sword high and with stiff arm and thrust it downward over the face of his opponent. No blinking, no step backward or to the side—that was only for the fainthearted. The idea was to conquer fear and accept pain stoically.

Duels were arranged by an elaborate code of insults by which the degree of satisfaction was determined. The most usual term

was *"dumme Junge"* ("stupid fellow"). Any student pledged to
a dueling fraternity *(schlagende Verbindung)* as a fox *(Fuchs)* or
freshman was expected to fight a certain number of duels against
opposing fraternity men before he was entitled to full membership. The *Fuchs* could be recognized by his rounded cap, which
he wore during his provisional membership. If he showed his
courage and never stepped from his position, he was elected to
full membership and allowed to wear the regular visored cap
(Mütze) of his fraternity.

Students boasted of their scars. Often their faces were man-
gled. From their viewpoint, disfigurement was evidence of Spar-
tan courage, of personal fearlessness. They proudly wore their
scars for the rest of their lives. The public seemed to prefer
doctors, dentists, or lawyers who had permanent facial scars.

Added to the dueling *Mensur* was the beer-drinking *Kneipe*,
sessions during which fraternity members drank themselves into
unconsciousness. Those who could hold their beer the longest
were regarded as superior human beings.

All this was of enormous attraction for young Skorzeny. He
fought his first duel in 1926, the year he enrolled in the university. To him it was not nerve-wracking but great fun, as he later
described it in his memoirs: "I could feel my heart beat rapidly.
I could scarcely see the face of my opponent through the steel
grill of my mask. Blade against blade! . . . After the seventh
round *(Gang)* I felt a short, sharp blow on my head. Surprisingly
enough, it did not hurt. My only fear was that I had flinched."

The enthusiastic fraternity man fought thirteen more duels.
Although an able bladesman, like others he made certain to win
the all-important scars *(Schmisse)* that would stay with him for
the rest of his life. For him it meant that he had gloriously passed
the tests of discipline and acceptance of pain.

During his student years, Skorzeny joined a *Freikorps* (Free
Corps) unit. These freebooters of the early post-World War I
years, were rightist paramilitary groups later to become a force-
in-being for the formation of the new German army. They were
composed of former officers, veteran enlisted men, militant ad-
venturers, and restless, unemployed students. Dedicated to the
cause of nationalism, they sought out those whom they regarded
as traitors. For energetic Skorzeny, membership in the *Freikorps*
meant adventure and excitement. Later he joined the *Heimwehr*,
the Home Guard.

After leaving the university, Skorzeny began his career as an engineer. His first job was business manager for a building contractor. In 1930 he joined the Austrian Nazi Party. He went into business for himself and soon built up a successful engineering firm. In the involved negotiations that ended with *Anschluss*, union between Germany and Austria effected by Hitler, Skorzeny, unlike many other Austrians, heartily supported the merging of his own country with the Third Reich.

For the always active but discontented engineer the outbreak of World War II was exactly what he wanted. He would go off joyously to combat. Austria was expected to contribute her share of fighting men and he was happy to be included among them.

The thirty-one-year-old Skorzeny could not wait to be drafted. Because he had done some flying on his own, he volunteered for the *Luftwaffe*. After several months of the training, he was told that he was just too old to be a successful pilot, but that he would be accepted for routine ground duties.

Routine? That was a veiled insult. Disappointed by what he deemed to be a slight to his sense of manhood, he volunteered for the elite *Leibstandarte*, the SS unit acting as Hitler's bodyguard. The regiment was overwhelmed with applications—only twelve men were to be accepted. Skorzeny was one of them—the oldest of the dozen.

Skorzeny speedily established a reputation as a leader in the special SS unit. He was promoted first to noncommissioned officer and then to *Fähnrich*, an officer-cadet who was expected to prove himself before he was admitted to full officer status. The former engineer was not altogether satisfied with routine military life—that was not for him. He was bored by the business of going through channels as well as by the ennui of barracks life. He soon got into trouble with his superior officers by his unconventional and sometimes eccentric conduct.

Nevertheless, Skorzeny managed to hold on. He served in the Balkans, took part in campaigns in Rumania and Hungary, and after the invasion of the Soviet Union in mid-1941 was stationed on the Eastern Front. As an engineering officer his main job was to keep the tanks of his division moving. He was awarded medal after medal for personal heroism in combat.

In the German offensive of late winter 1941, Skorzeny was chatting with some comrades several hundred yards from the front when suddenly he felt a blow on the back of his head. Hit by a fragment of a Russian artillery shell, he was knocked unconscious. When he regained his senses, he refused any attention other than an aspirin and a glass of whiskey. The wound, however, was a serious one—he was evacuated to Germany for treatment. Despite his protests he was ordered to a hospital train and taken through Poland back to the Reich. From there, in a weakened condition, he was sent to Vienna. For years thereafter he was to be tormented by blinding headaches.

Then it came—an order to report to the headquarters of the *Waffen-SS*, the military arm and largest of the major branches of the *SS*. The *SS* man, Hitler had said, must be hard, unemotional, fiercely loyal. "His basic attitude must be that of a fighter for fighters' sake; he must be unquestionably obedient and become emotionally hard; he must have contemptuous regard for racial inferiors, and for those who do not belong to the order; he must feel the strongest bonds of comradeship with those who do belong, particularly his fellow soldiers, and he must think nothing impossible."

These words made sense to Skorzeny, who in his happy-go-lucky way thought nothing impossible. Reporting for duty, he was told by a high-ranking officer that technically trained men were needed for special duties. He was delighted. Now he had a chance to get out of the boring life at the depot.

There were further explanations. The British had initiated an irregular type of warfare and they were good at it. The Germans would now do the same thing. Most of their army was bottled up at Stalingrad. It was necessary to strike elsewhere with specially trained commando troops. In this way, some of the heat could be taken off from the embattled veterans at Stalingrad.

Skorzeny was not told that he had been offered the post because few regular officers would even consider touching it. This was special duty for an irregular rather than a *Wehrmacht* officer, for one who had a devil-may-care attitude toward life or death, one who would take joy in adventure and danger.

On April 18, 1943, Skorzeny was named head of a special unit called the *Friedenthaler Jagdverbände* (Hunting Club), named after Friedenthal, its training base near Berlin. The small company was at first equipped only with captured enemy weapons. The combat-wise men were eager for adventure in their new calling. The unit was composed of men of varied background. Among its personnel were Karl Radl (Skorzeny's fellow student at Vienna), several volunteers of the *SS* Parachute Battalion, enlisted men from the *Waffen-SS*, and linguists from all corners of Europe. Enthusiastic and able soldiers, they enjoyed the vigorous training.

Skorzeny made a careful study of British commando tactics. Learning that Allied planes crossed over each night to drop supplies for the Dutch underground, he contacted double agents in the Netherlands to supply him with equipment dropped by the British. This gave him special satisfaction. He accumulated supplies of plastic explosives, Sten guns, pistols with silencers, and radio sets. Later he would find use for this equipment in his commando raids.

Training at Friedenthal took place in a large park in the midst of acres of woodland. More and more volunteers, dissatisfied with their normal duties and attracted by the lure of adventure, joined the special unit. Skorzeny was pleased to get them—the more the better.

What to do? Skorzeny rejected several plans, including a raid recommended by Heinrich Himmler on the town of Magnitogorsky, several thousand miles away in the Urals. The commando chief, studying reconnaissance photographs of the Soviet industrial complex, decided that the proposed mission was impossible.

Then came the break that brought Skorzeny's name into headlines throughout the world. The operation was to bear all the hallmarks of a Hollywood thriller.

For Skorzeny the lure was Italy. For more than two decades the world had been fed stories about the gigantic accomplishments of the Fascist state. The great Mussolini had cleaned up the country's mess. He had made the trains run on time. He had chased beggars from the streets. He had taken a soft and easygoing people by the scruff of their necks and had brought them, newly disciplined and efficient, into the 20th century.

All exaggeration and lies. Better than anyone else in the world, Italians were aware of the nature of the political monstrosity spawned by their Sawdust Caesar. The Fascist state ruled by dictator Mussolini was rooted in quicksand, so shot through with graft, corruption, nepotism, and inefficiency, that it was unable even to feed its armies in the field. Far from helping Hitler in his war, Italian arms proved to be a hindrance to the Nazi war effort.

By the summer of 1943, vulnerable Italy was being blasted to rubble by enemy war power. Allied aircraft, unopposed, flew deadly sorties over the country. Rail traffic was disrupted. Strikes and riots broke out in the northern industrial cities. The *Duce* was in critical trouble.

On July 24, 1943, the Fascist Grand Council met for the first time since 1939. Mussolini, in a weary replay of the same old record, tried to bluff his way to domination. He assumed responsibility for the country's predicament. He would throw out all traitors who, he charged, had brought the country to the edge of doom.

No way. This time the *Duce* was voted out of power.

The next day Mussolini called on King Victor Emmanuel II in a final effort to win support. It was a painful interview. "No longer any use," said the diminutive king. "Italy has gone to bits. Army morale is at rock bottom. The soldiers don't want to fight any more. At the moment you are the most hated man in Italy."

As he left the palace, disappointed Mussolini was surrounded by police, placed in a motor ambulance, and driven off to internment on the island of Ponza. The king announced the *Duce's* resignation, assumed command of the armed forces himself, and ordered Marshal Pietro Badoglio to form a new cabinet. Mussolini was then brought to Maddalena, off the Sardinian coast. At the end of August he was again moved, this time to a small mountain resort in central Italy.

Sensation at Hitler's Wolf's Lair. As soon as he received the news, the *Fuehrer* decided that he was not going to allow the fall of the *Duce*, who was in his eyes "the incarnation of the ancient grandeur of Rome." He would keep faith with his old ally and friend. He would see to it that Mussolini would not fall into the hands of the enemy.

Astonishing news for commando Skorzeny. On July 25, 1943, he was informed that the *Fuehrer* wanted to see him. A plane was waiting for him at Tempelhof. After a speedy flight he arrived at Hitler's field headquarters and was ushered into the *Fuehrer's* presence. Several other officers were there.

Hitler asked the group what they knew of Italy. Five of the six gave the usual response: "Our loyal Axis partner." "Our ally." Skorzeny, as was to be expected, was different. He snapped: "I am an Austrian, my *Fuehrer*!" Bulls-eye! Those were words

Hitler understood. As a native Austrian, he, too, resented Italy's annexation of South Tyrol, sacred Austrian territory.

Although he had no idea about what was at stake, Skorzeny's reply had won Hitler's approval. The *Fuehrer* informed him that the rescue of Mussolini was vital for the outcome of the war. It was a risky business, but it must be done quickly and efficiently. Would Skorzeny try it with his special commandos?

Skorzeny would. Rescue Operation Mussolini was under way.

At Friedenthal, Skorzeny selected his officers and men, including several trained in intelligence. The unit flew to Rome. The first and basic task was to locate the whereabouts of Mussolini. For several weeks Skorzeny was frustrated as the *Duce* was moved from one spot to another to avoid any possible rescue operation. There were false trails and incorrect rumors.

Then a spot of luck. German agents intercepted a governmental message from Rome: "Security measures around Gran Sasso completed."

So it was the Gran Sasso in the Apennines.

The giant Austrian flew over the area in a reconnaissance plane. He decided that the *Duce* was being held at the Hotel Campo Imperatore on a small plateau surrounded by steep, snow-covered crags. Nearby was a small green meadow just right, even if dangerous, for small planes to land. A ground attack was inadvisable, for all roads leading to the area were heavily guarded.

A plan of action began to form in Skorzeny's mind. He would land glider troops on the meadow, overcome the *Carabinieri* (police guards) and then take off with Mussolini in a small *Fieseler-156 Storch* (Stork) plane. He would need just a hundred men to face the two hundred Italian guards, an indication of what he and many Germans thought of Italian fighting capacity.

At one o'clock on the morning of September 13, 1943, Skorzeny's gliders were airborne. He had ordered an unenthusiastic Italian general, virtually kidnapping him, to come along in one of the gliders. He was pleased—this was the kind of action he craved.

A half dozen gliders landed safely, one very close to the hotel. One of them, caught in a sudden gust of wind, plummeted down, crashed, and disintegrated. All ten occupants were severely wounded. Prisoner Mussolini watched incredulously from a balcony window of the hotel. Most of the defending force, astounded by what they believed to be an impossible operation, took to the hills. The few remaining guards quickly surrendered.

Pushing his captive officer ahead of him, Skorzeny shouted: "Don't shoot! Don't fire on an Italian general!" He warned the local commander that Mussolini was already in his hands and that the hotel was occupied by his troops. He gave the commandant just one minute to surrender.

Within minutes an overjoyed Mussolini was hustled into the tiny plane. After a perilous take-off from the rock-strewn meadow, he was flown to Rome and from there, that same evening, to Vienna in a *Luftwaffe* transport plane.

Sensation! Immediate attention on the front pages of the world's press. It was, indeed, one of the most daring feats of the war. There was praise for the commando chief, who by careful planning and daring action had succeeded in making a rescue against great odds.

Hitler was ecstatic. "This mission will go down in history. You have given me back my old friend." He ordered that Skorzeny be promoted and decorated with the Knight's Cross of the Iron Cross, the most coveted German medal. It was a first. Never before in German military history had such a medal been awarded the same day as the action it recognized as heroic.

In Berlin, Skorzeny was feted as the new social lion. Festivities went on for days. A huge rally was held in his honor at the *Sportpalast*, during which he pinned medals on members of his unit.

In London, even Prime Minister Winston Churchill, admirer of gallantry, gave the House of Commons a full report of the rescue: "The stroke was one of great daring and conducted with heavy forces. It certainly shows that there are many possibilities in this kind of warfare."

Well and good for the Viennese giant. But the restless soldier of fortune wanted more action, not annoying social honors.

Skorzeny returned to Friedenthal a national hero. Plans were already under way for more commando missions. One suggestion—he would lead his special unit to France to kidnap Marshal Henri Pétain, who was suspected of wanting to desert to the Allies. Skorzeny would take his men to France and prevent Pétain from leaving the country. Great idea, but somewhere along the chain of command the suggested mission was aborted.

The next scheme was equally attractive. Something had to be

done about guerrilla leader Tito, for whom too many German troops had to be kept in Yugoslavia at a time when they were needed on the Eastern Front. Orders went to Skorzeny: "Get Marshal Tito, dead or alive."

The Tito mission ended in failure, though Skorzeny risked his life by moving through Partisan territory armed with a machine gun and accompanied by two sergeants. An overconfident corps commander refused to work with Skorzeny's staff and, looking for glory for himself, without adequate preparation launched a full-scale attack on Tito's headquarters. The glory-seeker, imitating Skorzeny at Grand Sasso, used parachutists and glider-borne troops. The operation was unsuccessful and Tito escaped. Skorzeny returned to Friedenthal for a rest.

Skorzeny was a bit discouraged by these two missions gone wrong. More action! More action! On September 10, 1944, he was again summoned to Hitler's headquarters. Here he found an angry *Fuehrer* denouncing Hungarian Regent Admiral von Horthy. "We have secret information," Hitler told Skorzeny and others of his intimate military circle, "that Hungarian Regent Admiral von Horthy is seeking to make contact with the enemy in order to achieve a separate peace for Hungary. That would mean the loss of our armies in Hungary. He is not only trying to negotiate with the Western Allies, but he is also trying to arrange talks with Russian leaders."

The yes-men audience reacted with proper shock and indignation. The *Fuehrer* would not allow that to happen. He turned to hero Skorzeny. He ordered the commando chief to prepare his men for a military occupation of the Burgberg (Castle Hill), Horthy's residence. His unit would have a squadron of gliders, two paratroop battalions, and a formation of battle-hardened officers.

Skorzeny expressed his pleasure. Here was a chance to duplicate his world-famous feat on the Gran Sasso.

Assuming the identity of a "Dr. Wolf," Skorzeny within a few days was in Budapest. He learned that Horthy was under the influence of his son Miklos ("Miki"), the black sheep of the Horthy family, known for his wild parties and devil-may-care lifestyle. This was important information for Skorzeny. Moreover, he heard that Miki had already begun negotiations with Tito and his Partisans to surrender to the Russians. He would stop Miki with his own "Operation Mickey Mouse." He would kidnap young Horthy and then capture the old man.

On October 15, 1944, the day on which young Horthy had agreed to meet the Yugoslavs, Skorzeny, still posing as Dr. Wolf, led his commandos against the building where he presumed the meeting was going to take place.

This time there was a reaction as Hungarian troops responded with a burst of gunfire. Skorzeny's commandos chased them away, stormed the house, and captured young Horthy at pistol point. The struggling Miki was taken to an airfield to be flown to a concentration camp.

The entire action took just ten minutes.

The elder Horthy was informed that his "traitor son" would be shot. The old man nearly broke down under the strain. Nevertheless, he went on national radio to announce that Germany had lost the war and that Hungary would make peace with the Russians. Hostilities, he said, would cease at once.

Angry outburst from the *Fuehrer*. The next day, Skorzeny and his commando force moved up the steep sides of the Burgberg. Pushing forward despite heavily mined roads, they used *Tiger* tanks to smash defensive barriers.

Within a short time, Skorzeny was talking to the Hungarian commandant guarding the castle, and Regent Horthy was his prisoner. He sent the Hungarian leader back to Germany as a "guest" of Adolf Hitler. Horthy's abdication was announced.

The burly Viennese commando had won again. With this coup he kept Hungary in the war during its last nine months. Hitler installed Count Szalasi as puppet ruler of Hungary.

There was other work for the always active Skorzeny. He played an important role in the immediate aftermath of the July 20, 1944, attempt on the life of Hitler at a war conference held in the guest barracks at Rastenburg in East Prussia. In Berlin, the upper brackets of the High Command remained loyal to Hitler after the bomb explosion. And it was here in the Bendlerstrasse, location of the War Ministry, that Skorzeny helped frustrate the plot against Hitler.

At 6 P.M. on that fateful day, unaware that a plot against Hitler was under way, Skorzeny boarded the night express in Berlin for a trip to Vienna. He was paged on the train when it stopped at a suburb and ordered back to Security Service *(SD)* headquarters.

There, Skorzeny found *SD* officers almost paralyzed and in a hysterical state. Cold-blooded as always, he took charge. He persuaded several tank formations to remain loyal to the *Fuehrer*. Then, accompanied by several *SS* officers, he set out for the Bendlerstrasse. His first task was to prevent the summary execution of the conspirators, for as an expert he knew that it would be a mistake to kill those plotters who could be tortured into naming their comrades and exposing the entire business.

Skorzeny and his men handcuffed their prisoners and sent them off to *Gestapo* prison. He then ordered that all incriminating papers, which the conspirators had not had time to destroy, be collected for future use.

In his memoirs Albert Speer told how, as he was about to turn in to the Bendlerstrasse, he was ordered to stop at the curb. Almost unrecognizable in the darkness were Ernst Kaltenbrunner, *Gestapo* chief, and Skorzeny, surrounded by numerous subordinates. Speer expected the two to denounce the army, which they had always regarded as their rival, or at any rate to gloat over its defeat. But both replied in fairly indifferent tone that whatever happened was the army's business. "We don't want to get involved."

Skorzeny brusquely took over the War Ministry in the Bendlerstrasse. For the following thirty-six hours, until the arrival of Heinrich Himmler, he acted as commander-in-chief of the Home Army.

Once again Skorzeny had demonstrated his loyalty to Hitler. He had added weight to his credibility and status: he had done important work in saving the Nazi regime at a moment of crisis. Hitler would not forget it.

There was one more major operation for the Viennese adventurer. It came during the climax of the war at a time when Germany was on the verge of collapse. Again, it was a planned commando operation.

On October 21, 1944, came the familiar call. Skorzeny was ordered to report to headquarters at the *Wolfsschanze*, Hitler's Wolf's Lair at Rastenburg. He was warmly received. The Allies, Hitler told him, had managed to obtain a foothold on the Continent at Normandy only because of superior air power. He would strike back with his new jet fighters at a time when the weather would be in his favor. Objective: the Ardennes.

Hitler went on: Skorzeny's commandos would play an important part in the coming offensive. As an advance guard they would be expected to capture one or more bridges on the River Meuse between Liège and Namur. German troops in American uniforms would carry out the operation. Using captured enemy tanks, the disguised Germans would misdirect traffic, cut communications, and in general create havoc behind American lines. For the operation Skorzeny would be assigned the crack *Panzer* Brigade 1540, consisting of several units. Among them was the Captain Stalau group of eighty men, all of whom were supposed to speak from fair to passable English.

Expression of delight from Skorzeny. This was the kind of assignment he preferred. He would do precisely what the *Fuehrer* in his wisdom had ordered.

The critical Battle of the Bulge began in mid-December 1944. German guns went into action all along the Belgian-Ardennes Line. Three of Hitler's armies with twenty-five divisions moved against six American divisions. General Gerd von Rundstedt issued an emotional Order of the Day: "Soldiers of the Western Front! Your great hour has struck! Everything is at stake!" The weather was just as Hitler wanted it. After a massive artillery barrage, his troops moved forward on a 70-mile front.

Skorzeny's commandos also went into action. As planned, his trained units infiltrated into the American positions and began their acts of sabotage.

Chaos in the Allied lines. The attack was totally unexpected. The Americans were bewildered by Skorzeny's commandos dressed in American uniforms. Confused GIs began to arrest their own men. One American captain was taken prisoner when it turned out that he was wearing a pair of German boots.

Rumors spread through the American lines that the formidable Skorzeny was on his way to capture Eisenhower, Montgomery, and Bradley. There were also whispers that a Skorzeny suicide squad was on its way to kill Eisenhower.

American military police, ordered to seek out spies and saboteurs, took into custody one German after another in American uniforms. Despite their schoolboy knowledge of English, they got themselves into trouble when they were unable to tell their captors who had won the last World Series, or name Betty Grable's husband (trumpeter Harry James). Some who were caught were summarily shot.

Skorzeny, himself, nearly fell victim in the battle. In the

midst of combat a piece of shrapnel hissed through the air and struck him in the face. Blood streamed from his forehead. An army doctor, summoned my medics, sewed up the wound.

The strong German offensive was dangerous for the Allies, but it turned out to be all in vain. When the weather cleared, more than 5,000 Allied planes began bombing the Germans and crippled their supply system. Goering's *Luftwaffe* was notably absent, bringing further curses from the disgruntled *Fuehrer*. On the ground, the Germans were pounded by artillery shells equipped with proximity fuses. Hitler desperately threw into the gap more troops, mostly old men and ill-trained youngsters. It was too late. By January 1945 the Ardennes front was re-established at the point where it had been in mid-December 1944. Little had been changed despite Hitler's high hopes. His massive effort only delayed the end of the war.

Skorzeny's part in the Battle of the Bulge was over. He had tried his best with his commandos, but he had done little to throttle the Allied war effort. For the rest of the conflict he served as a conventional soldier on the Eastern Front. But he was bored by it all. His days of glory were now past.

American troops arrested Skorzeny on May 15, 1945, in Steiermark. In September 1947, after two years in a prisoner-of-war camp, he was brought before an American military tribunal at Dachau. He was charged with a number of offenses, including the alleged slaughter of captured American troops, a plan to assassinate General Eisenhower, mistreatment of American prisoners of war, ordering his commandos to wear American uniforms, and allowing the use of poisoned bullets by his men.

Skorzeny was fortunate in his assigned counsel, an American officer who presented an able defense. The man, said his attorney, was merely fighting a new type of warfare typical of the 20th-century technological revolution. As for the use of American uniforms, the lawyer presented a witness who testified that Allied soldiers, too, had operated legitimately in enemy uniforms.

Skorzeny was acquitted on all counts. Nevertheless, he was held in custody in a denazification camp. On July 27, 1948, he escaped by hiding in the luggage compartment of an automobile. For a year and a half he kept out of sight. Then, with the help of a Nansen Passport* issued by the Spanish Government, he moved to Spain.

In Spain, Skorzeny established a small engineering business that rapidly grew into a successful enterprise. Under the name of Robert Steinbacher, and supported by leftover Nazi funds, he founded a secret organization called *Die Spinne* (The Spider), which helped as many as 600 former *SS* men to escape from Germany. In 1959 he bought a summer estate in Kildare, Ireland, where he spent several months each year. He also has a house in Mallorca.

In 1970 Skorzeny was brought to Hamburg, where he was operated on for two tumors on the spine. He was paralyzed from the waist down and the prognosis was poor. Eventually, he recovered and was able to walk again. He died in Madrid on July 5, 1975.

Of all the rogues surrounding Hitler, Skorzeny was perhaps the least objectionable as a human being. Genial and courageous, he was respected by his enemies as a fighting machine. The Allies, too, had their Army and Marine Commandos and Long-Range Desert Troops, all trained in the type of warfare in which Skorzeny was expert. The Viennese giant, however, was not a regular soldier, but rather a gifted amateur. Ordered on special missions, he carried them out in the way he wanted to, not as others suggested. For him, kidnapping and even killing meant normal operating procedure on the theory that all was fair in war.

Rogue or hero? The estimate depends on locale. In Germany he was a hero to his admiring fellow countrymen. For his Allied foes he was a simple-minded, even if courageous, rascal. His military operations revealed that the line between patriot and scoundrel is often a very fine one. A fair estimate would call him part hero and part gangster.

In his memoirs, Skorzeny called himself "the liberator of Mussolini." He did not admit to being an ideological Nazi. There is no reference to National Socialism in his entire book—

---

*In 1921 Fridtjof Nansen, Norwegian Arctic explorer and humanitarian, was appointed by the League of Nations as high commissioner for Russian and Armenian refugees. He devised a so-called League of Nations Passport ("Nansen Passport"), a travel document recognized "in principle" by 53 states.

not a word of regret for Germany's defeat, the death of his *Fuehrer*, or the collapse of the Third Reich. He portrayed himself as merely a robot, who placed himself at the disposal of his master and who obeyed him without question.

The Viennese adventurer saw himself as a hero who tempted fate for the sheer hell of it, an Austrian version of Hollywood's Errol Flynn. But others judged him to be a brutal, sadistic monster, who well merits a place in Hitler's collection of scoundrels. Saintly hero in the Nazi cause? If we look at Skorzeny through the prism of historical judgment, for him that may well be a contradiction in terms.

INDEX

THE BEST IN WAR BOOKS

__DEVIL BOATS: THE PT WAR AGAINST JAPAN
William Breuer 0-515-09367-X/$3.95
A dramatic true-life account of the daring PT
sailors who crewed the Devil Boats—outwitting
the Japanese.

__PORK CHOP HILL S.L.A. Marshall
0-515-08732-7/$3.95
A hard-hitting look at the Korean War and the
handful of U.S. riflemen who fought back the
Red Chinese troops.
"A distinguished contribution to the literature
of war."—New York Times

__THREE-WAR MARINE Colonel Francis Fox Parry
0-515-09872-8/$3.95
A rare and dramatic look at three decades
of war—World War II, the Korean War, and
Vietnam. Francis Fox Parry shares the
heroism, fears, and harrowing challenges of
his thirty action-packed years in an
astounding military career.